MALAYSIA'S POLITICAL ECONOMY

For Evie and Eric

MALAYSIA'S POLITICAL ECONOMY

ECONOMY

Politics, Patronage and Profits

EDMUND TERENCE GOMEZ

Faculty of Economics and Administration
University of Malaya

and

JOMO K. S.

Faculty of Economics and Administration
University of Malaya

CAMBRIDGE
UNIVERSITY PRESS

PUBLISHED BY THE PRESS SYNDICATE OF THE UNIVERSITY OF CAMBRIDGE
The Pitt Building, Trumpington Street, Cambridge CB2 1RP, United Kingdom

CAMBRIDGE UNIVERSITY PRESS
The Edinburgh Building, Cambridge CB2 2RU, United Kingdom
40 West 20th Street, New York, NY 10011–4211, USA
10 Stamford Road, Oakleigh, Melbourne 3166, Australia

© Edmund Terence Gomez and Jomo K. S. 1997

First published 1997

Printed in China by L. Rex Printing Company Ltd.

Typeset in Baskerville 10/12 pt

National Library of Australia Cataloguing in Publication data
Gomez, Edmund Terence, 1961–.
Malaysia's political economy: politics, patronage and profits.
Bibliography.
Includes index.
ISBN 0 521 59996 2 (pbk.).
ISBN 0 521 59007 8.
1. Malaysia – Economic policy. 2. Malaysia – Economic
policy – Case studies. 3. Malaysia – Economic conditions.
4. Malaysia – Economic conditions – Case studies. I. Jomo
K. S. (Jomo Kwame Sundaram). II. Title.
338.9595

Library of Congress Cataloguing in Publication data
Gomez, Edmund Terence, 1961–.
Malaysia's political economy: politics, patronage and profits /
Edmund Terence Gomez and Jomo K.S.
p.   cm.
Includes bibliographical references and index.
ISBN 0-521-59007-8 (alk. paper). – ISBN 0-521-59996-2 (pbk.) :
alk. paper)
1. Malaysia – Economic conditions. 2. Malaysia – Economic policy.
3. Malaysia – Politics and government. I. Jomo, K. S. (Kwame
Sundaram) II. Title.
HC445.5.G65   1997
338.9595–dc21   97–3763

A catalogue record for this book is available from the British Library

ISBN 0 521 59007 8 hardback
ISBN 0 521 59996 2 paperback

Contents

List of Tables		vii
List of Figures		ix
Preface		x
Acknowledgements		xii
Note on Currency		xiv
List of Abbreviations		xv
1	Defining the Parameters	1
	Development, Authoritarianism and Patronage	1
	Rents, Rent-seeking and Rent Distribution	5
2	The Colonial Legacy	10
	Early Political Development	10
	Early Economic Development	12
	Post-Independence Economic Development	15
	Consociational Politics: From Alliance to Barisan Nasional	21
3	The New Economic Policy	24
	NEP Objectives and the Development of Political Patronage	24
	The Reduction of Poverty	27
	Restructuring and the Growth of State Capitalism	29
	Perbadanan Nasional Bhd (Pernas)	32
	Permodalan Nasional Bhd (PNB)	34
	Policy Implementation and Non-Bumiputera Discontent	39
	Bumiputeras and the NEP	49
	Case Study 1: Daim Zainuddin	53
	Case Study 2: The UMBC Saga	56
	Case Study 3: Capturing the Banking Sector	60
	Case Study 4: The Hong Leong Group	66

Case Study 5: Shamsuddin Abdul Kadir and the
    Sapura Group   72

4   Privatising State Assets   75
    Promoting Privatisation   75
    Forms of Privatisation   81
    Justifying Privatisation   86
    Questioning Privatisation   87
    Privatised Patronage   91
    The Politics of Privatisation   98
    Case Study 6: The MBO of Kumpulan Fima and Peremba   100
    Case Study 7: The Bakun Dam BOO   110

5   The 'New Rich'   117
    Mahathir and the Promotion of Malay Capitalists   117
    'Money Politics' and the 'New Rich'   120
    UMNO Factionalism and Money Politics   124
    The Politics of Money: the 1994 Sabah State Elections   130
    Politically Linked Non-Bumiputera Capitalists   137
    Case Study 8: Wan Azmi Wan Hamzah   138
    Case Study 9: Tajudin Ramli   148
    Case Study 10: Vincent Tan Chee Yioun   152
    Case Study 11: T. Ananda Krishnan   159

6   Liberalisation after 1990?   166

7   Politics, Policies and Patronage   177
    Rents, Redistribution and Restructuring   177
    Elections, Accommodation and Investments   181

Bibliography   185
Index   198

Tables

2.1	British Malaya: Ethnic Ownership of Estates, 1938	13
2.2	British Malaya: Percentage of Tin Produced by European and Chinese Mines, 1910–38	13
2.3	Peninsular Malaysia: Major Exports, 1951–69	18
2.4	Peninsular Malaysia: Ethnic Income Shares by Income Cohort, 1957, 1970	19
2.5	Peninsular Malaysia: Ownership of Share Capital of Limited Companies by Ethnicity and Industry, 1970	20
2.6	Peninsular Malaysia: Ethnic Composition of Employment by Industry, 1970	20
3.1	Malaysia: Year of Establishment of Major Public Enterprises and Trust Agencies	30
3.2	Malaysia: Number of Public Enterprises, 1960–92	31
3.3	Comparison of ASN and Other Unit Trusts in 1993	36
3.4	Dividends and Bonuses Declared by ASN (1981–94) and by ASB (1990–94)	37
3.5	Malaysia: Gross Domestic Product by Sector, 1960–93	41
3.6	Malaysia: Equity Participation of Ethnic Groups in Approved Manufacturing Projects, 1975–90	43
3.7	Distribution of Bumiputera Directors by Occupation, Rank Status and Political Affiliation	50
3.8	List of Local and Foreign Banks by Size of Assets, 1990	63
3.9	Comparison of Banking Data between Local and Foreign Banks, 1990	64
4.1	Malaysia: Mode of Privatisation	84
4.2	Malaysia: Major Privatised Projects, 1983–95	84
4.3	Kumpulan Fima Group Performance, 1989–91	104
4.4	Turnover of Kumpulan Fima, 1989–91	104

6.1 Malaysia: Incidence of Poverty by Ethnic Groups,
     1970, 1984, 1990, 1992   167
6.2 Malaysia: Employment by Occupation and Ethnic
     Group, 1995   167
6.3 Malaysia: Ownership of Share Capital of Limited
     Companies, 1970, 1990, 1995   168
6.4 Malaysia: Outline Perspective Plan Targets and
     Achievement, 1991–2000   175
7.1 Malaysia: Parliamentary Election Results, 1995   182

Figures

3.1   Shareholding Structure Involving YBB, PNB,
      ASN and ASB   36
3.2   Ownership Structure of UMBC After the Takeover
      by Datuk Keramat Holdings   58
3.3   Hong Leong Co. Group's Malaysian Operations
      Simplified Corporate Structure, 1993   71
5.1   Shareholding Structure of JPC Before and After the
      Reverse Takeover of R.J.R. Tobacco Co. (US)   144
5.2   Wan Azmi Wan Hamzah's Control of the Corporate Sector   147
5.3   Tajudin Ramli's Control of the Corporate Sector   151
5.4   Vincent Tan's Berjaya Group   159
5.5   T. Ananda Krishnan's Corporate Holdings   164

Maps

Sabah and Sarawak   xviii
Peninsular Malaysia   xix

Preface

Studies of Malaysia's political economy have been undertaken several times before, from different perspectives (see for example, Tan 1982; Khor 1983; Jomo 1988). But these studies have not given much consideration to the impact of party politics on the formulation and implementation of policy, or on economic development. In view of the constantly changing nexus between politics and business in the Malaysian context – despite claims to the contrary by government leaders – over the past quarter-century, a more political perspective of the economy is particularly useful. It allows for an analysis of the character of the state which helps to explain key economic policies and the manner in which they have been implemented. This is pertinent since a significant outcome of some key Malaysian economic policies has been the accumulation and concentration of wealth through political patronage. In addition, such a perspective facilitates dialectical insights across the academic disciplinary boundaries between politics and economics.

Given the strong association between politics and policy development and implementation, the concept of rent and the related concept of rent-seeking provide useful tools for study of the Malaysian economy. The use of these concepts here, however, departs from the mainstream to offer another perspective of their implications for development and related economic issues. Resource rents from mineral and other primary commodities have contributed much to economic growth; the allocation of rents, in various forms, to promote 'social' objectives has been important in securing legitimacy and support for the government; rents have also been created by the government to encourage industrialisation and to bolster investments. But the dissipation of some resource rents has weakened potential accumulation. Rents have also been allocated inefficiently as a result of political patronage. Yet while those who are

politically well connected try to capture rents for themselves, they also
have an interest in maximising their rents and may therefore seek to
raise efficiency and productivity. While not disputing that the existence
of rents often leads to rent-seeking, which may have adverse repercussions for the economy and for politics, this book also argues that
governments can achieve many political and economic goals through the
deliberate creation, allocation and deployment of rents. By minimising
the abuse of such rent creation and distribution, for instance by keeping
processes transparent and accountable, adverse consequences can be
reduced and positive consequences maximised.

After briefly reviewing the major developments that have shaped the
formation of the Malaysian economy and the factors that have permitted
the emergence of executive dominance, this volume concentrates on
how this has shaped policy implementation, particularly the New
Economic Policy and privatisation. The manner in which these policies
have served the politically well connected 'new rich' is consequently a
focus of this study. It is argued that such abuse of executive power will
not be effectively checked by the rapidly growing middle class's concern
with increasing political patronage alone. This has significant implications for politics and private sector efforts to establish a more level playing field, reflecting the resentment of less-favoured business interests, as
dealt with in the concluding chapters.

This study is organised and presented for easy reading and reference.
The sometimes esoteric jargon of the new political economy is kept
to a minimum, while the chapters are presented for readers who are
interested in relevant details of the Malaysian experience.We have therefore used case studies in most chapters in moving from the general to the
specific. To facilitate reading, for those less interested in such details,
these case studies appear at the end of the relevant chapters.

Covering only half a century, this study does not claim to be com-
prehensive. Instead it focuses on some of the most politicised aspects of
the Malaysian economy in the course of offering a historical review of the
major recent developments. Inevitably it highlights the background to
and implementation of government economic policies, as well as their
implications and consequences for Malaysian society. Many related areas,
for example the issue of poverty eradication, are better covered by other
studies and are not dealt with in depth here. Rather than rake over
ground covered by others in the hope of offering new insights, we have
chosen to concentrate on areas largely neglected by other studies of
Malaysia's political economy.

Acknowledgements

This volume was made possible with a Visiting Fellowship in Malaysian Studies at the Asian Studies Program at Murdoch University, Western Australia. The fellowship was commissioned with a grant from the Australian government's Department of Employment, Education and Training for the purpose of preparing a reader on the Malaysian economy.

During this year-long fellowship from early 1993 until January 1994, the head of the program, Associate Professor Jim Warren, and his predecessor, Associate Professor Tim Wright, ensured that I was provided with a conducive environment and the necessary facilities for research. I appreciate their flexibility in allowing me to write the book with as few constraints as possible and in ways convenient to my schedule.

Other academics at the program and at the University's Asia Research Centre showed a keen interest in the project, attending the seminar I presented and contributing ideas and suggestions on improving the structure and content of the volume. I wish in particular to thank Professor Richard Robison, Dr Garry Rodan, Dr Ian Chalmers, Dr Carol Warren, Dr David Hill, and Dr Malcolm Mintz, who were all also very hospitable hosts.

Professor Jomo K. S. was instrumental in persuading me to take up this fellowship and facilitated the preparation of the volume by agreeing to collaborate with me on this project. His expertise helped to crystallise the main theme of the volume, while his insights helped to define the perspective of the study.

I am grateful to our lawyers for their advice on the manuscript.

For Sharm, I reserve my deepest gratitude for her interest in the project and willingness to take on a greater share of our responsibility to our young children while I was busy at work on this book. Her support and understanding was crucial in ensuring its completion. Our children,

Evie and Eric, grew with this book. Eric was born just after the project began, while Evie was at her inquisitive best with questions about why things are as they are. This book, I hope, will provide adequate answers to the many questions she will ask years from now.

Jomo and I take sole responsibility for the opinions expressed in this volume as well as its shortcomings.

Terence Gomez

Note on Currency

The Malaysian ringgit (RM: ringgit Malaysia) is based on a bundle of international currencies, mainly the US dollar. Before the 1970s, it was pegged at RM 3 : US$1. Since the beginning of flexible exchange rates in the early 1970s, it has moved in the range of RM 2.4–2.7 to the US dollar.

Abbreviations

ABIM	Angkatan Belia Islam Malaysia (Malaysian Islamic Youth Movement)
Akar	Angkatan Keadilan Rakyat
ASB	Amanah Saham Bumiputera (Bumiputera Unit Trust Scheme)
ASN	Amanah Saham Nasional (National Unit Trust Scheme)
BCB	Bank of Commerce Bhd
BCIC	Bumiputera Commercial and Industrial Community
Bhd	Berhad (Limited)
BMF	Bumiputra Malaysia Finance
BO	build-operate
BOO	build-operate-own
BOT	build-operate-transfer
Celcom	STM Cellular Communications Sdn Bhd
CIC	Capital Issues Committee
CIMA	Cement Industries of Malaysia
CMS	Cement Manufacturers of Sarawak
DAP	Democratic Action Party
D&C Bank	Development & Commercial Bank Bhd
DUP	directly unproductive profit-seeking
EOI	export-oriented industrialisation
EON	Edaran Otomobil Nasional Bhd
EPF	Employees' Provident Fund
FCW	Federal Cables, Wires and Metal Manufacturing Bhd
FELDA	Federal Land Development Authority
FIC	Foreign Investment Committee
FIMA	Food Industries of Malaysia Bhd

GDP	gross domestic product
Gerakan	Gerakan Rakyat Malaysia (Malaysian People's Movement)
HICOM	Heavy Industries Corporation of Malaysia Bhd
IPP	independent power producer
ISI	import-substituting industrialisation
JPC	Juara Perkasa Corporation Bhd
KCT	Kelang Port Container Terminal
KKI	KK Industries Sdn Bhd
KLSE	Kuala Lumpur Stock Exchange
KLOFFE	Kuala Lumpur Options and Financial Futures Exchange
KSM	Koperasi Serbaguna (M) Bhd (Multi-Purpose Co-operative Society)
KUB	Koperasi Usaha Bersatu Bhd
LTAT	Lembaga Tabung Angkatan Tentera (Armed Forces Savings Board)
M	Malaysia
MADA	Muda Agricultural Development Authority
MARA	Majlis Amanah Rakyat (Council of Trust for Indigenous People)
MARDEC	Malaysian Rubber Development Corporation
MAS	Malaysia Airlines Bhd
MBf	Malayan Borneo Finance Bhd
MBO	management buy-out
MCA	Malaysian Chinese Association
MHS	Malaysian Helicopter Service Bhd
MIC	Malaysian Indian Congress
MIDA	Malaysian Industrial Development Authority
MISC	Malaysian International Shipping Corporation Bhd
MPHB	Multi-Purpose Holdings Bhd
MRCB	Malaysian Resources Corporation Bhd
MUI	Malaysian United Industries Bhd
NDP	National Development Policy
NEP	New Economic Policy
NFO	Numbers Forecast Totalisator Operation
NGO	non-government organisation
NLFCS	National Land Finance Co-operative Society
NSTP	New Straits Times Press Bhd
OCBC	Oversea-Chinese Banking Corporation
OPP	Outline Prospective Plan
OPP2	Second Outline Prospective Plan
PAS	Parti Islam SeMalaysia (Malaysian Islamic Party)

PBB	Permodalan Bersatu Bhd
PBS	Parti Bersatu Sabah (Sabah United Party)
Pernas	Perbadanan Nasional Bhd (National Corporation)
Petronas	Petroliam Nasional (National Petroleum Corporation)
PGU	Peninsular Gas Utilization
PIHP	Pernas International Hotels and Properties Bhd
plc	proprietary limited company
PMP	Pan Malaysian Pools
PMRI	Pan Malaysia Rubber Industries Bhd
PNB	Permodalan Nasional Bhd (National Equity Corporation)
PPP	People's Progressive Party
Proton	Perusahaan Otomobil Nasional Bhd
RIDA	Rural Industrial Development Authority
RISDA	Rubber Industry Smallholders Development Authority
SAPP	Sabah Progressive Party
Sdn Bhd	Sendirian Berhad (Private Limited)
SEDC	State Economic Development Corporation
Semangat 46	Parti Melayu Semangat 46 (Spirit of 1946 Malay Party)
SESCO	Sarawak Electricity Supply Corporation
6MP	Sixth Malaysia Plan
SNS	Satellite Network Services
SPK	Syarikat Permodalan Kebangsaan Bhd
SPPPB	Syarikat Permodalan & Perusahaan Perak Bhd
STM	Syarikat Telekom (M) Bhd
STMB	Sistem Televisyen (M) Bhd (TV3)
TDC	Tourist Development Corporation
TNB	Tenaga Nasional Bhd
TRI	Technology Resources Industries Bhd
UAB	United Asian Bank Bhd
UDA	Urban Development Authority
UEM	United Engineers (M) Bhd
UMBC	United Malayan Banking Corporation Bhd
UMG	United Merchant Group Bhd
UMNO	United Malays' National Organisation
UMW	United Motor Works Bhd
USNO	United Sabah National Organisation
WAMY	World Assembly of Muslim Youth
YBB	Yayasan Pelaburan Bumiputera (Bumiputera Investment Foundation)

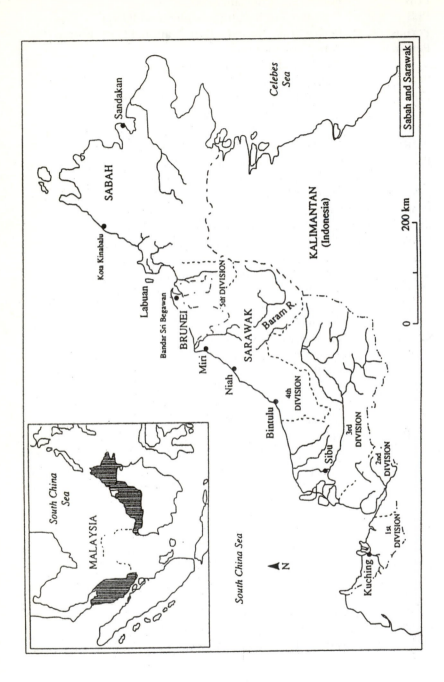

Sabah and Sarawak

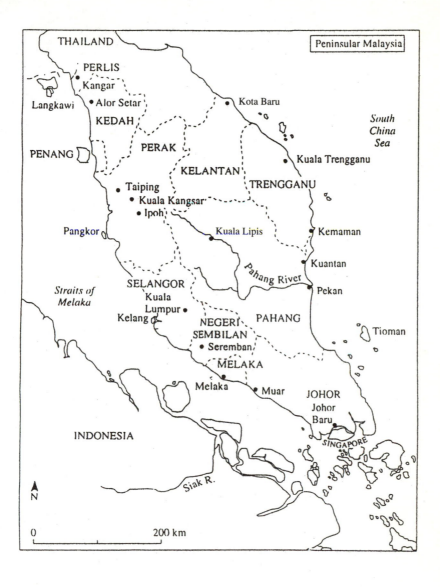

1

Defining the Parameters

Development, Authoritarianism and Patronage

As a major exporter of tin, rubber, palm oil, pepper, tropical timber and petroleum, and with a rapidly developing manufacturing sector, Malaysia has an open economy which is widely seen as being one of the most successful in the world. Access to considerable resource rents has undoubtedly facilitated economic growth and diversification. (An economic rent is 'a return to a resource owner in excess of the owner's opportunity cost' [Tollison 1987: 144]).Yet worrying problems have emerged, tainting Malaysia's commendable economic progress. For example, although the reforms instituted by the New Economic Policy (NEP) reduced poverty substantially and led to the growth of ethnic Malay middle and business classes, there has been growing concern over the influence of political patronage on the business sector, the increasingly inequitable distribution of wealth, and the apparent increase in corruption and other abuses of power. Controversy over these issues has grown with the implementation of the privatisation policy since the mid-1980s, which has enhanced private control of key economic activities and further concentrated ownership and control of corporate equity in the hands of a multi-ethnic, politically influential minority.

Many of Malaysia's problems are believed to stem from the multi-ethnic nature of its population, largely a legacy of British colonialism from the late eighteenth century to 1957, when independence was granted to British Malaya, now known as Peninsular Malaysia. Of Malaysia's 20 million people in 1996, indigenous Bumiputera, or 'sons of the soil', accounted for 61 per cent, while Chinese constituted about 30 per cent and Indians 8 per cent; the remaining 1 per cent was made up of other minor ethnic groups. Most political parties are ethnically based, encouraging ethnic political mobilisation and consciousness,

1

thus exacerbating the ethnic problem. This is only partly mitigated by the ruling Barisan Nasional (National Front) being a multi-ethnic, multi-party coalition. Comprising over a dozen parties, the Barisan Nasional is dominated by the United Malays' National Organisation (UMNO), while two other senior members of the coalition are also ethnically based parties – the Malaysian Chinese Association (MCA) and the Malaysian Indian Congress (MIC).

In spite of fairly regular multi-party elections and some other features requiring accountability of the regime, the Malaysian state has been authoritarian since the colonial period, though analysts have characterised the political system as semi- authoritarian (Crouch 1992, 1993a), semi-democratic (Case 1993), or quasi-democratic (Zakaria 1989). Although these qualified descriptions suggest that some democratic aspects and forms remain, most of the minimal conditions necessary for the practice of democracy in the Schumpeterian sense, particularly fair elections, adequate opportunities for independent political opinion-making and political organisation, and minimal protection for the individual from arbitrary state power, hardly exist in Malaysia (Schumpeter 1943: 269). Further, as Crouch (1992) points out, even the minimal civil liberties and democratic procedures that exist are only allowed as long as the position of the ruling elite is not seriously threatened, let alone undermined; he observes that such rights have been 'quickly modified or abolished when elite interests were threatened'. This has been true of amendments to the Federal Constitution and other legislation, as well as to the rules and regulations governing UMNO, which has increasingly enjoyed and deployed the powers and privileges of long-term incumbency since 1955 in a seemingly one-party state.

Some features of authoritarianism have been pronounced since Mahathir Mohamad became prime minister in 1981, and particularly during the late 1980s, when his own position was under threat. Since the 1980s, a pattern of incremental executive encroachment on the other branches of government has transpired. This has involved diminution of the powers of the (nine constitutional) monarchies, while the executive's encroachment on the independence of the judiciary has badly undermined public confidence in the judicial system's capacity to administer justice (see Lee 1995). The worst abuse of the Internal Security Act, which allows for indefinite detention without trial, during the Mahathir era probably occurred in 1987 (CARPA 1989). Draconian amendments to the Official Secrets Act have further reduced transparency, inevitably eroding public accountability in the process. Ownership of the docile press by politicians and politically influential businessmen and stringent government regulation have combined to similar effect. The government-controlled media have been used by the Barisan Nasional to promote and legitimise itself as well as to discredit political opposition and dissent more generally. All this has been accompanied by an intolerant official attitude towards opposition, dissent and independent criticism by largely ignoring and even discrediting public interest groups, non-government organisations and trade unions, which have been gradually emasculated through repression, legislation, regulation and manipulation. The absence of constitutional and other legislative constraints on the powers of the 'government of the day' holding a majority in parliament has probably accelerated these trends. Much of this has been legitimised by reference to the threat of ethnic conflict and the necessity of making such political sacrifices in the interest of political stability, ethnic harmony, economic redistribution, economic growth and accelerated modernisation, especially industrialisation.

It has been further justified on the grounds that the government has periodically renewed its mandate from the people through general elections since 1955. Federal and state elections have generally been held within constitutionally stipulated intervals, though municipal elections were discontinued from the mid-1960s, when it became obvious that the ruling coalition would continue to lose most urban councils to opposition parties backed by ethnic Chinese. Over the years, the Barisan Nasional government has introduced numerous restrictions which have undermined the capacity of the opposition parties to pose serious threat to the ruling coalition. Gerrymandering and other 'unfair' electoral practices are considered almost routine facts of life by an increasingly cynical populace unaccustomed to expect otherwise (see Mauzy 1979, 1983; Ismail 1979; Crouch et al. 1980; Chandra 1982; Sankaran and Hamdan 1988; Khong 1991; Crouch 1993b; Gomez 1996a). Such limitations on political participation have fostered a political culture with rather modest expectations of democracy, civic rights and public accountability.

Invoking different values for Malaysians in particular and Asians more generally, Prime Minister Mahathir has dismissed the assumption that the Malaysian political system should aspire to and evolve in the direction of a Western model of liberal democracy, often publicly deriding the procedural messiness and inertia of democratic institutions and practices. Instead he claims that Malaysia's political system should be based on a different, Asian conception of democracy which has yet to be fully elucidated. In so far as his arguments seem to parallel those of Singaporean 'strongman' Lee Kuan Yew, it has been suggested that its basic tenets have been elaborated by Lucien Pye (1985); in particular, Pye has argued that since 'Asian political culture' emphasises loyalty to the collectivity over individual freedom and needs, shuns adversarial relations and favours order over conflict, the Western understanding and practice of liberal democracy is inappropriate in the Asian context. Such arguments ignore the historical fact of suppression of political rights over time in the post-colonial era. This process has also gradually socialised Malaysians to accept and even appreciate authoritarian rule, norms and institutions.

The Mahathir regime has successfully achieved the greater central-isation of power in the executive arm of government, particularly in the hands of the top leadership, through repeated amendments to the Federal Constitution. The exercise of power by the executive has not only helped to channel state-created rents to well-connected business-men, but has sometimes also required them to deploy some of these rents in particular ways. Thus executive dominance has had significant consequences for the implementation of key economic policies, particularly the NEP – involving active state intervention to reduce inter-ethnic, especially Malay-Chinese, economic disparities – and privatisa-tion, which was started to roll back the state and trim the supposedly overblown and inefficient public sector. Despite the seemingly contradictory means and objectives of these two policies, both have involved political patronage in determining access to and allocation of rents.

The adverse consequences of such resource allocation cannot be denied and are often expected to impair economic development. Malaysia's impressive economic growth in spite of this, especially in the last decade, might seem paradoxical. The paradox, however, appears to be rooted in analytical presuppositions, most importantly that state-created rents will necessarily be dissipated by the resultant rent-seeking activity.

The government's deregulation initiatives since the mid-1980s en-hanced its efforts to attract investments, at first mainly from abroad and especially from East Asia. Renewed foreign investments and economic as well as cultural liberalisation in turn stimulated domestic private investments. By the mid-1990s the privatisation of infrastructure development had grown to include a new major international airport, highways, new and improved port facilities, major telecommunications projects including launching a new satellite, a huge dam, and increased energy supply. The resurgence of export-oriented manufacturing, coupled with heavy spending on infrastructure development, has enabled the economy to register average annual growth of over 8 per cent since 1988. Meanwhile the middle class has grown and full employment has been attained, resulting in real wages rising, social mobility increasing, and business opportunities expanding.

Executive dominance, which has contributed to greater political patronage involving abuses of power and conflicts of interest, has also enhanced the efficacy of the developmentalist role of the state – hence the basic contradiction of the *dirigiste* Malaysian state. Authoritarianism, and more specifically executive dominance, has enhanced the government's developmentalist capacity on the one hand as well as political patronage and other abuses of power on the other.

Yet with rapid economic growth since 1987, intra-ethnic income differences have become pronounced. Meanwhile some social consequences of rapid Westernisation have forced the government to try to check some of their most pronounced social consequences. Many rural Malays appear disgruntled that they have benefited little from the government's recent development emphases. Some even feel that the economic environment created by the government is not only culturally alien but also hostile to Malay interests (Gomez 1996a).

Moreover, since the state has slowly become a vital instrument for accumulation in Malaysia, through its ability to formulate and implement policies, regulate markets and otherwise distribute rents (for example, through privatisation, licences and contracts), this has meant that access to rents is increasingly contingent on political access and influence. This has contributed to growing political factionalism, especially among senior UMNO leaders. Such factionalism has raised serious concerns over its economic implications in view of the close links between politics and business. Thus the formulation and implementation of policies that shape the allocation of rents, and the economic and political consequences that emerge from them, are the main concerns of this book.

Rents, Rent-Seeking and Rent Distribution

While UMNO's hegemony in the Barisan Nasional and related political patronage have encouraged rent-seeking behaviour and certain abuses of administrative discretion in the allocation of rents, executive dominance of the state may actually have served to limit political access and rent-seeking associated with government intervention in Malaysia. Discretionary executive powers have enabled the political elite, particularly leading members of the UMNO hierarchy, to abuse their powers to capture government-created rents for themselves. Public knowledge as well as criticism and the factionalism such patronage has caused among UMNO members have served to check such abuses, but they have also made them more covert. These developments, together with other factors leading to the privatisation policy, have led to new forms and modes of rent-allocation, favouring businessmen who are politicians and other politically well-connected businessmen, who have all grown in number and influence, especially since the mid-1980s (see Gomez 1994).

Political patronage thus perpetuates rent-seeking activities by those seeking to induce government decision-makers to allocate various state rents in their own favour in return for economic and political support. In many cases the rents secured through influential politicians have to be shared with others to get the job done (through joint ventures, re-sales, etc.). Needless to say, the basis for the award of such business opportunities invariably compromises the quality of the goods or services involved, though it should also be pointed out that the rentier has a strong interest in efficiency since this will maximise the available rents and profits.

Directly unproductive profit-seeking (DUP) behaviour, which includes rent-seeking behaviour as a subset, has been defined as 'ways of making profit (that is, income) by undertaking activities which are directly unproductive' (Bhagwati 1982). Public choice theorists assert that DUP activities – for example direct political activity, lobbying, and bribes – increase in markets where competition is artificially limited by government. The contention is that with government intervention in the economy, the competitive market forces which eliminate rents are undermined and rendered irrelevant. In these circumstances DUP activities are encouraged as companies expend resources to obtain rents; in competitive circumstances, it is argued, such resources would instead be used for productive activities. It is often presumed that the existence and hence pursuit of rents in such circumstances tends to undermine economic development (Shapiro 1990: 127). It has also been argued that public concern about the adverse effects of certain types of rent-seeking has reduced some of the more politically unacceptable adverse consequences of such distortions which could precipitate destabilising political backlashes (Brawley 1993).

Elaborating on the adverse consequences for growth and development, Rowley (1985: 133) asserts that rent-seeking generates 'social waste rather than social surplus, not infrequently as a consequence of government-imposed entry barriers and market regulation'. He argues that such interventions occur 'in response to effective political rent-seeking by special interest groups, who recognise their significance for market rent- seeking'. He also claims that once conceded, rent-creating interventions may not be easily withdrawn even by a determined government, not least because of resistance by the rentiers concerned.

Rent-seeking theorists also argue that when wealth can be redistributed through political intervention, interest groups and individuals will be inclined to organise themselves and pursue initiatives to secure interventions to benefit themselves, or, more defensively, to minimise anticipated losses that arise from such state policies, legislation, and initiatives (McChesney 1988: 179). While the state often seeks legitimacy by depicting itself as a neutral arbiter standing above society, certain political groups, individuals or institutions usually have much more influence on or even hegemony over the state than others, particularly when state access is acknowledged to be uneven (Brawley 1993).

But uneven influence on or control over the state may also imply unequal access to opportunities for capturing rents. This has various possible consequences including limits to rent-seeking behaviour because this behaviour is seen as not necessarily successful. In this case it is likely that those seeking a rent will limit their (unproductive) expenses and efforts according to what they see as the value of the rent and the likelihood of securing it.

In view of UMNO hegemony and executive dominance in Malaysia, rent-seeking is in most cases unlikely to be very competitive, because of the often clandestine, illegal, covert, exclusive or otherwise inaccessible ways of capturing rent. In other words there is no reason to presume total dissipation of rents through perfectly competitive rent-seeking after state intervention has allegedly undermined perfect competition. This has most certainly limited rent-seeking, thus keeping down its costs and hence the dissipation of rent. Businessmen who are more competent but not well-connected often find it worthwhile and not too costly to work with and through the better-connected to secure rents. This suggests that the existence of rents in itself does not necessarily result in enough rent-seeking behaviour to eliminate the rent created, for example if the distribution or allocation of the rent is known beforehand or believed to have been predetermined such that new efforts cannot expect to secure access to the rents.

Although the usual rent-seeking argument regards all resources expended in rent-seeking as dissipated, and hence wasteful, rent-seeking may only involve transfers of wealth (for example, bribery), which does not constitute waste in the same sense, that is a social cost in the economic sense. Hence the real waste in rent-seeking involves the transaction costs incurred in securing and transferring rent claims (for example property rights), not the actual wealth transfers themselves. Failure to distinguish between these two elements of rent-seeking costs has tended to exaggerate perception and estimation of the social waste attributable to rent-seeking (see Chang 1994: Chapters 1 and 2).

Moreover, the rent-seeking welfare losses may well be more than offset by the dynamic gains of productivity growth which the rent facilitates, for example by serving as an incentive to induce particular investments, increasing opportunities for learning by doing, as in the case of the protection of an infant industry, or by encouraging firms to invest in research and development. So while rent-seeking activities may be 'directly unproductive', they may well constitute transaction costs which indirectly facilitate productivity gains (Chang 1994).

Thus while there may have been considerable seeking, capture and transfer of rents, the rents may not have been completely dissipated by unproductive activities, but may also have contributed to capital accumulation, besides inducing desirable productive investments. Nevertheless, as this book will also show in some detail, these rents could have been better deployed to accelerate growth and to generate productivity gains. More careful analysis of rents in Malaysia can go a long way to reconciling the apparent paradoxes (to neo-liberals) of state intervention and rapid economic growth on the one hand as well as authoritarianism and political competition (wrongly identified with democracy) on the other.

The following chapter begins by summarising the impact of British colonialism on Malaya, particularly how it contributed to the creation of a multi-ethnic society and an economy based on tin-mining and rubber production dominated by British interests and how it inhibited the development of an indigenous business class. The discussion of economic development is interspersed with a review of the political developments that led to the 'consociationalist' domination of the post-colonial government by a multi-ethnic elite coalition and how this affected economic development after Independence in 1957 until the watershed developments of May 1969. A 'consociationalist' government is one which seeks consensus between different groups in a political system by bringing leaders of different parties into the governmental process (Lijphart 1977).

Chapter 3 deals with the implementation of the New Economic Policy, introduced in response to the crisis culminating in the events of May 1969. Particular emphasis is given to changing ownership patterns, specifically by tracing how restructuring led to virtual monopolisation of certain economic sectors by state-owned agencies. Some attention is also given to industrialisation efforts as government leaders continued to seek diversification of the economy. Chapter 4 surveys Malaysia's privatisation experience, especially the manner in which state assets have been transferred to politically influential businessmen at heavily discounted prices, ostensibly to address several problems while continuing to promote Bumiputera businessmen.

These two key policies are emphasised because although the NEP involved greater state intervention in the economy, while privatisation entailed efforts to reduce the state's role, yet these apparently contradictory policies have both been significant means for accumulation by rentiers which have compromised other, more developmentalist, state interventions, for example industrial policy. A major emphasis in this book will therefore be on the consequences of different kinds of state intervention, partly in relation to policy goals but also in view of incompatibilities in policy. Malaysia's development experience will therefore be judged not only on the basis of the targeted achievement of growth, diversification and redistribution goals.

Chapter 5 focuses on how political patronage through the NEP and privatisation has created a new business class while also exacerbating factionalism in UMNO, electoral irregularities, and 'money politics'. This discussion traces how the political ambitions of senior UMNO leaders have generated greater political patronage, thus consolidating the mutual dependence of the burgeoning new business class and the political elite. The deployment of most rents to create this new breed of businessmen and to bolster their rapid rise has contributed to capital accumulation in general and strengthened certain political interests, but has not directly contributed much to export-oriented industrial-isation, technological upgrading and other structural changes desired by developmentalist states. Thus the Malaysian experience illustrates the dilemma of a developmentalist state torn between competing – though not completely incompatible – priorities: industrial progress versus inter-ethnic parity.

Chapter 6 assesses Malaysia's political economy after 1990, reviewing the major economic policies introduced after the end of the NEP's first Outline Perspective Plan period (1971–90), while Chapter 7 focuses on the impact on the country's future of rent-seeking, patronage and factionalism in UMNO. With continued abuses in rent allocation, mainly arising from the government's commitment to promoting Bumiputera wealth, the book concludes with a discussion of why the manner of rent distribution may have significant implications for the future of authoritarianism, political patronage, and development in Malaysia.

2

The Colonial Legacy

Early Political Development

When Malaya gained independence in 1957, apart from a formally
Westminster style of government it inherited an economy largely shaped
by British colonial business interests, built around the export of tin and
rubber. Malaya was long the major world producer of both these commodities, causing the country to develop rapidly during the first half of
this century to become Britain's single most profitable colony, and
contributing more foreign exchange in the critical immediate post-war
years than the rest of the empire. British colonialism contributed to the
ethnically heterogeneous population by allowing, even encouraging,
Chinese and Javanese immigration, and organising Indian immigrants
to work in the nascent public and plantation sectors, resulting in a
close identification between race and economic function. Many of the
country's existing economic and political institutions and problems
are rooted in the colonial experience, including the reforms in the
1950s to win hearts and minds from the communist-led anti-colonial
insurgency.

For example, although the ruling coalition has always been multi-
racial in composition, the character and constitution of most Malaysian
political parties are ethnically based and heavily influenced by the multi-
ethnic feature of its population and its colonial legacy. The formation of
the tripartite Alliance in the early 1950s comprising the Malay-based
UMNO, the Chinese-based MCA and the Indian-based MIC was linked
directly to the British colonial government's development of the Malayan
economy. Despite the formation of a plural society in Malaya with the
mass migration of Chinese and Indians into the country, there was
very little integration and only limited interaction among the ethnic
communities. That the majority of Chinese were mainly involved in the

urban-based tin mines, the Indians cloistered in self-contained semi-rural plantations, and most Malays serving as and largely remaining peasants in rural areas meant that the communities were largely kept apart and separated by the fact of economic specialisation. There was also no felt need for integration among the immigrant populations since the general perception of many of the Chinese and Indians was that their stay in Malaya was only temporary. Since they were to return 'home' to China or India after accumulating enough savings, they naturally conceived of Malaya as a transition land rather than as their new homeland.

In 1946, after the British returned to reclaim control over Malaya following the surrender of the Japanese in World War II, they proposed a unitary Malayan Union scheme which involved placing under one government all the nine Malay states and the Straits Settlements of Penang and Malacca; Singapore, the other remaining Straits Settlement, was to be left out of the Union. The Malays, however, were vehemently opposed to the idea of the Union, renouncing it as a British ploy to abolish the Malay Sultanate. They also objected to the Union's goal of providing citizenship with equal political rights to all Malayans, irrespective of race, as long as they professed loyalty to and regarded Malaya as their home (Funston 1980).

In May 1946 a myriad Malay clubs, associations and political organisations converged to form UMNO, with the primary purpose of opposing the Union. Led by Malay aristocrats and helped by its galvanising of the indigenous Malay political structure – from the Malay rulers down to the village headmen – UMNO managed to marshal widespread Malay opposition to the Union (Chandra 1979; Funston 1980). UMNO's key role in contesting the Malayan Union made the party the leading political force in Malaya, with its support base in rural areas. Even now, in the 1990s, despite a membership totalling almost 2.4 million, making the mass-based UMNO the largest local political party, its bastion of support still remains the rural Malays.

Although the British had collaborated with the predominantly Chinese-based Malayan Communist Party during the war – the party had gained a reputation among Malayans for its role in opposing the Japanese – they were fearful of the growing impact of the party and the influence of other 'left-leaning' organisations on the Chinese. As tension mounted between the British and the Communist Party – the party was eventually banned – and the Emergency was declared over the entire country in 1948, the need for an alternative Chinese party that was conservative yet pliant to British interests became imperative. This need paralleled British hesitation to negotiate independence with a single, communally based party such as UMNO. To initiate the formation of such an alternative Chinese party, the British turned to leading Chinese businessmen who, like them, would have vast interests in the economy to protect after independence was gained. When the Malayan Chinese Association was established in February 1949, the main preoccupation of its leadership – which comprised leaders of the anti-communist Guomindang and some of the wealthiest Chinese businessmen in the country – was to ensure that their economic interests would be protected through political involvement (Heng 1988: 57). However, in view of the bourgeois nature of the MCA leadership and its subservient role to UMNO in the ruling coalition, the party has always had much difficulty in galvanising and sustaining the support of the working-class and middle-class Chinese.

The Malayan Indian Congress was formed in August 1946 after Indians were encouraged by visiting Indian Prime Minister Jawaharlal Nehru to remain in Malaya (Stenson 1980). Originally led by left-leaning, middle-class, non-communal members, the MIC displayed a preponderance of multi-racial political organisations. But when it became apparent that multi-racial parties received little electoral support, the MIC in 1954 became the third partner in the Alliance, a coalition which UMNO and the MCA had first formed in an *ad hoc* manner two years earlier to contest municipal elections. The MIC's entry into the Alliance was precipitated by fears over its political survival since the party represented a small fraction of the community (Indians constitute approximately 8 per cent of the population) which was well dispersed in the electorate (Stenson 1980; Arasaratnam 1980).

When the Alliance was officially formed in 1954, it was not only to meet one of the colonial government's conditions that independence would only be granted to a multi-ethnic leadership, but also because of the apparent electoral appeal of a multi-racial coalition of parties as opposed to that of a single multi-racial party. The coalition formula was expedient for a number of other reasons as well. UMNO, whose members then mainly comprised peasants and teachers, was heavily dependent on the wealthy MCA for financial support, while the MCA, with its limited support even among the Chinese, needed UMNO to secure victory for its candidates during elections. The MCA needed UMNO to win seats because although Malays comprised only 49 per cent of the population in 1955, they made up more than 80 per cent of the electorate (Ness 1967: 56–7). By participating in the coalition, the three parties were able to retain their communal identities and bases while achieving elitist, multi-ethnic co-operation.

Early Economic Development

Integrated into the world economy, the colonial Malayan economy grew around the international trade in tin and rubber, which was controlled by the British and to a lesser extent the Chinese (see Puthucheary 1960). By 1938 Europeans dominated the plantation sector (Table 2.1), while British involvement in the tin-mining industry increased progressively at the expense of the Chinese (Table 2.2). The rubber industry proved extremely lucrative, generating enormous dividends for investors, especially in the early years; in 1910, for example, companies paid dividends ranging between 225 and 375 per cent, while dividends declared during that decade averaged around 225 per cent (Bach 1975: 467). By 1938 almost 93 per cent of British capital in Malaya was in plantations and mines (Junid 1980: 18).

By the early 1940s heavy British investment in rubber plantations and tin mines had resulted in a specialised economy. With little expansion in production of food and consumer goods, Malaya was heavily dependent on imports (Parmer 1969: 288). In the 1950s, before Independence, European companies had control of 65 to 75 per cent of the export trade

Table 2.1   British Malaya: Ethnic Ownership of Estates, 1938

Ethnic group	5,000 acres and over	1,000–4,999 acres	500–999 acres	100–499 acres
Europeans	47	467	237	245
Chinese	1	47	94	911
Indians	–	5	21	343
Others	5	13	10	63

Source: Khoo 1980: 202

Table 2.2   British Malaya: Percentage of Tin Produced by European and Chinese Mines, 1910–38

Year	European	Chinese
1910	22	78
1915	28	72
1920	36	64
1922	38	62
1924	45	55
1926	44	56
1928	49	51
1930	63	37
1932	66	34
1934	66	34
1936	67	33
1938	67	33

Source: Khoo 1980: 198; Yeoh 1987: 37

and 60 to 70 per cent of the import trade, while Chinese firms owned around 10 per cent of the import agencies; Indian ownership of companies involved in trade amounted to around 2 per cent, while Malay ownership was virtually non-existent. European companies also controlled 60 per cent of tin output, while the remaining 40 per cent was in Chinese hands. About 83 per cent of plantation acreage was European-owned, while the Chinese share amounted to 14 per cent (Puthucheary 1960: xiv–vi; Yeoh 1987: 24). Far from contributing to capital formation in Malaya, the net outflow of profits between 1955 and 1961 amounted to RM844 million, or 60 per cent of gross domestic capital formation; between 1961 and 1970 the outflow of profits had increased to RM1.8 billion, while foreign investment during this period amounted to only RM1 billion (*Far Eastern Economic Review* 13/4/77).

Malaya's economic development priorities after Independence were largely influenced by the considerations behind the formation of the Alliance among UMNO, the MCA and the MIC, and the understanding its leaders reached with the British to achieve independence. The MCA leaders felt little threat to their economic interests in a private enterprise system which they helped to protect by participating in the Alliance. While the British were assured of no nationalisation of their vast investments in their former colony, UMNO leaders may have favoured a large foreign stake in the economy to limit the expansion of Chinese capital (Golay et al. 1969: 346–7). Generally the Alliance government subscribed to the view that British investments in Malaya were crucial to ensure economic development.

The 1955 recommendations of the World Bank for the post-colonial development of the Malayan economy also espoused limited government intervention in the economy and promotion of development led by the private sector, with government provision of better infrastructure and favourable fiscal and monetary policies to generate investment, both foreign and local. Most such proposals for the country's future development coincided with the interests of the Alliance leadership and the British.

Some emphasis was given to rural development, especially since UMNO derived the bulk of its political support from rural areas, where most of the voters, primarily Malays, were situated (Snodgrass 1980: 167). The government also had to contend with the problems of Malay poverty and limited involvement in the modern capitalist economy. The Malays were thus granted special privileges in public service employment, land reservation, and the award of scholarships, education grants, licences and permits. Though the magnitude of Malay poverty justified increased state involvement to elevate their economic position, by Independence the number of public enterprises established for the promotion of Malay

welfare was still limited to two: the Rural and Industrial Development Authority (RIDA) and the Federal Land Development Authority
(FELDA).

RIDA, established in 1950 to help enhance Malay participation in
business, was probably the first institutionalised effort to develop Malay
entrepreneurs by providing them with access to credit facilities and
business training. In 1954 RIDA was converted into a public corporation
and given enlarged responsibilities and funds, though its efforts in
promoting Malay capitalism were not very successful. Golay et al. (1969:
366) noted that 'in terms of enterprises initiated, credit granted and
repayment experience', RIDA's accomplishments were 'modest', while
'the capital fund, which served as a revolving credit fund, tended to
become immobilized in illiquid loans'.

Established in 1956, FELDA has been a major development scheme
responsible for opening up, developing and distributing land to landless
peasants for the cultivation of cash crops, mainly rubber and oil palm. By
the early 1970s, around 250,000 hectares of land had been opened up in
almost 150 FELDA schemes (Pollak 1980: 269). The rate of settlement in
FELDA schemes, however, was far less than the number of families desiring such land; between 1956 and 1970, for example, only around 20,700
families had been resettled under the scheme (Kasper 1974: 55–6).

Among the schemes introduced to help develop Malay capitalism were
'special privileges', such as allowing Malay quotas to be imposed in the
award of business licences, government employment and educational
access. The government also had 'assistance' schemes, which provided
facilities in the form of credit, training and business premises, and an
'acquisition' strategy to expand Malay ownership of the corporate
economy (Gomez 1990: 4–5). These strategies to create a Malay middle
class and to facilitate Malay capital accumulation had limited success.
Malay acquisition of shares in corporations remained insignificant, even
after the government sponsored the creation of an investment company
in 1961, Syarikat Permodalan Kebangsaan (SPK) Bhd (Golay et al. 1969:
382). Only a few of the shares in public limited companies reserved for
Malays were acquired, mainly because of insufficient funds. Although the
Malays were generously awarded government permits, licences and bank
loans to facilitate their entry into business, few competent Malay
entrepreneurs emerged (Horii 1991: 290–1).

Post-Independence Economic Development

At the time of Independence in 1957, Malaysia enjoyed one of the
highest standards of living in Asia (Rao 1980). In that year the primary
sector (agriculture, forestry and mining) accounted for 45 per cent of

GDP, the secondary sector (manufacturing and construction) for 11 per cent, and the tertiary sector (services) for 44 per cent. Mainly because of the export earnings from tin and rubber, the average annual GDP growth rate in Peninsular Malaysia during 1957–70 was 6.4 per cent (Khor 1983: 2). By the late 1960s, however, there had been little structural change in the economy. After sharp fluctuations in the prices of primary commodities during the 1960s, and in anticipation of the inevitable exhaustion of tin deposits and the long-run decline of natural rubber prices because of advances in synthetic rubber technology, diversification of the economy appeared imperative. Oil palm and then cocoa production were encouraged, with many incentives from the early 1970s; Malaysia went on to become the world's largest producer and exporter of palm oil (Kasper 1974: 11; Anuwar 1992).

Besides preserving the open, export-oriented economy after Independence, Malaysia also encouraged import-substituting industrialisation (ISI) by offering infrastructure and credit facilities as well as tariff protection to the mainly foreign manufacturing companies seeking to secure or increase their market. British investors, particularly anxious to preserve if not expand their market shares from the colonial period, took good advantage of such opportunities. Public development expenditure for infrastructure, particularly in transport, power and communications, increased. In fact under the First and Second Malaya Plans (1955–65) and the First Malaysia Plan (1966–70), almost half of total public development expenditure was invested in developing such infrastructure (Schatzl 1988: 35). The most important incentive, however, was the tariff protection offered by the government to investors in import-substituting manufacturing.

In 1958 the Pioneer Industries Ordinance was introduced, offering tax relief allowances on profits for 'pioneer firms' – mainly new import-substituting manufacturing firms – with the length of relief dependent on the size of the company's investments. With such lucrative opportunities, foreign capital investment in the country grew (see Junid 1980). While the pioneer industries legislation offering tax incentives reflected arguments about the protection of infant industries and was legislated to be temporary (though in practice it could be extended by various means), tariff protection tended to be more lasting in nature. The incentives tended to favour large, capital-intensive, usually foreign companies, besides reducing government tax revenue. Meanwhile the development of domestic industry remained limited, mainly by the continued commitment to economic openness and perhaps by Malay concern that ethnic Chinese would be the primary beneficiaries of protected domestic industrialisation. Thus the extent of domestic capital participation in ISI initiatives in the 1960s was rather small, mainly involving ethnic Chinese in fairly simple food, plastic and wood-based industries. With limited incentives and support from the government, the manufacturing and technological base developed by Malaysians then continued to remain small and often dependent on foreign technology (Khor 1983: 25). But as far as local communities were concerned, the government was also aware that

> import-substitution was not politically disruptive but on the contrary tended to strengthen the democratic status quo because it provided benefits to significant political groups without imposing deprivation on others ... It also helped the government to consolidate elite support through the distribution of patronage to Chinese business people and their Malay associates through the granting of 'pioneer' status, various licences and tariff protection. (Crouch 1994: 20)

Despite the promotion of large, capital-intensive industries, most foreign companies participating in ISI merely established subsidiaries for assembling, finishing and packaging goods produced with imported materials for profitable sale within the protected domestic market. The motor-car assembly industry, for example, replaced imports of completely built-up units with imports of completely knocked-down packs to be assembled locally. Furthermore, since the materials and technologies were generally imported from parent companies abroad, they were poorly linked to the rest of the national economy and usually more suited to foreign conditions. Though wage rates in these capital-intensive industries rose, the industries tended to generate relatively little employment, thus not helping very much to reduce unemployment. Also, the size of the local market was limited by the level and distribution of income (Jomo 1990: 12).

By the mid-1960s the problems of ISI had become quite apparent. In 1965 the Federal Industrial Development Authority, FIDA – now known as MIDA, the Malaysian Industrial Development Authority – was set up to encourage industrial investment. By this time too, many transnational corporations were beginning to relocate their more labour-intensive production processes abroad to reduce production costs, often in East Asia. Foreign experts and international consultants were also encouraging the Malaysian government to switch to export-oriented industrialisation (EOI), which it did from the late 1960s.

As in the rest of East Asia, therefore, with the exhaustion of ISI, the government began to promote EOI, although no significant attempt was made to reduce or remove the incentives provided during its active promotion of ISI. In 1968, the more employment and export-oriented Investment Incentives Act was introduced, which provided tax holidays to approved firms for a maximum of eight years. Among the other incentives under the Act were company income tax exemptions to encourage employment, exemption from import duty for capital equipment and raw materials for export-oriented production, investment tax credits, other export incentives and accelerated depreciation allowances; a new tariff policy on imported consumer goods was also adopted to continue to protect the domestic market for import-substituting industries (Khor 1983: 48).

Under the Free Trade Zone Act of 1971, new industrial estates or export-processing zones known as free-trade zones were established to encourage investments, particularly by companies manufacturing for export. The Act provided exemptions from customs regulations for free-trade zone companies importing and exporting equipment, inputs and outputs for export-oriented industries; later, licensed manufacturing warehouses were introduced to allow greater flexibility in the location of such export-oriented industries. Within a decade, firms in these free-trade zones came to dominate Malaysian manufactured exports, overtaking the resource-based industries processing raw materials for export.

With the new policy direction, the government would rely even more on foreign capital to promote industrialisation, especially since it was wary that growth would otherwise probably contribute more to the accumulation of wealth by ethnic Chinese (Bowie 1991). Unlike ISI, domestic capitalists had even fewer opportunities to benefit from EOI. Foreign firms in the free-trade zones mainly used imported equipment and materials for production and were not under pressure from the government to set up joint ventures with domestic firms unless they produced for the domestic market. Thus foreign firms continued to dominate these industries, especially with their control over technology and marketing (Jomo and Edwards 1993: 6–7).

Despite some industrialisation and the uncertainties posed by over-dependence on tin and rubber production for the economy, primary commodities remained the open economy's mainstays at the end of the

Table 2.3   Peninsular Malaysia: Major Exports, 1951–69 (percentages)

Item	1951–55	1956–60	1961–65	1966–69
Rubber	64	63	50	44
Tin	21	17	25	25
Iron ore	1	4	6	4
Timber	1	2	2	5
Palm oil	2	2	3	4
Other	11	12	14	18

Source: Lim 1973: 122

1960s (Table 2.3). From 1951 to 1969, in spite of declining rubber export earnings due to falling prices, among other factors, rubber and tin still accounted for almost 80 per cent of Malaya's gross export earnings (Lim 1973: 122). David Lim (1973: 51) has also noted that 'the spread effects from the export sector' were negligible, with development concentrated in urban, rubber plantation and tin-mining areas, largely ignoring other rural areas.

Thus despite fairly steady and relatively high economic growth and low inflation for over a decade after Independence, income inequalities increased and poverty remained widespread. Inter-ethnic income differences were reduced slightly, while intra-ethnic differences grew, especially among Malays (Table 2.4). Between 1957 and 1970, according to one estimate, the lowest 20 per cent of households registered an average fall in real income of around 30 per cent. Among the predominantly Malay rural households, the decline (40 per cent) was sharper compared to the mainly Chinese urban households (15 per cent) (Pang 1983: 317).

Despite the government's efforts to promote Bumiputera capitalism, Malay ownership of assets in the corporate sector had not increased appreciably. By 1970 Bumiputera ownership of shares in all major sectors of the economy was still insignificant (Table 2.5). Although Chinese ownership of the economy amounted to 22.5 per cent, foreign control was almost three times more, at 60.7 per cent. Even with the inclusion of shares owned by government agencies in trust on their behalf, Bumiputera ownership stood at a meagre 2.4 per cent.

Malays remained disproportionately poor and were largely to be found outside the modern, urban and corporate sectors, with very few entrepreneurs or corporate managers among them; they continued to be concentrated in low-productivity peasant agriculture and the public

Table 2.4 Peninsular Malaysia: Ethnic Income Shares by Income Cohort, 1957, 1970 (percentages)

Income Cohort	Malays			Chinese			Indians		
	1957	1970	(Diff)	1957	1970	(Diff)	1957	1970	(Diff)
Top 5%	18.1	24.6	(6.5)	19.6	25.3	(5.7)	19.5	28.2	(8.7)
Next 5%	9.5	11.6	(2.1)	11.9	11.8	(−0.1)	10.0	11.4	(1.4)
Next 10%	14.9	16.3	(1.4)	15.3	15.5	(0.2)	14.2	14.6	(0.4)
Next 40%	38.0	34.8	(−3.2)	36.2	33.5	(−2.7)	36.6	31.5	(−5.1)
Bottom 40%	19.5	12.7	(−6.8)	18.1	13.9	(−4.2)	19.7	14.3	(−5.4)

Source: Tan 1982: 120

Table 2.5 Peninsular Malaysia: Ownership of Share Capital of Limited
Companies by Ethnicity and Industry, 1970 (percentages)

Sector	Malay	Chinese	Indian	Foreign
Agriculture, Forestry & Fisheries	0.9	22.4	0.1	75.3
Mining & Quarrying	0.7	16.8	0.4	72.4
Manufacturing	2.5	22.0	0.7	59.6
Construction	2.2	52.8	0.8	24.1
Transport & Communications	13.3	43.4	2.3	12.0
Commerce	0.8	30.4	0.7	63.5
Banking & Insurance	3.3	24.3	0.6	52.2
Others	2.3	37.8	2.3	31.4
	1.9	22.5	1.0	60.7

Source: Low 1985: 26
Note: The shares owned by the ethnic groups in each sector do not include
the shares held by government agencies and nominee companies.

sector (Table 2.6). Between 1957 and 1970 there was an overall increase
in income inequality among all Peninsular Malaysians, and also among
all major ethnic groups (Low 1985: 25).

Instead of fostering social stability, economic development seemed
to be exacerbating social inequalities and frustrating growing Malay
aspirations. Extremists in the various ethnic communities argued that the
ethnically based ruling political parties professing to represent ethnic
interests were too accommodating of others in the Alliance to represent
their interests effectively. This exacerbated popular discontent with the

Table 2.6 Peninsular Malaysia: Ethnic Composition of Employment by
Industry, 1970 (percentages)

Industry	Malay	Chinese	Indian
Agriculture, Forestry & Fishing	68	21	10
Mining	25	66	8
Manufacturing	29	65	5
Construction	22	72	6
Utilities	48	18	33
Transport & Communications	43	40	17
Commerce	24	65	11
Services	49	36	14

Source: Snodgrass 1980: 96

ruling Alliance coalition, resulting in its worst electoral performance
ever in the 1969 general elections.

Consociational Politics: From Alliance to Barisan Nasional

In the elections of 10 May 1969, the Alliance gained the support of only
about half the Malay electorate and a third of the non-Malay vote. The
Alliance, however, managed to retain control of the federal government
for several reasons, including the divided nature of the opposition, the
rural and other biases of the gerrymandered electoral constituency
system, and the inability of the opposition in Peninsular Malaysia to forge
meaningful links with possible allies in Sabah and Sarawak, despite the
discontent in East Malaysia then. The states of Kelantan and Penang
nevertheless fell to the opposition, while the Alliance barely secured
majorities in the Selangor, Perak and Terengganu legislatures.

Several developments in the economy had probably contributed to
the events of May 1969. Despite steady growth, diversification and low
inflation, unemployment had been growing and ethnic tensions grew as
inequalities were increasingly perceived in ethnic terms and attributed
to the 'ethnic other' – the ubiquitous urban Chinese businessman or the
Malay-dominated government, as the case may be.

Ironically, while the government's accommodative policy towards
Chinese and foreign capital was increasingly unacceptable to the expanding Malay middle class with its rising expectations, there was growing
concern among the Chinese over increasing government intervention,
the form of regulation, and new public enterprises, which they felt would
reduce the economic opportunities open to them. With rising Malay
economic expectations by the late 1960s, and mounting frustration over
the modest changes in ownership and control of the economy since
1957, the UMNO leadership came under severe criticism, even from
within its own ranks, for the government's essentially non-interventionist
or *laissez faire* policy. A number of government-owned enterprises were
established to enhance Malay capital accumulation, from the mid-1960s,
among the most important of which were a Malay bank, Bank Bumiputra
(M) Bhd, and Perbadanan Nasional Bhd (Pernas). RIDA was recon-
stituted as Majlis Amanah Rakyat (MARA) in the same spirit, while a
Bumiputera Stock Exchange was introduced in 1969 to promote Bumiputera participation in business. Meanwhile there was growing Chinese
dissatisfaction with the MCA as the party was blamed for not checking the
growing government role. These dissatisfactions with the government's
policies were reflected in the electoral rejection of the Alliance,
especially in Peninsular Malaysia, with the MCA sustaining the greatest
losses, reflecting its declining popularity among the Chinese electorate.

Such developments also contributed to the outbreak of ethnic clashes on 13 May 1969, resulting in the proclamation of a state of emergency, which led to the suspension of parliament, and a 'palace coup' by UMNO's Young Turks against Prime Minister Tunku Abdul Rahman's more conservative ruling clique and style. The incident of 13 May exposed the vulnerability of the supposed multi-racial unity that was believed to prevail in Malaysia. Tunku's deputy, Abdul Razak Hussein, succeeded him as party and government leader and significantly changed the form and style of government.

Razak embarked on a round of discussions with all major political parties to regroup the Alliance into an enlarged coalition, the Barisan Nasional, which was registered as a party in June 1974. Most opposition parties, including the main Malay opposition party, Parti Islam SeMalaysia (PAS, or Malaysian Islamic Party), the Gerakan Rakyat Malaysia (Gerakan, or Malaysian People's Movement) and the People's Progressive Party (PPP), were co-opted into the Barisan Nasional. Their leaders were convinced by Razak's argument that warring political parties needed to stop 'politicking' and instead transcend their ideological differences to come together to forge a nation that had been torn asunder by racial strife.

Moreover, UMNO's ostensible accommodationist attempt, through the system of consociationalism provided by the Barisan Nasional, meant that the huge Chinese support enjoyed by the Gerakan and the PPP had eroded into the MCA's influence. Meanwhile the incorporation of PAS, which was very influential in the east coast of the peninsula, enhanced Malay electoral support. UMNO's refusal to allow PAS to increase the number of seats it contested in the subsequent general election of 1974 further strengthened UMNO's hegemony in the coalition. PAS eventually returned to the opposition in 1977, emerging later as a serious threat to UMNO's electoral base in rural Malay areas.

In the post-1969 period, the hegemonic position of the new, more Malay-oriented leadership in the Barisan Nasional was enhanced through amendments to the Constitution. It was, for example, prohibited, even in parliament, to question 'ethnically sensitive' issues, which included any reference to Malay special rights, non-Malay citizenship, the status of the national language, Islam, and the constitutional provisions pertaining to the Sultans. Thus this attempt at power-sharing within the Barisan Nasional, as Mauzy (1993: 110–11) noted, was in effect 'accommodation on essentially Malay terms'. In subsequent years, UMNO leaders would openly assert that the party could rule alone, but preferred to 'share' power in the interests of national unity. Ironically the government insisted that it was precisely this system of consociationalism, or power-sharing, within the Barisan Nasional which enabled them to manage and resolve ethnic problems, thus contributing to ethnic co-existence. Malay hegemony within this political arrangement, however, was justified on the grounds that it represented the interests of the largest ethnic community (Chee 1991).

This contributed to the creation of a pronounced Malay perception of policies by the party leadership. This was represented in the ideology of 'Bumiputeraism' (Brown 1994), reflected especially in the post-1969 New Economic Policy. UMNO's enhanced dominance of the Barisan Nasional provided Razak with greater leverage to implement the NEP; this entailed partial abandonment of the previous *laissez faire* style of economic management in favour of greater state intervention. Besides the eradication of poverty, the policy mandated extensive state intervention for ethnic affirmative action, including the accelerated expansion of the Malay middle class, capital accumulation on behalf of the Malay community and the creation of Malay capitalists.

3

The New Economic Policy

NEP Objectives and the Development of Political Patronage

The primary objective of the New Economic Policy, announced in 1970, was to achieve national unity by 'eradicating poverty', irrespective of race, and by 'restructuring society' to achieve inter-ethnic economic parity between the predominantly Malay Bumiputeras and the pre-dominantly Chinese non-Bumiputeras. This second prong basically involved affirmative action for the Malays to reduce inter-ethnic economic differences, especially with the Chinese community. In the early 1970s, an Outline Prospective Plan (OPP) for the period 1971–90 was announced for implementing the NEP. Essentially redistributive in intent, the government expected to achieve the goals of the NEP on the basis of sustained economic growth.

The attention given to eradicating poverty ensured minimal political opposition as well as legitimacy and broad support for the NEP. From the outset, however, the keenest interest in implementing the NEP was clearly on restructuring wealth, particularly on creating a Malay business community and achieving 30 per cent Bumiputera ownership of the corporate sector by 1990. To meet the NEP objectives, the government increased state intervention and public sector expenditure and sought to ensure continued economic growth based on export-oriented industrialisation.

In so far as the NEP seemed to respond to the problems of poverty, unemployment and inter-ethnic economic imbalances that had emerged before May 1969, it was received favourably and widely seen as a sincere attempt to transcend problems created by colonialism and perpetuated by *laissez faire* policies after Independence. The emphasis on wealth-restructuring, however, and actual implementation of the

24

NEP soon became grounds for criticisms. Some observers – like Adam and Cavendish (1994) and Yoshihara (1988) – have suggested that implementation of the NEP hindered economic growth:

> While real GDP growth had been impressive (during the two decades of the NEP) and the standard of living of the Bumiputeras as a whole had improved dramatically, the overall performance of the economy had not been outstanding by regional standards. It has been widely argued that growth was hampered by the NEP. When it was introduced, Malaysia ranked third only to Japan and Singapore among East Asian nations in terms of GDP per capita; by 1990, it had fallen behind South Korea, Taiwan and Hong Kong as well. Had growth not been constrained by the NEP, it is argued, the economic performance and welfare of the Bumiputera would have been even more greatly enhanced. (Adam and Cavendish 1994: 15)

Among the problems which Adam and Cavendish suggest have hindered faster growth has been the emergence of what they term 'cronyism', or the distribution of rentier opportunities to companies controlled by politicians, retired bureaucrats, parties in the ruling coalition and politically well-connected businessmen, which in turn 'raised concerns about the transparency of government policymaking and implementation' (Adam and Cavendish 1994: 15). For Yoshihara, crony capitalists were rent-seeking 'private-sector businessmen who benefit enormously from close relations' with government leaders by obtaining 'not only protection from foreign competition, but also concessions, licences, monopoly rights, and government subsidies (usually in terms of low-interest loans from government financial institutions)', resulting in 'all sorts of irregularities' in the economy (Yoshihara 1988: 3–4, 71). There is much justification for such criticism since patronage networks, especially in UMNO, grew under the NEP; it is through the NEP that rents have been created, captured and disbursed, ostensibly as part of the government's policy of 'restructuring' to attain greater inter-ethnic wealth parity and to develop Bumiputera entrepreneurs.

The growth of the public sector and regulation, which increased power in the hands of ruling politicians and the bureaucracy, was crucial for the development of patronage networks. This political-bureaucratic power, coupled with UMNO's growing hegemony over the state, was exploited by some party leaders who found it politically expedient to use the expanded state machinery and the party's access to economic resources to patronise groups and individuals in return for support within the party. The mushrooming of patronage networks in UMNO was facilitated by the encouragement of a 'subsidy mentality' among Malays, who viewed the state as a protector of their interests (Chandra 1979; Mehmet 1988). Since such political patronage led to the emergence of a group of politically influential 'new rich', including many Malays, intra-ethnic inequality grew (see Chapter 5). Among the most prominent of this 'new rich' who emerged with much government patronage is former Finance Minister Daim Zainuddin, currently the government's economic adviser and probably the most influential capitalist in Malaysia, with significant control over the corporate sector through his numerous business protégés (see Case Study 1, p. 53).

As the Barisan Nasional was returned to power in subsequent national elections and as UMNO's hegemony increased, the control of these 'new rich' over the national economy grew. NEP implementation was seen to be contributing greatly to the consolidation of the 'new rich', some of whom were reputed to be proxies of prominent politicians. Since their close ties with influential politicians had given them access to government rents to develop their corporate holdings, these business-men were expected, in turn, to fund their political patrons. Such funding, normally covert, was facilitated by the very limited disclosure requirements under Malaysia's election regulations on sources of funding for political parties (see Gomez 1996b).

Since the principal beneficiaries of government policies were politi-cally linked businessmen, involvement in politics increasingly came to be viewed by Bumiputeras as a quick means to obtain profitable business opportunities, and other rents, in view of UMNO's control over the allocation of resources and determination of policies. Inevitably this use of political patronage to establish power bases reaching down to the grass-roots level led to rancorous infighting and bickering that has deeply divided UMNO and most other Barisan Nasional component parties. In vying for power, each party faction – with its own sources of funding and business proxies – often operated quite independently.

Apart from heightening factionalism, the development of patron-age networks and emergence of Malay businessmen led to a gradual change in the composition of UMNO's grass-roots leadership. Domin-ated mainly by rural teachers since the party's formation in 1946, by the 1980s businessmen had begun to gain control over party branches and divisions. In 1981, just a decade after the implementation of the NEP, although teachers still made up 41 per cent of the delegates to UMNO's annual General Assembly, this dropped to 32 per cent in 1984, and declined further to 19 per cent in 1987. Meanwhile businessmen con-stituted 25 per cent of the delegates in 1987, while elected represen-tatives made up 19 per cent (Hasan 1990: 308). By 1995 almost 20 per cent of UMNO's 165 division chairmen were millionaire businessmen-cum-politicians (*Wawancara* December 1995). The rise in UMNO of such rentier elements and the increasing use of money to secure positions in the party hierarchy contributed to the development of 'money politics' (see Gomez 1990, 1991a, 1994, 1996b), blurring the distinction between corporate and political power. This pattern of clientelism involved much unproductive deployment of economic resources, growing political corruption and cronyism, and the increased use of money in party, state, and federal elections (see Gomez 1996b). Despite the debilitating impact of political patronage on intra-party politics and the corporate sector, government leaders maintained that such patronage and the preferential award of government contracts and other government-allocated rents to select individuals was necessary to create Malay businessmen.

But the insulation of such politically linked businesses – and public enterprises – from market competition and their apparently unlimited access to finance undermined the possibly disciplining experience of business management. Moreover the speed with which this new breed of politically influential, often Bumiputera, businessmen moved in the corporate world probably undermined their 'learning by doing' as limited success soon led to greater opportunity in an often dizzying spiral of politically accelerated ascent.

There have also been many criticisms that this emphasis on 'wealth-restructuring' has meant that the other NEP objective of eradicating poverty has been compromised, with the substantial decline in poverty mainly due to factors besides government efforts, rather than the NEP itself (Jomo 1989).

The Reduction of Poverty

The government has viewed poverty in absolute terms (in relation to a poverty line), rather than in relative terms, for example inequality. With such a conception of poverty, income inequality could grow even as the poverty rate declined if the economy registered high growth (Jomo 1994: 4–5). In fact, unlike the period 1957 to 1970, when the lower-income groups experienced declining real incomes as inequalities grew, it appears that during the 1970s the average real income of the bottom 40 per cent increased while overall inequalities continued to grow (Jomo 1994: 4–5).

The OPP projected a reduction in the official poverty rate in Peninsular Malaysia from 49 per cent in 1970 to 16 per cent in 1990, with the poverty line apparently then defined at RM33 per capita per month in 1970 (Anand 1982). By 1989, even before the close of the NEP period, the official poverty rate for Peninsular Malaysia was down to 15 per cent, while a rate of 17 per cent was registered for the whole country. In fact, when considered per capita rather than by household, the official poverty rate in Peninsular Malaysia had been reduced to

1.3 per cent by 1987. Official poverty rates for Sabah and Sarawak in 1987 remained much higher, at 35.3 and 24.7 per cent respectively. They were, however, probably also much higher in 1970 to begin with, meaning that the official poverty rate for Malaysia as a whole was probably higher than 50 per cent in 1970.

While there is little doubt that poverty in Malaysia, as measured by the official poverty line, has been significantly reduced since 1970, because of tremendous economic growth and trickle-down from the massive increase in public expenditure under the NEP's auspices, there is still some scepticism over the official figures. It appears, for example, that the official poverty line was reduced by about 8 per cent from RM33 per capita per month in 1970 to the equivalent of RM30 in 1987 in 1970 price terms, that is after discounting for inflation, as measured by the increase in the official Consumer Price Index.

Criticism of NEP public expenditure has focused attention on the efficacy of government expenditure for eradicating poverty. By its own admission, the Malaysian government claims that only 40 per cent of the RM30 billion spent on poverty eradication under the NEP until 1988 actually reached the target groups, with the balance covering administration and infrastructure costs. It is probably unlikely that much of this RM12 billion actually reached the poor since the main beneficiaries of many government poverty eradication programs were not actually poor.

For instance, when the government withdrew the diesel price subsidy in 1983, it admitted that only 1 per cent of the diesel was bought by fishermen, the ostensible beneficiaries of the subsidy. The larger boat-owners benefited more from the diesel subsidy since poor fishermen either used small petrol engines or no engines at all, or else worked for boat and gear owners. As for rice farmers, the guaranteed minimum price scheme provided greater benefits to those able to market more rice, which invariably meant big farmers rather than poor ones. Similarly, input subsidies, such as fertilisers, are distributed on the basis of the extent of land owned, again benefiting the well-to-do much more than the poor.

Unfortunately, available official information does not allow us to determine precisely the extent to which government expenditure on eradicating poverty actually benefited the poor. There is now, therefore, widespread recognition of the need for targeting if poverty eradication measures are to be more effective and cost-efficient. It is also widely recognised that government expenditure for poverty eradication has been increasingly politicised over the years, encouraging political nepotism and patronage in the process, especially at the grass-roots level. It is unclear how these problems will be overcome without undermining the political system and the dominant interests which have been consolidated over the years. So it seems unlikely that fundamental reforms will be forthcoming.

It should also be recognised that much of the reduction in poverty has been due to economic growth and increased productivity, rather than more equitable redistribution of capital or land. Without such redistributive measures, poverty reduction measures are mainly based on growth and productivity since the basically inequitable pattern of asset distribution has not been affected by government policies. In fact the present pattern of asset distribution, especially of agricultural land, continues to exacerbate inefficient and sub-optimal use of peasant land, which stands in the way of greater productivity gains and a more efficient and dynamic agricultural sector. It appears unlikely that the reforms needed to bring about desirable change in this sector will be introduced without fundamental changes in the political regime and concomitant changes in the distribution of economic resources.

Restructuring and the Growth of State Capitalism

Although the NEP restructuring involves redistribution of corporate stock ownership, employment and education (with the latter two often considered together), it is this restructuring that has generated most interest, despite the small number of corporate owners among the population (Lim 1981; Tan 1982; Gale 1985; Yeoh 1987; Mehmet 1988; Gomez 1990, 1991a, 1994). Such concern with ownership is significant for it reflects the increasing influence of elite minorities in defending their own interest in ownership and control of economic wealth under the guise of advancing ethnic or communal interests.

With the government emphasising wealth-restructuring under the NEP, the number of government-owned enterprises participating in activities involving all sectors of the economy increased considerably during the 1970s. These public enterprises can be classified into three major categories. First, departmental enterprises, mainly those responsible for providing public services, such as water supply, telecommunications, civil aviation and refuse collection. Second, statutory bodies established by law at federal and state levels, for example, the Malaysian Industrial Development Authority, the Tourist Development Corporation (TDC), the Urban Development Authority (UDA), Petroliam Nasional Bhd (Petronas), the Muda Agricultural Development Authority (MADA), the Malaysian Rubber Development Corporation (MARDEC), and the various state economic development corporations (SEDCs). In the third category are government-owned private or public limited companies established under the Companies Act (1965), whose equity holdings are either fully or partially held by the government;

among the more prominent public enterprises are the Heavy Industries Corporation of Malaysia (HICOM), property developer Peremba Bhd, and Food Industries of Malaysia (FIMA). Many public enterprises in the latter two categories were developed to accelerate Bumiputera participation in commerce and industry.

Among these public enterprises are the Bumiputera trust agencies, ostensibly accumulating wealth on behalf of the entire community, since they were responsible for advancing the Bumiputera share of corporate equity by purchasing and holding shares on behalf of the community.

Table 3.1   Malaysia: Year of Establishment of Major Public Enterprises and Trust Agencies

Public Enterprise	Year
Federal Land Development Authority (FELDA)	1956
Selangor SEDC	1964
Penang SEDC	1965
Terengganu SEDC	1965
Bank Bumiputra (M) Bhd	1965
Johor SEDC	1966
Federal Land Consolidation and Rehabilitation Authority (FELCRA)	1966
Majlis Amanah Rakyat (MARA, Council of Trust for Indigenous People)	1966
South Kelantan Development Authority (KESEDAR)	1967
Kelantan SEDC	1967
Kedah SEDC	1967
Melaka SEDC	1967
Negeri Sembilan SEDC	1967
Perak SEDC	1967
Bank Pertanian Malaysia (Agricultural Bank of Malaysia)	1969
Pahang Investment & Industrial Company Ltd	1969
Perbadanan Nasional Bhd (Pernas, National Corporation)	1969
Lembaga Padi dan Beras Negara (LPN, National Padi and Rice Authority)	1971
Pahang Agricultural Development Authority (PADA)	1971
Pahang Tenggara Development Authority (DARA)	1971
Urban Development Authority (UDA)	1971
Selangor Agricultural Development Authority (SEADA)	1972
Johor Tenggara Development Authority (KEJORA)	1972
Perlis SEDC	1973
Pahang Trading Company (PTC)	1973
Johor Port Authority (JPA)	1973
Farmers' Organisation Authority (FOA)	1973
Terengganu Tengah Regional Development Authority (KETENGAH)	1973
Food Industries of Malaysia (FIMA)	1972
Permodalan Nasional Bhd (PNB, National Equity Corporation)	1974
Heavy Industries Corporation of Malaysia Bhd (HICOM)	1980

Source: Horii 1991: Tables 3 and 4

Some of the major trust agencies incorporated for this task include Perbadanan Nasional Bhd or National Corporation (Pernas), Permodalan Nasional Bhd or National Equity Corporation (PNB), and its wholly owned subsidiaries, Amanah Saham Nasional or the National Unit Trust scheme (ASN) and Amanah Saham Bumiputera or the Bumiputera Unit Trust scheme (ASB) (Toh 1989: 245).

While there were only 23 public enterprises in 1957 – of these, only two, the Rubber Industry Smallholders Development Authority (RISDA) and FELDA, had redistributive objectives – by 1969 54 more had been established, including SEDCs in almost all states (Ismail 1991: 598). While the primary emphasis of most public enterprises in the pre-NEP period was on rural and infrastructural development, enterprises established after 1969 participated much more in 'modern sector' activities such as finance, commerce and industry, previously the exclusive domain of private enterprise (Table 3.1). During the next two decades the total number of enterprises owned by federal and state authorities grew considerably, totalling 1,149 by 1992 (Table 3.2).

This, inevitably, resulted in soaring public development expenditure during the early 1970s. Under the First Malaysia Plan, 1966–1970, for example, the allocation was RM4.6 billion, which more than doubled to RM10.3 billion under the Second Malaysia Plan, 1971–1975. With the Third Malaysia Plan, 1976–1980, the allocation for public development expenditure tripled to RM31.1 billion; although a similar rise in expenditure was projected under the Fourth Malaysia Plan, 1981–1985, the actual increase was only around RM8 billion. Under the Fifth Malaysia Plan, 1986–1990, however, although RM74 billion was allocated for public development, the figure was later revised downwards to RM57.5 billion (Jomo 1990: 111).

Table 3.2   Malaysia: Number of Public Enterprises, 1960–92

Industry	1960	1965	1970	1975	1980	1985	1992
Agriculture	4	5	10	38	83	127	146
Building & Construction	2	9	9	33	65	121	121
Extractive Industries	0	1	3	6	25	30	32
Finance	3	9	17	50	78	116	137
Manufacturing	5	11	40	132	212	289	315
Services	3	6	13	76	148	258	321
Transport	5	13	17	27	45	63	68
Others	0	0	0	0	0	6	9
Total	22	54	109	362	656	1,010	1,149

Source: Rugayah 1993

Since the government felt that the Bumiputeras' lack of propensity to save was a major impediment towards achieving the NEP objectives, public enterprises were supposed to mobilise resources and accumulate capital on behalf of the Bumiputera community. Backed by government legislative and regulatory power and financial resources, these enterprises could gain control of strategic segments of the economy. In the process, new economic projects and businesses could also be created, which could be later divested to Bumiputeras. Apart from these roles, the government also presumed that public enterprises would provide human resource development and transfer technology to Bumiputeras. Public enterprises could also develop joint ventures with foreign and other private corporations (Low 1985: 63–5).

The funds allocated under the five Malaysia plans for the development of equity ownership led to a swift increase in Bumiputera ownership of the corporate sector. Bowie (1988) noted that 'there was a 50 per cent growth rate in Malay equity participation under the Second Malaysia Plan (amounting to 8 per cent of total shares in 1975)'. But this was not the only means of remedying the disproportionate distribution of wealth. Under the NEP there was also discriminatory dual pricing in the allocation of shares; Bumiputera individuals or institutions were allotted shares at par value, or charged only nominal premiums. Such methods of share and hence rent allocation contributed to the growth of two of the government's most successful agencies: Pernas and PNB. With much government funding, both these agencies quickly became among the country's leading owners of corporate stock.

Perbadanan Nasional Bhd (Pernas)

Incorporated in 1969 with a paid-up capital of RM116 million, Pernas is controlled by the Ministry of Finance Incorporated, the Treasury's holding company. Functioning primarily as a holding company, Pernas began acquiring some of the country's major publicly listed companies, particularly those under foreign control. Pernas also controlled resource-based industries, export manufacturing businesses, strategic trading and some high-technology investments (Low 1985: 107). Among its more noted acquisitions was its 1975 purchase of London Tin (now the Malaysia Mining Corporation Bhd), the country's leading tin-mining concern; the next year Pernas gained control of Sime Darby Bhd, the plantation-based conglomerate. By the end of the 1970s, within just one decade, Pernas also had controlling interests in other major companies such as Goodyear (M) Bhd, Island & Peninsular Bhd, Highlands & Lowlands Bhd and Kontena Nasional Bhd. With control of such lucrative assets, Pernas continued to chalk up profits which peaked at RM179 million in 1981 (*Malaysian Business* 1/5/91).

Pernas' growth, however, was affected by the government's next major investment holding company, PNB, established in 1978; soon after, Pernas was compelled to transfer thirteen of its more lucrative major companies, including Sime Darby and the Malaysia Mining Corporation, to PNB at cost. This caused Pernas to register losses for a number of years, a situation exacerbated by the economic recession of the mid-1980s and some questionable deals such as the purchase in 1986 of a 40 per cent stake in Malaysia's third largest bank, the United Malayan Banking Corporation Bhd (UMBC), from then Finance Minister Daim Zainuddin for almost RM350 million with off-shore loans it could ill afford (see *Asian Wall Street Journal* 31/5/88). Daim had acquired a majority stake in UMBC in 1984, just before he was appointed Finance minister. In 1986 he sold his UMBC equity to Pernas, ostensibly to comply with Prime Minister Mahathir's directive that all cabinet members divest their corporate holdings (Gomez 1990: 41–2). Pernas has also sold some of its more profitable concerns under questionable conditions: it sold 40 per cent of its 100 per cent equity in Perbadanan Nasional Shipping Line Sdn Bhd to a company ultimately owned by Technology Resources Industries Bhd, a listed entity controlled by Tajudin Ramli, a Daim protégé (*Malaysian Business* 1/5/91).

Pernas has since been revitalised, in part because it has benefited when non-Bumiputera companies have had to 'restructure', as required by the NEP, to allow for at least 30 per cent Bumiputera ownership. One example was when Pernas was designated by the government to acquire a 30 per cent stake in the then Singapore-controlled newspaper publishing company Nanyang Press Bhd, when the latter's ownership was restructured in the mid-1980s; Pernas eventually divested its stake in Nanyang Press for handsome returns. The company was subsequently publicly quoted in April 1989.

By the end of 1990, Pernas still had, among its assets, four major publicly listed companies – Malayawata Steel Bhd, Tradewinds (M) Bhd, United Malayan Flour Mills Bhd, and Pernas International Hotels and Properties Bhd (PIHP) – and had expressed its intention eventually to seek listing on the Kuala Lumpur Stock Exchange (KLSE) (*The Star* 28/8/90). Although Pernas had an interest in more than 70 companies involved in a diverse range of activities, such as plantations, manufacturing, hotel and property development, its major investment was its 85.7 per cent stake in UMBC, which constituted about 74 per cent of its total assets in the early 1990s (*The Star* 14/9/88; *Business Times* 2/8/91). Despite this, Pernas desperately sought to divest its stake in UMBC; the burden of the massive loans taken to acquire the bank and the poor returns on this investment had meant that Pernas had never considered the bank a lucrative asset. Pernas eventually sold UMBC in 1992, without open tender, and in circumstances which gave rise to questions of political patronage and abuse of state enterprises by the executive. This undermined the credibility of the Mahathir administration, particularly when UMBC was sold just three years later, in late 1995, after allegations of mismanagement and suspect transactions by the bank's new owners, for a handsome profit (see Case Study 2, p. 56). The current owner of UMBC is, ironically, Sime Darby, the publicly listed, but government-controlled, plantation-based conglomerate which Pernas had acquired in 1976 before being forced by the government to divest to PNB in 1978.

Permodalan Nasional Bhd (PNB)

Despite the accelerated transfer of corporate assets to Bumiputeras and repeated appeals to Malays to seize business opportunities created for them by the government, the 'individual Bumiputera' share of total Bumiputera equity dropped sharply from 60 per cent in 1970 to 34 per cent in 1980 (Hing 1984: 312). This transpired during a period when the annual growth rate of individual Bumiputera equity increased by 23.5 per cent per annum, while Bumiputera trust agencies registered an average 39 per cent per annum growth between 1971 and 1980 (Means 1991: 69–70). Concerned that divestments by Bumiputeras were going primarily to ethnic Chinese, the government introduced the 'owner-ship-in-trust' concept by establishing the unit trust scheme (ASN), managed by PNB. PNB was placed under the jurisdiction of the Yayasan Pelaburan Bumiputera (YBB), or Bumiputera Investment Foundation, established by the government in 1978 and headed by the Prime Minister. In March that year YBB incorporated PNB to act as its investment house and fund manager by purchasing shares in companies to be held in trust by PNB itself or through its wholly owned subsidiary ASN, for individual Bumiputera investors (Zainal 1991: 370). This allowed the government to accommodate Bumiputera demands for greater individual ownership and to expand Bumiputera ownership of equity capital while also ensuring that these assets remained with Bumiputeras.

Incorporated in May 1979 and launched in April 1981, ASN was set up to help ensure wider dispersion of share ownership. By 1989, for example, PNB had transferred to ASN sizeable stakes in a number of listed entities, including the Malaysia Mining Corporation, KFC Holdings Bhd, Cement Manufacturers Sarawak Bhd, Malaysian Tobacco Company Bhd, Rothmans of Pall Mall Bhd, Petaling Garden Bhd and Malaysian Plantations Bhd (*The Star* 22/4/89). Since PNB could only divest to ASN, the government effectively ensured that the acquired equity remained under its control.

To facilitate PNB acquisitions, the government provided large grants and interest-free loans through YBB. Of the RM3.7 billion loan to PNB outstanding in 1983, for example, only RM0.5 billion bore interest (Limlingan 1986: 209). In addition to such funding and investments by Bumiputeras in ASN, PNB's rapid growth was also attributable to the transfer of shares at cost by Pernas, the SEDCs, and various other statutory bodies (*The Star* 7/9/88). Like Pernas, PNB was also a major beneficiary when non-Bumiputera companies were restructured under the NEP.

On 1 January 1990 the Bumiputera Unit Trust Scheme (ASB) was launched to take over the role of ASN. As required under the terms and conditions of the trust scheme, the price of the ASN units was left to the market from January 1991. Henceforth ASN shareholders had to bear the risks of transacting their shares at market prices, although there was little possibility of much depreciation in the unit price since ASN and PNB had interests in some of Malaysia's most lucrative corporate stock. However, since ASN assets primarily comprised quoted companies, the fate of the local bourse as a whole affected the value of ASN units. Since trading of ASN units commenced on 2 January 1992, it has been conducted through PNB (*Malaysian Business* 1/1/90). Since the ASN was legally committed to transact its shares in the open market at market prices after 1990, the ASB was set up alongside it for those investors who preferred the old ASN arrangements of a fixed price with annual returns. Thus, like the old ASN, the price of each ASB unit was fixed at one ringgit, and investors could continue to expect generous returns with minimum risks (*Malaysian Business* 1/1/90). All ASN unit-holders had their investments automatically transferred to ASB unless they specifically indicated otherwise. By 1992, 3.54 million Bumiputeras had invested almost RM13.46 billion in ASB, while there were still approximately 1.34 million ASN unit-holders who had invested almost RM1.01 billion in the scheme (*Investors Digest* July 1992; *New Straits Times* 25/7/94). As in the case of ASN, ASB's assets comprise those transferred to it by PNB. ASN only holds stakes in listed companies while the ASB portfolio includes stakes in both quoted and unquoted companies. Figure 3.1 indicates the current shareholding structure involving the YBB, PNB, ASN, and ASB.

By the end of 1990 ASN had almost 2.4 million investors (44 per cent of an estimated 5.4 million eligible investors!) who had invested around RM6.2 billion in the scheme, with which ASN had developed an impressive investment portfolio of 67 listed companies (*New Straits Times* 17/2/91). ASN thus represented an effective means of mobilising

Figure 3.1   Shareholding Structure Involving YBB, PNB, ASN and ASB

Bumiputera savings and providing liquidity for equity acquisition by PNB. To limit excessive accumulation through the trust scheme, the purchase limit for each individual investor was 50,000 one-ringgit units for ASN and 100,000 for ASB. ASN's growth was so rapid that by 1993, only twelve years after its incorporation, it had become the largest unit trust in the country (Table 3.3).

Since their inception, the ASN and ASB have consistently been declaring high returns, well above the prevailing savings and fixed-deposit interest rates. Table 3.4 shows the dividends and bonuses

Table 3.3   Comparison of ASN and Other Unit Trusts in 1993

Unit Trust	Number of funds	Size of funds (million units)
Amanah Saham Nasional	2	1,600
Kuala Lumpur Mutual Fund Bhd	3	600
Amanah Saham Mara Bhd	14	360
Pelaburan Johor Bhd	2	305
Asia Unit Trusts Bhd	6	300
BBMB Pacific Trust Management Bhd	2	160
Arab-Malaysia Unit Trust Bhd	2	150
BHLB Pacific Trust Management	1	100
DCM-RHB Unit Trust Management Bhd	1	100
MBf Unit Trust Management Bhd	1	100
Mayban Management Bhd	1	50
MIC Unit Trusts Bhd	3	16
Amanah Saham Pahang Bhd	1	4

Source: Malaysian Business 16/1/94

Table 3.4   Dividends and Bonuses Declared by ASN
(1981–94) and by ASB (1990–94)

Year	Dividends & Bonuses (percentages)	Value (RM million)
Amanah Saham Nasional (ASN)		
1981	20.0	75.4
1982	18.0	96.9
1983	18.0	159.8
1984	17.2	252.2
1985	17.2	361.7
1986	14.0	419.3
1987	13.0	494.1
1988	13.2	587.0
1989	14.5	852.6
1990	12.5	836.0
1991	6.25 (dividend only)	161.0
1992	8.25 (dividend only)	165.0
1993	12.5 (dividend only)	200.0
1994	14.0 (dividend only)	182.0
Amanah Saham Bumiputera (ASB)		
1990	14.0	72.0
1991	12.5	1,040.0
1992	12.5	1,361.2
1993	13.5	1,703.9
1994	13.5	2,146.7

Sources: *Investors Digest* December 1990; *The Sun* 25/11/94;
New Straits Times 1/1/95

declared by ASN between 1981 and 1994 and by ASB between 1990 and 1994. In view of the lucrative returns to investments offered by ASN, however, it was estimated that about 35 per cent of investments in the scheme in 1989 were made with bank loans (*The Star* 22/4/89).

PNB's initial portfolio was mainly from the transfer of some of Pernas' most important investments between 1982 and 1985 for a nominal RM350 million, though the market value of these investments was then over a billion ringgit (*Malaysian Business* 1/5/91). Later, other government entities – such as MARA, UDA, and its former wholly owned subsidiary, Peremba, and some SEDCs – were also compelled to transfer some important assets to PNB. This enabled PNB to develop strategic stakes in major sectors of the economy, such as the financial sector, through its acquisition of important institutions like Malayan Banking, Komplek Kewangan (M) Bhd, and subsidiaries of Bank Pembangunan (M) Bhd (Low 1985: 227; *The Star* 7/9/88).

This also helped PNB to become the country's largest institutional investor and an important player on the local stock exchange. In September 1981 PNB gained prominence with its famous 'dawn raid' to acquire a 50.41 per cent stake in the then British-controlled Guthrie Corporation, Malaysia's largest plantation company. The speed of PNB's expansion was stunning: of the share ownership of the top 145 companies listed on the bourse in 1983, just five years after incorporation, PNB was already the country's single largest shareholder, with ASN the third largest (Mehmet 1988: 111–17).

By the end of 1990 PNB held shares in 162 companies, 107 of which were publicly listed (*New Straits Times* 11/6/91). Together with ASN, PNB's assets in 1990 included 55 per cent of Malayan Banking Bhd, Malaysia's largest banking group, 93 per cent of Kumpulan Guthrie, 65.5 per cent of Golden Hope Plantations Bhd (formerly Harrisons Malaysian Plantations), 28 per cent of Sime Darby, 55 per cent of Island & Peninsular, and 50.5 per cent of the Malaysia Mining Corporation. Other major publicly listed plantation companies in which PNB had an interest during this period included Consolidated Plantations Bhd, Batu Kawan Bhd, Kuala Lumpur-Kepong Bhd and Austral Enterprises Bhd (*The Star* 18/7/89; Cheong 1990a: 174). By 31 December 1993 PNB had 26 per cent of the financial sector, 26 per cent of the hotel industry, 57 per cent of the manufacturing sector, 5 per cent of the plantation sector, 6 per cent of the property sector, and 6 per cent of the tin-mining sector (*New Straits Times* 8/6/94). Just as Pernas had an interest in a major bank, UMBC, which the public enterprise eventually had to divest, PNB also had a major stake in Bank Bumiputra, then Malaysia's largest banking group, but eventually divested its stake to Petronas in late 1984, after the enormous losses the bank incurred in the infamous BMF scandal. BMF (Bumiputra Malaysia Finance) was a Hong Kong-based subsidiary of the government-owned Bank Bumiputra, which ran up these losses allegedly because its funds had been mismanaged for speculative purposes. The scandal implicated senior members of Mahathir's administration, and Bank Bumiputra eventually had to be bailed out by Petronas, the government-owned petroleum corporation. Petronas took control of Bank Bumiputra in 1984, when it pumped in more than RM2 billion to prop up the bank. Petronas paid PNB RM1 billion and took over BMF-related loans at a write-down value of RM1.25 billion (*New Straits Times* 10/10/89).

The government needed Petronas to absorb Bank Bumiputra's losses rather than adversely affect the politically sensitive PNB's performance. The rehabilitation of Bank Bumiputra after the BMF scandal had cost RM1.5 billion by 1987. Almost all of BMF's bad loans had to be written off (*Asiaweek* 22/2/87). In 1990 Petronas had to inject another RM982.4

million into Bank Bumiputra when the bank registered a record loss of RM1.06 billion at the end of December 1989 (*The Star* 4/10/89). If ASN returns had been badly affected, adverse political repercussions for UMNO could have been expected.

By the end of 1991 ASN's investments in 67 publicly quoted companies amounted to RM2,428.73 million, while ASB's total investments were valued at RM9,791.83 million, comprising 53 listed entities and 25 unquoted companies (*The Star* 18/8/92). By the end of 1992 the value of corporate stock owned by PNB – including those owned by ASN and ASB – amounted to RM22.654 billion, making it the second largest owner of stock listed on the local bourse. By this time the largest owner of such stock was the Treasury's holding company, the Ministry of Finance Incorporated, which owned RM62.196 billion worth of listed equity. Listed as the eighth largest owner of quoted stock was another government enterprise, HICOM Holdings Bhd, listed on the Kuala Lumpur Stock Exchange in early 1994; HICOM Holdings then owned RM3.204 billion worth of listed equity (*Malaysian Business* 1/12/93).

Such implementation of the NEP through government-owned enterprises initially resulted in greater concentration of economic resources in the hands of the state. Even the extensive ownership by agencies like Pernas and PNB reflected only a fraction of the extent of actual state control of the national economy, particularly in key sectors like plantation agriculture, finance and mining. The Gerakan, a member of the ruling Barisan Nasional coalition, estimated that between 1983 and 1984, Bumiputera – including Bumiputera trust agencies – ownership of companies involved in plantation agriculture was 45 per cent, while the figure for tin-mining exceeded 50 per cent (Toh 1989). Even the strategically important banking sector, long dominated by foreigners and Chinese before the 1970s, saw remarkable changes by the early 1980s (see Case Study 3, p. 60). This inevitably led to growing discontent among the non-Bumiputeras – and much concern among those in the business community – over implementation of the NEP.

Policy Implementation and Non-Bumiputera Discontent

Even though the NEP's stated objective was the eradication of poverty irrespective of race, the weak official commitment to addressing the problems of poor Chinese in new villages and the predominantly Indian workers in the plantation sector has drawn criticism even from within the ruling Barisan Nasional coalition. By the late 1980s the Malaysian Indian Congress had even gone so far as to propose that a new positive discrimination policy be established specifically for Indians since the

Indian condition had deteriorated rapidly under the NEP (Gomez 1994: 277). The proportion of non-Bumiputera employment in the public sector declined dramatically under the NEP, while no efforts were made to restructure peasant agriculture to reduce overwhelming Malay dominance in the sector. Complaints were rife about the NEP's pro-Malay bias, even among non-Malay Bumiputeras; the Orang Asli – the aboriginal communities of which there are at least nineteen distinct tribal groups in Peninsular Malaysia – and some indigenous communities in Sabah and Sarawak claimed that they had been overlooked by the government's poverty eradication initiatives under the NEP.

Furthermore, although the government had declared that no particular group would experience any loss or feel any sense of deprivation with the implementation of the NEP, many non-Malays felt otherwise. Such fears were exacerbated when public enterprises – especially Bumiputera trust agencies – began to dominate key economic sectors, heightening non-Bumiputera and foreign business concerns about their own diminished prospects. Chinese businessmen and politicians tried unsuccessfully to steer the attention of public enterprises to business areas controlled by foreigners (Jesudason 1989: 128–32). Meanwhile foreign businessmen were concerned with the public enterprises' rapid takeover of major foreign companies, particularly those in the plantation and mining sectors. Although there was some hesitancy in taking over ethnic Chinese companies in view of the political implications, some important concerns came under state if not private Malay control; among them were two major Chinese-controlled banks, Malayan Banking (in 1966) and the UMBC (in 1976), taken over after runs on the banks. In these circumstances Chinese businessmen feared increasing uncertainty, encouraging many to prefer short-term investments offering quick returns (see Jesudason 1989: 163–4: Yoshihara 1988: 90–1; Tan 1993). Many non-Bumiputera businessmen began actively to court influential Malay politicians and senior bureaucrats to gain state access through them.

As noted earlier, the Chinese were also aware that the government's promotion of export-oriented industrialisation in the late 1960s – after coming against the limits of import-substituting industrialisation – was leading to even greater reliance on foreign capital to promote industrialisation (Jomo and Edwards 1993: 11; Fong 1989: 202–3). With limited access to technology, international markets, and capital, domestic capitalists, especially the Chinese, participated less in EOI compared to ISI, allowing foreign firms expanded control over industries (Jomo and Edwards 1993: 6–7; Crouch 1994: 21).

With the rents provided to promote manufacturing, especially EOI, the average annual growth rate of manufacturing output exceeded

Table 3.5   Malaysia: Gross Domestic Product by Sector, 1960–93
(percentages)

	1960[a]	1970	1980	1990	1993
Agriculture	40	31	23	19	16
Mining	6	6	10	10	8
Manufacturing	9	13	20	27	30
Others	45	50	47	44	46
Total	100	100	100	100	100

Note: [a] Peninsular Malaysia only
Source: Alavi 1987: 14; Ministry of Finance 1989: xii, xiii

10 per cent between 1970 and 1980, before declining to an average of 4.9 per cent during 1981–85, and then recovering to double-digit rates after 1986. By the end of the 1980s manufacturing had become a major net foreign exchange earner, reducing Malaysia's previously heavy dependence on primary exports (see Table 3.5). Within two decades, from 1970 to 1989, manufacturing's share of Malaysia's GDP doubled from only 13 per cent to 26 per cent, before increasing to 30 per cent in 1993 (Jomo and Edwards 1993: 25–8).

Given the easier profitability of protected industrial production for the domestic market and the increasing involvement of the state in the economy, investors became more interested in gaining access to government-created rents by lobbying influential Malay politicians and bureaucrats; a common method was to offer them heavily discounted stock options and directorships on the boards of companies. Such enhanced political clout provided better access to profitable business opportunities in the state-protected national economy not subject to international competition. Under these circumstances, the expenditure of resources by Chinese and foreign investors to capture such government-created rents became increasingly widespread.

The development of rent-seeking activities may therefore partly be attributed to the implementation of regulatory legislation to realise NEP objectives. In 1974 and 1975 the government enacted the Petroleum Development Act and the Industrial Coordination Act respectively, both of which were condemned by foreign and Chinese business interests. Foreign oil companies were upset with the Petroleum Development Act, which would put the country's petroleum industry under the control of the national oil agency, Petronas. The Industrial Coordination Act, ostensibly promulgated to implement the government's industrialisation policies and to ensure the orderly development and growth of industries, alarmed non-Bumiputera investors, particularly the Chinese, who perceived it as an attempt to advance Malay interests in the country's manufacturing sector at the expense of the investors and entrepreneurs. The Act's ruling that unexempted companies ensure at least 30 per cent Bumiputera participation in their ventures drew the most protests. Meanwhile the Investment Incentives Act, instituted in 1968, was also used by the government to get foreign companies to adhere to NEP guidelines on Bumiputera equity participation and employment. As Chinese protests against the Industrial Coordination Act mounted, even the MCA objected to the haste with which it was bulldozed through parliament (see *Asiaweek* 15/9/78). Although this Act was amended, first in 1977, and on several subsequent occasions, with a few more concessions each time, many Chinese investors remain adamant that it should be repealed.

Besides such legislation, in 1968 the government set up a regulatory body, the Capital Issues Committee (CIC), to regulate the growth of the capital market. By the 1970s the CIC had obtained much more clout to advance the 'indigenisation' of corporate stock in line with the NEP. CIC approval, for example, was required before companies could obtain public listing and before quoted companies could change their equity structure or their operations (Low 1985: 88). In 1992 the CIC was replaced by the Securities Commission, which possesses even more wide-ranging powers, but these have not been deployed so heavy-handedly for NEP purposes. The Foreign Investment Committee (FIC) was established to oversee foreign investments, particularly to ensure conformity to NEP guidelines. Non-Bumiputeras have also complained that other policy instruments – licensing, allocation of concessions for logging and mining, land alienation, protective tariffs and import controls – have constrained and hindered their business prospects (Low 1985: 83).

After implementation of the Industrial Coordination Act, Bumiputera participation in government-approved manufacturing projects grew between 1975 and 1985, even after such investments declined in the early 1980s, with equity participation always above 40 per cent, surpassing half on two occasions (Table 3.6). The declining Bumiputera share of such investments since 1986 is attributable to the more liberal investment policies following the mid-1980s recession. The liberalisation initiatives, including some deregulation, introduced by the government to address the recession, attracted much foreign and then domestic investment from the late 1980s.

Among the deregulation measures used by the government to attract foreign investments was the relaxation of restrictions on foreign equity in manufacturing. Between 1984 and 1985 the 30 per cent ceiling on shareholdings by foreigners was raised significantly, especially for export-oriented industries. For example, the government permitted up

Table 3.6   Malaysia: Equity Participation of Ethnic Groups in Approved
Manufacturing Projects, 1975–90 (percentages)

Year	Bumiputera	Public Enterprises	Non-Bumiputera	Foreign
1975	41.8	–	30.7	27.5
1976	40.3	–	34.8	24.9
1977	42.2	–	27.7	30.1
1978	33.3	–	29.7	37.0
1979	46.1	–	14.4	39.5
1980	40.4	–	26.7	32.9
1981	44.5	–	26.5	29.0
1982	56.3	–	16.2	27.5
1983	47.4	–	26.9	25.7
1984	42.5	–	34.8	22.7
1985	54.4	–	27.8	17.8
1986	37.6	–	34.5	28.0
1987	29.4	–	21.5	49.1
1988	12.1	11.6	18.4	57.9
1989	9.8	2.8	13.5	73.9
1990	16.4	3.5	15.7	64.3

Source: Yasuda 1991: 340–1

to 80 per cent foreign shareholding for companies producing 80 per
cent or more for export, while companies producing between 51 and
80 per cent for export were allowed to have foreign shareholdings up
to their actual export shares; where the percentage of production for
export was between 20 and 51 per cent, up to 51 per cent of the firm's
stock could be owned by foreigners. The 30 per cent ceiling then only
applied to companies exporting less than 20 per cent of its products
(Yasuda 1991: 346).

Recognising that legislation such as the Industrial Coordination
Act and regulatory bodies like the CIC and the FIC were meant to
pressure the private sector to comply with the NEP employment and
ownership objectives, many Chinese investors tried to conceal the extent
of their investments by setting up diverse and widespread cross-holding
networks. Some, especially those who owned listed vehicles, had little
choice but to restructure, contributing to a spate of rights issues in
the late 1970s. A number of prominent Chinese businessmen such as
Robert Kuok, Lim Goh Tong, Tan Chin Nam and Khoo Kay Peng by-
passed the state by diversifying their operations overseas (Tan 1993: 88).
Small, predominantly manufacturing enterprises were most affected by
the government's new constraints.

As Chinese dissatisfaction with the NEP mounted, there was a corresponding reluctance to invest in the economy. The Industrial Coordination Act resulted in a significant drop in domestic private investment and presumably encouraged capital flight. According to a Morgan Guaranty estimate, total capital flight during 1976 to 1985 amounted to US$12 billion (Khoo 1994: 165).

This situation was compounded by the MCA's declining influence within the ruling Barisan Nasional coalition. Having fared very badly in the 1969 general elections and lost influence within the expanded Barisan Nasional as the coalition incorporated a number of opposition parties with Chinese support, the MCA's standing in the eyes of the Chinese business community diminished. As greater power gravitated to the UMNO-dominated state with the implementation of the NEP, the MCA's influence within the executive also diminished. MCA leaders were no longer appointed to head the powerful Finance and Trade & Industry ministries in the 1970s; of almost two dozen cabinet ministers, barely half a dozen were non-Bumiputeras. Realising the limited capacity and ability of the MCA to protect and advance their interests with the government, Chinese businessmen – particularly the 'old' Chinese capitalists, but also newly emerging, politically influential Chinese businessmen like Loy Hean Heong, Alex Lee and Khoo Kay Peng – began recruiting Malay politicians or politically influential Malays as company directors; some businessmen even began funding UMNO or certain Malay leaders.

Since the MCA was aware of its increasing alienation from the Chinese community and perturbed by its own growing irrelevance to leading Chinese capitalists, the party sought to stem its eroding influence. Aware that small- and medium-scale Chinese businesses were most adversely affected by the NEP and that they hardly had any links with the Malay political elite, the party began to mobilise small Chinese capital. This attempt, popularly known as the corporatisation movement, was championed by politically ambitious Chinese businessmen like Tan Koon Swan and Kee Yong Wee, who cultivated their ethnic constituency into a political business movement in response to the NEP (see Gale 1985; Yeoh 1989; Gomez 1991a, 1994). Despite the MCA's involvement in the Barisan Nasional, the group's main premise was that Chinese capitalism had to be reorganised to function effectively in the increasingly politicised economy. Among the weaknesses cited by the MCA leaders as having a debilitating effect on the development of Chinese capital was the individualistic nature of much Chinese business activity. For them, 'self-help' had to be undertaken at the community level by pooling financial resources and investing strategically in the politicised business environment of the NEP (Gale 1985; Yeoh 1989;

Gomez 1991a, 1994). As small Chinese businesses began to feel that their economic interests and prospects for business development were progressively threatened by the NEP and legislation such as the Industrial Coordination Act, they became increasingly receptive to the call to pool their resources for the purposes of modernisation and consolidation.

The MCA's main vehicle to pool Chinese resources was Multi-Purpose Holdings Bhd (MPHB), incorporated in 1975 and controlled by the MCA-backed co-operative Koperatif Serbaguna (M) Bhd (KSM). MPHB, however, was only one of approximately 50 investment holding companies and co-operatives incorporated during the corporatisation movement; like MPHB, most of these businesses were also controlled by MCA leaders (see Gomez 1994: 175–239).

This was not the first time a Malaysian political party had ventured into business in a major way, ostensibly to protect the economic interests of the community it claimed to represent. The MCA had started to operate a welfare lottery in 1949 (just months after it was established), which greatly contributed to the strengthening of the party and its coffers (Heng 1988: 104). The lottery was a means of raising funds for the welfare of Chinese squatters who had been forcibly relocated in new villages during the Emergency (1948–60) to isolate the rural communist insurgency. The RM1 million-prize lottery, which was only open to members, rapidly increased the MCA's membership. However, after complaints by other parties that the lottery gave the MCA an unfair financial advantage, it was discontinued by the British authorities in 1953 (Khong 1984: 174). In 1968 the MCA had established KSM when UMNO members were calling for increased state intervention, which led to the incorporation of several public enterprises to advance Malay economic interests.

Before the MCA, UMNO had attempted to go into business in 1946, merely months after its formation, by establishing companies involved in banking, transportation and trading, purportedly to benefit the Malays. Because of the party's lack of business acumen and expertise, however, these ventures failed to develop (Funston 1980: 85–7).

The MIC helped establish the National Land Finance Cooperative Society (NLFCS) in 1960. This co-operative was meant to pool the resources of Indian plantation workers to acquire estates sold by foreign owners who were fearful that their estates would be nationalised after Independence. These estates had been acquired by local businessmen fairly cheaply, fragmented, and then sold, usually for huge profits; in the process, unemployment among plantation workers increased substantially. The MIC claimed that the NLFCS would be able not only to resolve the unemployment problem but also to enable Indian plantation workers to become landowners (Gomez 1994: 248–54). This helped substantially to raise support for the MIC from working-class Indians; they remain the party's most important source of support. During the 1970s at least three other cooperatives, all linked to various MIC leaders, were also established. None of them, however, emerged as major business enterprises (see Gomez 1994: 248–54).

Although the MCA's involvement in business did not make a major impact immediately, things began to change in the 1970s after the implementation of the NEP, as MPHB began to use its large financial base and access to bank loans to acquire a number of publicly listed companies. With these acquisitions under MPHB, by 1982 – within just seven years – the company had become the second largest company on the local stock exchange, with interests in many sectors of the economy, including gaming, wholesaling, manufacturing, shipping, property development and finance (Gale 1985; Yeoh 1989; Gomez 1994: 198–223). Although MPHB was at first a phenomenal success, after mismanagement of the company's funds by its directors, including Tan Koon Swan, who became the MCA president, the company came very close to bankruptcy. MPHB was eventually taken over by Kamunting Bhd, controlled by T. K. Lim and his family, who had close ties with Daim's family (Gomez 1994: 211–19).

Observing the apparent success of the MPHB and the failure of the MIC-related co-operatives to make significant inroads into the corporate sector, Maika Holdings Bhd was launched by the party in the early 1980s as a vehicle for the expansion of Indian corporate wealth. After much publicity, Indians, particularly those from the lower middle and working classes, poured their savings into Maika Holdings, an unlisted public company; taking a cue from Malays who had borrowed to buy ASN units, many Indians borrowed to invest in the company. With its large capital base, Maika Holdings managed to obtain stakes in companies involved in banking, insurance, manufacturing and the electronic media. After the privatisation policy was introduced, Maika Holdings also benefited, gaining interests in the government-controlled and publicly listed Malaysia Airlines Bhd (MAS), Malaysian International Shipping Corporation Bhd, Edaran Otomobil Nasional Bhd (EON), and Syarikat Telekom (M) Bhd (STM), when their equity was sold to the public. Unlike the MCA, which had never enjoyed such opportunities, the MIC's Maika Holdings had some limited access to government patronage. Despite cautious involvements in the corporate sector, Maika Holdings has been mainly a loss-making concern, except when it sold its assets. It still functions primarily as a holding company, and has yet to fulfil its much touted objective of being the vanguard of Indian capital accumulation (see Gomez 1994: 240–86).

The involvement of non-Bumiputera political parties in business can therefore be attributed to the need to be seen to be responding to the NEP and UMNO efforts at capital accumulation ostensibly on behalf of the Malays. Reference to the NEP and such pro-Malay efforts was therefore invoked to mobilise and secure ethnic support for the Barisan Nasional parties among the Chinese and Indian communities.

Maika Holdings, for example, managed to raise more than RM100 million at a time when the Malaysian economy was in recession. The company even managed to attract funds from the Indian middle class, who had long been wary of the MIC's caste and communal politics. In the case of the MCA's MPHB, most of its funds were obtained from working- and middle-class Chinese, many of whom had previously refrained from supporting what they perceived to be a bourgeois party.

Despite the decline of domestic private investment after the Industrial Coordination Act, and capital flight in response to uncertainties over the future of Chinese capital in Malaysia, the proportion of non-Bumiputera stock ownership in 1980 rose to 40.1 per cent, from 30.4 per cent in 1971. In spite of the absolute and relative increase in Chinese capital, Chinese access to state power was generally more circumscribed compared to the 1960s, hence necessitating new business strategies.

Thus Chinese businessmen have increasingly co-opted influential UMNO politicians and Malay ex-civil servants as directors of their companies. Among the prominent former government employees to emerge as directors of Chinese-controlled publicly listed companies in 1994 were the former inspector-general of police, Haniff Omar, and the former attorney-general, Abu Talib Othman. Haniff is currently a director of the major gaming entities Genting Bhd and Resorts World Bhd, controlled by Lim Goh Tong, while Abu Talib is a director of Tan Chin Nam's construction and property development concern Tan & Tan Bhd, and chairman of Malaysian French Bank Bhd, controlled by T. K. Lim's Multi-Purpose Holdings Bhd (*New Straits Times* 5/9/94). Prominent UMNO leaders also have close ties with Chinese companies; Tengku Adnan Tengku Mansor, an UMNO Supreme Council member and former treasurer of UMNO Youth, is a director and shareholder of Berjaya Singer Bhd, controlled by Vincent Tan Chee Yioun, while Mohd Tamrin Abdul Ghafar, the son of ex-Deputy Prime Minister Ghafar Baba and a former member of parliament himself, is also a director of Malayan United Industries (MUI) Bhd, controlled by Khoo Kay Peng (Cheong 1993: 38–40, 180–2).

By the 1990s even medium-scale Chinese companies were beginning to incorporate influential Bumiputeras as directors. Haniff Omar, for instance, is also chairman of the publicly listed General Corporation Bhd, controlled by Low Keng Huat. Ghafar Baba was appointed chairman of Union Paper Bhd, a Chinese-controlled toilet-paper manufacturer listed on the second board of the KLSE. Other former senior UMNO ministers like Hamzah Abu Samah and Mohamed Khir Johari are directors of Malayan Flour Mills Bhd and MUI respectively (Cheong 1993: 167–80). Tengku Adnan is also a director of a number of other smaller Chinese companies, among them EMC Logistics Bhd, Minho Bhd, Topgroup Holdings Bhd, and Unza Holdings Bhd (*New Straits Times* 1/6/94; *The Star* 1/5/94).

Mutually lucrative ties between Chinese businesses and the Malay political elite appear to have been forged by subtle means. Some Chinese businessmen have, for instance, been known to finance ambitious politicians as a means of gaining access to government patronage. In fact, as UMNO experienced increasing factionalisation in the mid-1980s and again in the 1990s, the support of some Chinese businessmen became crucial for some factions to raise funds for their political campaigns. The Hong Leong Group, for example, controlled by Quek Leng Chan, appears to have attained a mutually profitable quid pro quo relationship with senior political leaders (see Case Study 4, p. 66).

Thus while small- and medium-sized Chinese companies probably still adhere to the notion of Chinese unity and the mobilisation of community resources for mutual economic benefit, the orientation of the individual corporate leaders is one which appears to be moving away from the Chinese community in a quest for Malay patronage and, more recently, overseas business opportunities. By distancing itself from its communal roots, this group may be inclined to identify itself more closely with the interests and needs of Bumiputera capitalists and the requirements of a Bumiputera-dominated state. To the extent that these leading corporate figures are distant from the Chinese political leadership, it is difficult for the MCA to exercise influence at the political centre, thus enhancing UMNO hegemony.

One of the implications of this is that Chinese business leaders appear to have decided that networking with other Chinese businesses and with the socio-economic and political institutions of the community has little to offer them in terms of either financing, social status or political influence. Rather, leading Chinese business groups appear to have chosen a two-pronged strategy: working closely with Bumiputera political patrons to achieve business success in Malaysia, while at the same time building relations with non-Malaysian – preferably other so-called 'Overseas Chinese' – capital that can serve as a potential source of wealth should conditions in Malaysia deteriorate (Heng 1992). Yet even while Malay political patronage is crucial for successful business activities, the Chinese businessman is always on an uncertain footing, for his patrons can easily be swept aside by shifting political tides. For example, some Chinese businessmen who were closely linked with Razaleigh Hamzah, the influential former Finance Minister and a front-runner for the premiership who eventually formed a new opposition Malay party, found themselves alienated from both Malay and Chinese businessmen.

Bumiputeras and the NEP

Since the 1980s, government policies to assist Malays have tended to favour larger business interests rather than smaller companies. Larger, politically well-connected enterprises have enjoyed better access to government-created rents as business size and political influence have interacted as part of the new Malay idiom of power in contemporary Malaysia. In addition, commercial banks have also been more inclined to provide credit to large establishments.

These and other problems have restricted the capacity of small businesses to accumulate capital, in turn limiting their voice and political influence and hence access to government patronage. Lack of technological capacity and skilled labour, market limitations and competition have also kept their turnover and profits low, thus inhibiting their ability to accumulate further. There have been, for instance, frequent conflicts between small Malay contractors and public enterprises like Pernas, the SEDCs, and the UDA. The government, however, has been able to control them to some extent by appearing to be responsive to their complaints and demands. In fact since a significant number of public enterprises had emerged within a short time, mainly in the 1970s, there was also some competition among them.

In addition, small Malay enterprises have to compete with companies owned or controlled by politicians which are generally assured of favourable government treatment, particularly in the award of licences and contracts, and in terms of access to finance and information. This has enabled their enterprises to do well in areas of business in which political patronage is crucial, such as real property, construction, transport, supplies, logging, mining and finance. As Table 3.7 shows, by the late 1980s politically linked Bumiputera businessmen figured prominently as corporate leaders and shareholders of major publicly listed companies. Not surprisingly, UMNO members involved in business complained that 'elected representatives should not use their position to do business to the extent that they affect opportunities for other Bumiputeras' (*The Star* 31/10/88).

A 1992 study of corporate stock ownership by directors of publicly listed companies disclosed that only two Bumiputeras were among the top ten owners of such equity in the country, with the rest being

Table 3.7   Distribution of Bumiputera Directors by
               Occupation, Rank Status, and Political Affiliation

	Percentage
Occupation	
Businessmen	27
Professionals	16
Politicians	20
Civil servants	22
Army/Police	5
Royalty	8
Rank Status	
With titles	55
Without titles	45
Political Affiliation	
With	90
Without	10

Source: Low 1985: Tables 4.13 and 4.14

Chinese. However, the two listed Bumiputeras – Halim Saad, at number two, and his wife Noraini Zolkifli at number ten – collectively owned almost RM2.4 billion worth of corporate stock, almost RM380 million more than the value of the equity held by the director with the largest shareholdings, Quek Leng Chan of the Hong Leong Group. Halim Saad, a close associate of former Finance Minister Daim Zainuddin, had publicly acknowledged in 1987 that he held corporate equity in trust for UMNO, though party leaders have subsequently denied that UMNO still has corporate assets. Halim had significant interests in five publicly listed entities – Renong Bhd, the Faber Group Bhd, Kinta Kellas plc, TV3, and the New Straits Times Press Bhd (NSTP) – while his wife owned shares in Renong; all of these companies are closely linked to UMNO and had been, until the early 1990s, directly owned by the party. Also figuring prominently in the study, at thirteenth spot, was Halim's former right-hand man, Anuar Othman, who had also publicly announced that he was acting as UMNO's business proxy; Anuar owned RM453.27 million worth of corporate stock in Renong and United Engineers (M) Bhd (UEM), another major UMNO-related listed company (see *Malaysian Business* 16/4/92). By early 1994 Anuar Othman had relinquished his interests in Renong and UEM, reportedly after a disagreement with Halim Saad. It is uncertain, however, to whom Anuar divested his interests in the two companies, though it is probable that Halim took control of the equity.

There appears to be a common thread in the mode of development of new Bumiputera capitalists like Halim Saad. A number of them have thrived with great assistance from the government and by acting as proxies for political patrons; though professing to be independent, many of those in the latter category remain crony capitalists. This has given them greater access to rent opportunities distributed by the government, such as privatisation opportunities and contracts, for the expansion of their businesses. Most new Bumiputera capitalists have inevitably been criticised for being rentiers, rather than genuine entrepreneurs – although, as Schumpeter has recognised, entrepreneurs have also captured rents – (see Yoshihara 1988; Clad 1989; Mehmet 1990; Gomez 1994). In Malaysia their methods of accumulating wealth are rarely characterised by long-term productive investments for exports, that is, facing international competition. Instead, short-term rentier activities in the state-regulated national economy have been the norm for such accumulation.

Moreover, most rentiers who have had access to government patronage have abused or wasted all the rents made available to them by the government. If well deployed or used, such rents can be the basis for entrepreneurial activity and further accumulation, even without government assistance, though this has tended to be exceptional in the Malaysian experience. The example of Shamsuddin Kadir of Sapura Holdings Sdn Bhd suggests such productive use of rents (see Case Study 5, p. 72).

Shamsuddin Kadir, who has become a leading figure in the telecommunications industry by deploying well the captured rents to develop Sapura Holdings is not, however, representative of how most other well-connected Bumiputera businessmen have accumulated wealth in the corporate sector. Some would even argue that he represents the exception that proves the rule. Rather, the rampant abuse of political patronage has encouraged much unproductive business activity. Such rentier interests seldom stay in a particular field of business, but instead seek to capture available rentier opportunities virtually regardless of previous experience or expertise unless the likelihood of capture of such rents is remote. Hence the conglomerate style of growth has become the mode of expansion for many such Malaysian companies. In most instances, such conglomerates have been developed via publicly listed vehicles. Financial requirements have been reduced by market manoeuvres such as reverse takeovers, equity swaps and shares-for-property swaps, while the necessary funds have often been provided by government-controlled banks (see Gomez 1990; 1991a; 1994).

Such patronage has also characterised UMNO's involvement in business. UMNO, through its holding company, Fleet Holdings Sdn Bhd (and its wholly owned subsidiary, the Fleet Group), began acquiring considerable equity from around 1972. Its initial target was to gain control of the main newspaper company, NSTP, then controlled by Singaporeans and British. It was also hoped that Fleet Holdings would generate enough funds to reduce UMNO's financial dependence on the MCA and on Chinese businessmen (Gomez 1990: 52). After Mahathir became the president of the party in 1981 and appointed Daim Zainuddin chairman of Fleet Holdings, the company became a major corporate player (see Gomez, 1990, 1991a, 1994). With state intervention to enhance Malay wealth a key premise of the NEP, state access became an increasingly important means of such accumulation. Individual Malay businessmen strengthened their ties with UMNO leaders to gain better access to business opportunities. However, as UMNO's ownership of the corporate sector increased substantially, many individual ambitions were frustrated by direct UMNO involvement in the corporate sector besides having to contend with other politically linked companies and, increasingly rarely, with public enterprises for government contracts, licences and other such business opportunities.

Thus the emergence of the new Malay middle and business classes through political patronage led to increased friction over access to rents. UMNO was torn between its own financial needs, the ambitions of those ostensibly acting on behalf of the party, and its obligations as 'protector' to and 'patron' of Malays desiring to accumulate. Access to lucrative business opportunities became increasingly scarce as competition among Malays grew.

In 1991, through a complicated series of share swaps, takeovers and mergers, Fleet Holdings became the holding company of publicly listed Renong Bhd, which had emerged as one of Malaysia's largest conglomerates with a total group capitalisation of between RM6 and RM7 billion (see Gomez 1994). Through an intriguing network of cross-holdings involving a number of private and publicly listed companies, the previously ailing Renong had, by mid-1991, obtained significant interests in the media, construction and financial sectors, led by a coterie of young Bumiputera executives, which included Halim Saad and Anuar Othman, who had been groomed by Daim from the early 1980s (Gomez 1991a: 8–11). The rapid conglomeratisation of the Renong Group and its dominant if not near monopoly position in some important economic activities is clearly attributable to executive patronage. It is quite possible that actual accountability to the UMNO leadership in these affairs is a fiction.

It has been speculated that to conceal the actual extent of the empire that he had built up, both for UMNO and for himself, Daim had placed these holdings under the control of trusted third parties (see Case Studies 1, p. 53 and 8, 9, pp. 138–52). It is still unclear, however, to what extent the companies Daim's proxies control are held for him, UMNO, or some other interests. These links between politics and business have become increasingly apparent, but also complex, especially with intensifying factionalism and power struggles within UMNO (see Chapter 5).

Thus the NEP's 30 per cent Malay wealth ownership target (often invoked as an ethnic cudgel to advance particular Malay business interests), has enabled influential Malay politicians and businessmen with close links to UMNO leaders to amass wealth for themselves. NEP privileges – claimed in the name of the mass of ordinary Bumiputeras – have mainly been appropriated by the better connected in the Bumiputera community.

Such concentration of wealth among select Bumiputera individuals is evident in corporate ownership figures. Bumiputera ownership of corporate equity steadily increased from 1.5 per cent in 1969 until the early 1980s; by 1980 this figure had increased to 12.5 per cent, before rising to 18.7 per cent in 1983 and then almost levelling off to 20.3 per cent in 1990. However, a significant change in share ownership among Bumiputeras has occurred since 1980 with the private individual's share of the Bumiputera stake increasing phenomenally from 39 per cent in 1983 to 68 per cent in 1990. This change is a reflection of the new emphasis on private Bumiputera wealth accumulation under Mahathir's leadership instead of the previous mode of accumulating trust agencies on behalf of the community.

The centralisation of political power among top UMNO leaders and the related rise of authoritarianism in the 1980s have contributed to the concentration of wealth among politically well-connected Bumiputeras. In such a situation, continued factionalism within UMNO raises questions about how conflicts among these factions affect the corporate sector. This state of affairs also contradicts the free-market rhetoric propounded by Mahathir and impedes the development of a more dynamic, entrepreneurial and progressive form of capitalism in Malaysia.

Case Study 1: Daim Zainuddin

Daim Zainuddin, born in 1938 in Kedah, worked as a teacher before studying law in England in the late 1950s. He began his career as a lawyer with a private firm in Kelantan, then worked as a government prosecutor and magistrate, before turning to the private sector. His first commercial activity, the production of table salt and plastics, which he ventured into in the late 1960s, was a failure. It was only in 1973, when he acquired a lucrative piece of land on the outskirts of Kuala Lumpur, apparently obtained because of his close association with certain UMNO leaders, that his business fortunes improved appreciably. According to *Asiaweek* (27/7/82), it was Daim's close association with the then Mentri Besar (Chief Minister) of Selangor, Harun Idris, that enabled him to acquire the land.

Daim also became a close associate of Mahathir – though both of them reputedly hail from the same urban quarter of Alor Setar, the considerable gap between their ages meant that they did not get to know each other until much later in life – who as Deputy Prime Minister appointed him first chairman of Peremba in 1979; Peremba was then owned by the government's Urban Development Authority. After becoming UMNO president and prime minister in 1981, in 1982 Mahathir appointed Daim chairman of UMNO's investment arm, Fleet Holdings Sdn Bhd, which operated through its wholly owned subsidiary the Fleet Group Sdn Bhd. Daim's appointment was also attributed to Mahathir's apparent desire to promote the growth of Fleet Holdings through more active management, which could then serve as an example of how a Bumiputera company could progress (see *Asian Wall Street Journal* 9/8/82). Acting in this triple capacity as private business-man, government appointee and party trustee, Daim was involved in a myriad business activities involving companies he controlled in his different capacities (Gomez 1990: 37–43).

In April 1983 Daim secured control of publicly listed Raleigh Bhd (now renamed the Berjaya Group) through a part-cash, part-share swap deal; he exchanged his total equity in his family property development concern, Taman Bukit Maluri Sdn Bhd, for a 33.27 per cent stake in the listed company and RM30 million cash. Later, in May 1983, through Seri Iras Sdn Bhd, a company owned and controlled by him and his close associate Tajudin Ramli, Daim increased their stake in the Berjaya Group by another 33.33 per cent. One month later, in June 1983, the publicly listed Faber Group Bhd, a company controlled by UMNO's Fleet Group, acquired part of the large land bank owned by Taman Bukit Maluri, which was by then wholly owned by the Berjaya Group. This enabled the Berjaya Group to recover a substantial portion of the payment made to purchase Taman Bukit Maluri from Daim. At the time of these transactions, apart from his personal stake in the Berjaya Group and his control of Faber through Fleet Group, Daim also owned equity in Faber; Daim's stake in Faber was later sold to the Fleet Group (Gomez 1990: 38–40).

In 1982, in another major corporate transaction, the government-owned Peremba had a 33 per cent stake in the publicly listed Sime UEP Bhd, which was developing Subang Jaya, a major 646-hectare residential and commercial development area. In December 1982 Baktimu Sdn Bhd, owned by Daim, bought a 33 per cent stake in Sime UEP from Bandar Raya Developments Bhd, the property development arm of the then MCA-controlled Multi-Purpose Holdings Bhd, for RM75 million cash. Part of the loan for the acquisition, amounting to RM40 million, was obtained from the Singapore branch of the Union Bank of Switzerland; the loan was approved by the Union Bank only after the government-owned Bank Bumiputra issued a guarantee on Baktimu's behalf as security for the credit (*Asian Wall Street Journal* 24/8/84). Since Daim now had, through Baktimu and Peremba, almost 66 per cent control of Sime UEP, assets owned by UEP were sold to Faber in May 1984 in a shares-for-assets swap; UEP obtained an 11 per cent stake in Faber by selling its entire equity in the Subang Merlin Hotel to Faber for an allegedly over-valued price of RM56.25 million (see *New Straits Times* 23/4/87).

In June 1984 Daza Sdn Bhd (later renamed Tekal), another Daim-owned company, acquired for RM74.81 million a 20 per cent stake in the publicly listed NSTP from Times Publishing Bhd of Singapore; at that time the UMNO-owned Fleet Group had a substantial stake in NSTP. Around the same time, rights and bonus issues were announced, for which Daza had to get further loans. Daza eventually incurred a huge debt of RM70.65 million from its acquisition of the shares and the rights issue. Despite this, Fleet Trading & Manufacturing Sdn Bhd, a wholly owned subsidiary of UMNO's Fleet Group, acquired Daza for RM1 million in August 1984. Now with almost 76 per cent of equity in NSTP, the Fleet Group attempted to sell a 25 per cent stake in the listed company to Faber for a massive RM141.9 million. The deal, however, was later aborted as Faber – badly affected by economic recession, poor performance and large, unserviced loans – could not honour the payment (Gomez 1990: 84–8).

In most of Daim's major deals, a number of his close associates have figured prominently, namely Halim Saad, Mohd Razali Mohd Rahman, Wan Azmi Wan Hamzah and Tajudin Ramli. Apart from the fact that all these men had worked with Daim in Peremba, Halim Saad was also linked with Daza. Mohd Razali also had associations with Daza, Taman Bukit Maluri, and Baktimu. Tajudin Ramli was connected to Seri Iras, Taman Bukit Maluri, the Fleet Group and Fleet Trading & Manufacturing, while Wan Azmi had worked with Daza, the Fleet Group, NSTP and Sime UEP. Wan Azmi was also responsible for negotiating the NSTP acquisition from the Singapore-based Times Publishing (Gomez 1990: 43–5; see also Case Studies 8 and 9, pp. 138–52).

Despite having no previous ministerial experience, but probably because of his limited grass-roots support and apparent lack of political ambition, Daim was appointed Finance Minister and UMNO treasurer by Mahathir in 1984. In the light of an increasingly fractious UMNO, following the two contests for the deputy presidency between party stalwarts Musa Hitam and Razaleigh Hamzah, it seemed important for Mahathir that the powerful Finance Ministry be entrusted to someone 'reliable' and personally loyal; although Mahathir had openly supported Musa for the deputy presidency, it later became clear that the UMNO president did not fully trust his deputy. Although Daim later resigned as Finance Minister in 1991, he remains UMNO treasurer, and was appointed government economic adviser. He is also considered an influential power-broker, mainly because he enjoys Mahathir's trust and remains his closest political confidant.

When appointed to the Treasury in 1984, the value of Daim's stock listed on the local bourse was estimated at US$151 million, while his total net assets were estimated at around US$259 million (Lent 1991: 41). Following a cabinet directive in 1986, Daim reportedly divested his vast business interests, which included, by his own admission, interests in important companies such as United Malayan Banking Corporation, Sime Darby, Technology Resources Industries (TRI), Sistem Televisyen Malaysia (TV3), Cold Storage, Guthrie Ropel, Malayan Banking, Tasik Cement, Oriental Holdings, Bolton Properties, Idris Hydraulic, Malayan Flour, Industrial Oxygen, SPK and Syarikat Permodalan & Perusahaan Perak Bhd (SPPPB). Though not all these companies were publicly listed, they were involved in virtually all the key sectors of the economy such as banking, broadcasting, plantations, manufacturing, retailing, property development and construction (Gomez 1990: 43). According to one 1992 estimate, the total value of corporate assets owned by Daim was approximately RM1 billion. This included assets he owned in Australia, Britain, Mauritius and the United States (*The Star* 19/5/92). Although Daim claims that he does not actively participate in corporate activities, he is widely regarded as the most powerful figure in the Malaysian corporate scene.

Case Study 2: The UMBC Saga

The United Malayan Banking Corporation Bhd (UMBC), Malaysia's third largest bank in terms of assets, was once controlled by Chang Ming Thien, who sold, in June 1981, a significant stake in the bank to Multi-Purpose Holdings Bhd, a publicly listed company then controlled by UMNO's leading partner in the Barisan Nasional, the MCA. Earlier, when UMBC directors were suspected of diverting bank funds to themselves in 1976, Bank Negara had intervened to restructure the ownership and management of UMBC. Pernas was then brought in as a

30 per cent shareholder (Jesudason 1989: 93, 107). When Multi-Purpose Holdings acquired its 41 per cent stake in UMBC in 1981, Pernas increased its share to the same level, giving them both joint and equal control of the bank. This, however, led to policy and management disagreements, and when it was disclosed that Petronas had also acquired a 9 per cent stake in UMBC, Multi-Purpose Holdings realised that its attempt to control the bank was futile. The MCA holding company's interests in UMBC were subsequently divested in 1984 to companies controlled by Daim Zainuddin, soon to be Finance minister, for RM125 million cash and a 51 per cent controlling stake in the Malaysian French Bank, then a relatively minor bank. In late 1986 Daim divested his stake in UMBC to Pernas for a profit (see *Asian Wall Street Journal* 31/5/88). Finding the holding costs of its interests in UMBC too high to absorb, Pernas was open about its desire to liquidate its interests in the bank.

A highly profitable merger with the Development & Commercial (D&C) Bank was proposed in early 1991, but eventually fell through when the terms set by Pernas for the takeover could not be met. Later, although it was reported that PNB was interested in acquiring UMBC, the takeover did not materialise.

Among the other companies apparently also interested in UMBC were UMNO-linked entities like Idris Hydraulic (M) Bhd, and some companies controlled by Bumiputeras with close ties to top UMNO leaders, such as Land & General Bhd (run by Wan Azmi Wan Hamzah, who also has an indirect stake in the D&C Bank), Advance Synergy Bhd (controlled by Ahmad Sebi Abu Bakar, a close associate of both Daim and Deputy Prime Minister Anwar Ibrahim), and Setron (M) Bhd (in which Kamaruddin Jaafar, probably Anwar's closest confidant, has an interest) (*Malaysian Business* 1/2/92).

In spite of the interests of some major companies in UMBC, in July 1992, a minor, ailing British-controlled publicly listed company, Datuk Keramat Holdings Bhd, involved in tin-smelting and without previous banking experience, acquired the bank. Majority control of Datuk Keramat Holdings was with a Bumiputera company, Meridien Best Sdn Bhd. In the multifaceted transaction, Bakti Kilat Sdn Bhd, a wholly owned subsidiary of Meridien Best, initially acquired a 20 per cent stake in UMBC. Bakti Kilat was then sold to Datuk Keramat Holdings via a share-swap which gave Meridien Best 30.3 per cent control of Datuk Keramat Holdings. Later Pernas also acquired a 20 per cent stake in Datuk Keramat Holdings, which gave it an indirect stake in UMBC. The reasons for this decision by Pernas have never been revealed by either the government or Pernas officials (see Figure 3.2). Meridien Best, interestingly, is owned by Mohamed Noor Yusof, popularly known as Mohamed Noor Azam, a former political secretary of Prime Minister

Mahathir, and currently also chairman of the listed UMNO-linked company TV3; he is reputedly also closely associated with Deputy Prime Minister Anwar (see *The Star* 20/7/92, 22/7/92). Mohamed Noor Yusof's acceptability to Anwar was implied when he retained the chairmanship of TV3 after the management buy-out of the company in early 1993 by supporters of the Deputy Prime Minister (see Case Study 4, p. 66).

By 1994 Bakti Kilat had been renamed UMBC Holdings Sdn Bhd, and Datuk Keramat Holdings' stake in UMBC, through this holding company, amounted to 60.33 per cent, which had been acquired for a total sum of RM600 million; in order to comply with the Banking and Financial Institutions Act 1989, however, Datuk Keramat Holdings was given five years by Bank Negara – after the central bank had unsuccessfully opposed the sale of UMBC to Datuk Keramat Holdings – to reduce its interest in the bank to 20 per cent; under the Act, a corporate shareholder of a bank can own no more than 20 per cent of its equity, while an individual shareholder's interest is limited to 5 per cent (*The Star* 20/9/93; *New Straits Times* 15/7/94). By early 1994 other major

Figure 3.2   Ownership Structure of UMBC After the Takeover by Datuk Keramat Holdings

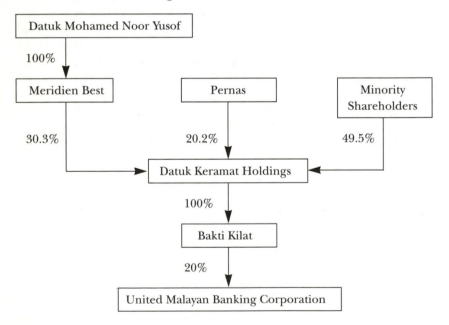

Source: *The Star* 24/7/92

shareholders of Datuk Keramat Holdings were Meridian Best, with 32.8 per cent of equity, and Pernas with 7.7 per cent, while UMNO's co-operative, Koperasi Usaha Bersatu Bhd (KUB) had obtained a 10 per cent stake in the company (*The Star* 20/9/93). By this time KUB, which has been an important beneficiary and tool of political patronage, had come under the control of Anwar's close associates.

The questionable sale of UMBC to Mohamed Noor Yusof and UMNO's eventual indirect stake in the bank is one of many cases of processes by which the interests of the political elite have been served by government decisions, ostensibly to redistribute wealth and create Malay entrepreneurs. In view of the limited business experience and entrepreneurial potential of those gaining this rent and the limited transparency in the sale of UMBC, it was probably inevitable that the bank's operations would become subject to allegations of corruption.

After the UMBC takeover by Datuk Keramat Holdings, although the bank registered a pre-tax profit of RM190.7 million at the end of 1993, it was involved in several banking irregularities, including the disbursement of questionable loans; it was alleged that loans to some prominent businessmen had been approved without following the proper procedures, and the bank had also violated banking regulations by channelling loans to related parties to enable Datuk Keramat Holdings to acquire the publicly listed George Town Holdings Bhd, a pharmaceutical and consumer products retailer (*Malaysian Business* 1/8/94). The chairman of George Town Holdings was Tunku Abdullah of the Melewar Group, a close friend of Prime Minister Mahathir, while another director of the company was Shuaib Lazim, a former senator from Kedah and a close associate of both Mahathir and Daim (KLSE 19 (II) 1993: 381–3).

The controversies involving UMBC heightened when it was further alleged that the bank was being run by an official who had not been approved by the central bank. Although these allegations precipitated an investigation by Bank Negara into UMBC's activities, no charges were ever filed by the authorities (see *Malaysian Business* 1/8/94; *Malaysian Industry* July 1995).

In July 1995, apparently after covert pressure from the government, Datuk Keramat Holdings proposed to divest its entire stake in UMBC to Sime Darby Bhd, the conglomerate controlled by the government through PNB (*New Straits Times* 13/7/95). It was expected that UMBC would be sold for between RM1 billion and RM1.4 billion, which would give Datuk Keramat Holdings a profit of between RM400 million and RM800 million for its brief – less than two years – investment in the bank (*Malaysian Industry* July 1995).

Case Study 3: Capturing the Banking Sector

Besides the predominantly British foreign banks, almost all local banks incorporated in Malaya before Independence were owned by Chinese. Most Chinese banks were established almost half a century after British banks had started operating. The first Malay bank, the Malay National Banking Corporation, was only incorporated in Kuala Lumpur in 1947, almost 50 years after the first Chinese bank was established, but ceased operations in 1952 (Lim Chong-Yah 1969: 233). Of the 26 banks in Malaya in 1959, only six were locally incorporated. By 1990, however, there were 39 commercial banks, of which sixteen were foreign-incorporated and 23 were locally domiciled (*Malaysian Business* 16/4/91). In 1970 Malay share ownership in banking and insurance came to only 3.3 per cent, while the Chinese held 24.3 per cent, Indians 0.6 per cent, and foreigners a dominant 52.2 per cent (see Table 2.5, p. 20). By 1986, however, ownership or management control of banking services by Bumiputeras and government agencies had increased to between 60 and 70 per cent (Hing 1987: 411).

Malayan Banking Bhd, currently Malaysia's largest bank in terms of assets – the relative sizes of banks vary when compared in terms of assets, shareholder funds or deposits – was first established and controlled by a prominent Chinese tycoon, Khoo Teck Puat. The son of a wealthy Singaporean landowner, Khoo joined the Oversea-Chinese Banking Corporation (OCBC) as a clerk in 1933 and worked himself up to the position of deputy general manager while simultaneously building up a sizeable stake in the bank. Since he could not get a place on the OCBC board after differences with Tan Chin Tuan, the bank's main share-holder, Khoo left the bank to establish Malayan Banking (*Far Eastern Economic Review* 4/12/86).

Incorporated on 31 May 1960 and publicly listed on 17 January 1962, Malayan Banking expanded so rapidly that within five years it had 109 branches, both locally and abroad (Gill 1985: 19). In 1966, however, after rumours that Khoo was channelling bank funds to his own companies, there was a massive run on Malayan Banking, which wiped out 40 per cent of its deposit base in just ten days (Yoshihara 1988: 204–5; *Far Eastern Economic Review* 4/12/86). In 1967 Bank Negara stepped in to restructure Malayan Banking, bringing it under direct control later that year. Majority ownership of Malayan Banking was later transferred to the government-controlled PNB, which has almost 55 per cent of the bank's equity, although it is a publicly listed company.

By 1992 Malayan Banking had a total of 287 branches, and had also acquired around 99 per cent of the once Chinese-controlled Kwong Yik Bank Bhd, the country's eighth largest bank. Malayan Banking has three financial subsidiaries, Mayban Finance, Mayban Finance (Singapore) and Kwong Yik Finance, as well as a 70 per cent interest in Aseam Bankers, a merchant bank. Malayan Banking has majority control of two insurance companies: a 70 per cent stake in Mayban Assurance and 51 per cent equity in Universal Life and General Insurance (*Malaysian Business* 1/4/90).

Bank Bumiputra Bhd, once seen as the flagship of Malay capital, was Malaysia's largest bank until the mid-1980s, when it was displaced by Malayan Banking. Although Bank Bumiputra has remained under government control since its inception in 1966, its equity has been shifted around among several government agencies. By 1985 Bank Bumiputra had 95 branches, both locally and abroad. In 1991 the bank was acquired from Petronas for RM1.15 billion by the Ministry of Finance Incorporated.

United Malayan Banking Corporation Bhd, the country's third largest bank, was established by a Chinese, but eventually fell under government control in 1976 after a run on the bank precipitated by allegations of mismanagement. After passing through the hands of a few state-owned and politically well-connected companies, by 1995, the government-controlled Sime Darby Bhd agreed to acquire Datuk Keramat Holdings' entire stake in UMBC (see *Malaysian Business* 1/7/95). By 1991 UMBC had 82 branches locally and nine branches abroad. Among its non-banking subsidiaries were UMBC Finance, UMBC Leasing, UMBC Nominees, UMBC Securities and a merchant bank, Asia Bank International Merchant Bankers (*The Star* 20/7/91).

The D&C Bank, the country's fifth largest bank, was established in 1965 by Henry H. S. Lee, a founding member of the MCA and the country's first Finance minister. Lee requested, and was given, a licence to establish the bank soon after he retired from government office. By the early 1980s control of the D&C Bank was equally balanced between the Lee family and Syed Kechik, who had made a fortune in Sabah as the right-hand man of the state's Chief Minister until 1976, Mustapha Harun. By 1984 the government-controlled PNB also had 10 per cent of the D&C Bank's equity. That same year Lee's son Alex, currently a Gerakan vice-president, a former deputy minister and close to Daim, was forced to resign as a director of the bank by Bank Negara, the central bank, after allegations of financial misappropriation. The Lee family transferred their 33 per cent stake in the D&C Bank to Roxy Bhd, a publicly listed company they had then just acquired. Alex Lee's personal interest in Roxy was financed by massive loans, some from Singaporean banks. Lee later had problems servicing these loans and apparently had to depend on his influential political contacts, including Mahathir and Daim, to avoid legal action.

Badly affected by the 1985–86 recession, which exacerbated its debt problem, Roxy sold 20 per cent of the D&C Bank's equity to a Singaporean company, United Industrial Corporation, which later sold this stake to the publicly listed stock-broking concern Rashid Hussain Bhd, controlled by the fast-rising and politically connected Rashid Hussain (Gomez 1991a). Roxy itself was later acquired by a Daim protégé, Tajudin Ramli, and renamed Technology Resources Industries (TRI). Among the D&C Bank's other major shareholders is Japan-based Mitsui Bank (with a 9 per cent stake), which also owns 20 per cent of the D&C Mitsui Merchant Bank Bhd, in which the D&C Bank also has an interest. The D&C Bank has 36 branches nationwide and owns a finance wing, D&C Finance, which has twelve local branches (*New Straits Times* 1/3/91).

In September 1990 Malaysia's sixth largest bank, the United Asian Bank Bhd (UAB), and the Bank of Commerce Bhd (BCB), the ninth largest bank, announced their merger through a share-swapping exercise. Renong Bhd, reputedly under UMNO control through businessmen closely associated with UMNO treasurer Daim Zainuddin, had a 64 per cent stake in BCB through two subsidiaries, Maika Holdings Bhd, a holding company controlled by the MIC, then reportedly held an 8 per cent stake in UAB.

UAB, once controlled by banks in India and associated with the Indian community in Malaysia, had passed into majority Malay ownership during the 1970s and come perilously close to receivership in 1986, when Bank Negara stepped in, injecting almost RM363 million to revive it. Bank Negara later made known its intention to divest its 74 per cent stake in UAB for cash if an acceptable bid was made (*Malaysian Business* 1/10/90). The UAB–BCB merger made the new concern – the name Bank of Commerce Bhd was retained – the fifth largest bank in the country. After the merger, Renong, through its subsidiaries, was believed to hold a controlling 33 per cent stake in BCB (*Malaysian Business* 1/10/90). Maika Holdings' stake shrank to 2.7 per cent after the merger, but in June 1991 it acquired another 11.17 million shares in BCB (*New Straits Times* 15/6/91).

Thus, within just two decades, eight of the top ten local banks, once primarily dominated by Chinese and foreign interests, were brought under the control of Bumiputera and government companies. The two exceptions were the publicly listed Public Bank Bhd, the fourth largest bank, and the Southern Bank Bhd, the tenth largest, both of which remain under Chinese control. The *Mid-Term Review of the Fifth Malaysia Plan, 1986–1990* (1989: 73) disclosed that Bumiputera interests in the commercial banking sector held more than 50 per cent of the equity in ten of the 22 domestic banks.

Since the increasing control over the financial sector implies corresponding access to lucrative bank profits largely assured by banking regulation and credit facilities as well as power in determining and enforcing conditions of credit, the desire to control the banking sector was consistent with NEP objectives. Moreover, by developing an oligopolistic bank ownership structure, indirect dominance over other sectors of the economy had been achieved (Herman 1982: 115–21).

Table 3.8 lists locally incorporated and foreign banks in terms of size of assets, while Table 3.9 gives a breakdown of banking operations controlled by local and foreign banks in 1990. In 1988 the five largest local banks accounted for 53 per cent of total bank resources, 55 per cent of total bank deposits, and 50 per cent of total bank loans (*The Star* 27/2/91). The top four foreign banks still have substantial operations in Malaysia, with sizable branch networks and deposit bases (Table 3.8). According to 1989 figures, the Hongkong Bank is the fourth largest bank in Malaysia in terms of assets. In 1990 all sixteen foreign banks had a total of 146 branches nationwide and held 24.3 per cent of total

Table 3.8   List of Local and Foreign Banks By Size of Assets, 1990

Number	Local Bank	Foreign Bank
1	Malayan Banking	Hongkong & Shanghai Bank
2	Bank Bumiputra	Standard Chartered Bank
3	UMBC	Citibank
4	Public Bank	Oversea-Chinese Banking Corp.
5	D&C Bank	Bank of Tokyo
6	UAB	Chase Manhattan Bank
7	Perwira Habib Bank	Chung Khiaw Bank
8	Kwong Yik Bank	Bank of America
9	Bank of Commerce	Overseas Union Bank
10	Southern Bank	Lee Wah Bank
11	MUI Bank	Algemene Bank Nederland NV
12	Malaysian French Bank	Bangkok Bank
13	Hock Hua Bank	Deutsche Bank AG
14	Pacific Bank	Bank of Nova Scotia
15	Oriental Bank	Security Pacific Asian Bank
16	Bank Islam	United Overseas Bank
17	Ban Hin Lee Bank	
18	Bank Utama	
19	Bank Buruh	
20	Sabah Bank	
21	Hock Hua Bank (Sabah)	
22	Wah Tat Bank	
23	Kong Ming Bank	

Sources: `Malaysian Business 16/10/91; Asian Wall Street Journal 10/7/89

Table 3.9 Comparison of Banking Data between
Local and Foreign Banks, 1990

Activity	Local Banks	Foreign Banks
Total deposits	RM62,047m	RM20,366m
Total loans	RM59,478m	RM21,285m
Loan–deposit ratio	95.9%	104.5%
Shareholder funds	RM5,818m	RM2,913m
Branch networks	852	146
Number of employees	34,169	10,079

Source: Malaysian Business 16/4/91

commercial bank assets and 25.6 per cent of total deposits in the banking system (*Malaysian Business* 16/4/91).

In 1986 the Banking Act (1973) was amended to limit the amount of equity ownership by individual companies in a bank to a maximum of 20 per cent, while a family-owned company or an individual person could own a maximum of 10 per cent in a financial institution; the amendments, however, did not apply to those who already owned more than the newly stipulated limits before the amendment (*New Straits Times* 29/10/86).

In 1989 the Banking and Financial Institutions Act was passed by Parliament, which required all foreign banks to incorporate Malaysian subsidiaries by September 1994. Although the local subsidiaries would be allowed to remain under total foreign control, they would not be allowed to open new branches if they did not Malaysianise their shareholdings (*Far Eastern Economic Review* 6/4/89). With this Act, Bank Negara also had extensive powers to supervise, regulate and investigate all financial institutions to try to ensure domestic monetary stability. The Act also prohibited banks from providing loans to companies in which their directors had an interest and required senior bankers to declare their assets (Ho 1990: 7).

Although most banks had incorporated local subsidiaries by 1994, not all had divested part of their equity to local investors. In June 1994 the Canadian-based Bank of Nova Scotia entered into negotiations with the publicly listed Idris Hydraulic Bhd for the sale of a majority interest in its locally incorporated branch; Idris Hydraulic is controlled by Ishak Ismail, a businessman-cum-politician with close ties to Finance Minister and Deputy Prime Minister Anwar Ibrahim (*New Straits Times* 16/6/94). Meanwhile the Singapore-controlled United Overseas Bank's branch in Kota Kinabalu was acquired by the publicly listed Linatex Process Rubber Bhd and merged with the ailing Cooperative Central Bank to form a new financial concern, the Newco Bank Bhd. MUI Bank was acquired by the Hong Leong group at the end of 1993 and was renamed the Hong Leong Bank, while 40 per cent of Bank Buruh's equity was acquired by the government-owned Bank Simpanan Nasional. Some other foreign banks have incorporated their Malaysian operations – among them the Standard Chartered Bank (M) Bhd, the Hongkong Bank (M) Bhd, Citibank Bhd, and the Bank of Tokyo (M) Bhd – though they have yet to relinquish any of their equity to Malaysian concerns (*Malaysian Business* 16/7/94).

Besides restrictions posed by the Banking and Financial Institution Act, banking licences have become increasingly difficult to obtain; the last new licence was issued in 1979. The official reason for not issuing banking licences is the presence of too many banks serving a small population. The government has even voiced its intention to further reduce the number of banks in the country and has been actively promoting the consolidation of existing financial institutions. Believing that there are far too many small banks in the financial market, the government is promoting mergers and hopes to eventually see the dominance of five or six major banks which, it claims, would help strengthen the banking system (see *Asiaweek* 21/6/91). Apart from these banks, by the end of 1990 Malaysia also had twelve merchant banks and 45 finance companies, with 486 branches nationwide, believed by many financial analysts and banking authorities to be too many for the country. Apparently this is another reason why Bank Negara has been encouraging mergers of financial entities in an attempt to develop Malaysia's financial market. The government has also been encouraging the larger Malaysian banks to invest in a wide range of financial services such as stockbroking, equity and property trust management, and nominee services (see *The Star* 11/7/91). In fact the Sixth Malaysia Plan anticipated considerable financial reform; for example, the Securities Commission Act 1992 was promulgated to establish the Securities Commission in March 1993 to oversee the development of Malaysia's capital market and to help develop the Kuala Lumpur Stock Exchange into a sophisticated international market (*Far Eastern Economic Review* 25/7/91; Awang 1992: 120–1).

The importance of control of the banking sector in Malaysia's financial system cannot be overemphasised. According to the Sixth Malaysia Plan, the financial sector expanded by 8.4 per cent between 1986 and 1990. Its share of the GDP increased from 8.8 per cent in 1985 to 9.7 per cent in 1990. The plan also noted that the total resources of the financial system grew at an average of 13.7 per cent per annum from RM169 billion at the end of 1985 to RM320 billion in 1990. The banking industry alone accounted for about 56 per cent of the total assets of the financial system at the end of 1990 (*New Straits Times*

11/7/90). More importantly, the big banks shape and influence invest-ment and economic activity more generally.

Case Study 4: The Hong Leong Group

Though the Hong Leong Co. is owned by the Singapore-based Kwek family, its Malaysian operations are controlled by Quek Leng Chan. Hong Leong's vast interests in the Malaysian corporate sector are held through three publicly listed companies: Hong Leong Credit Bhd, Hong Leong Industries Bhd, and Hume Industries Bhd. A fourth com-pany, the Guoco Group, controls Hong Leong's overseas invest-ments, particularly in the United Kingdom, Hong Kong, China and the Philippines. These three Malaysian listed companies have an interest in a number of other publicly quoted companies, including OYL Industries Bhd, Nanyang Press Bhd, Bedford Bhd, Mycom Bhd, Malaysian Pacific Industries Bhd, Hong Leong Bank Bhd, and Zalik Bhd. Apart from these companies, Hong Leong owns and controls over 200 other companies, which collectively posted revenue earnings of RM3.3 billion in 1993 (*Malaysian Business* 16/7/91 and 1/3/94).

Hong Leong's links with UMNO gained prominence in April 1989 when one of its listed entities, Hume Industries, made a RM1.13 billion bid to take over the ailing Multi-Purpose Holdings, the quoted con-glomerate originally developed by the MCA. The Hong Leong Group's simultaneous announcement that the UMNO-controlled UEM had awarded Hume Industries a RM500 million supplies contract for the privatised North–South Highway project led to speculation that there would be a tie-up between UEM and Hume Industries. The issue of such a tie-up arose when Hong Leong did not declare its intention to take up its entitlement in the three-for-two rights issue that Hume Industries had proposed to facilitate its takeover of Multi-Purpose Holdings. Many in the Chinese community were concerned that if Hong Leong Co. relinquished its rights to a third party representing UMNO, control of Multi-Purpose Holdings would fall into the hands of the Malay party (Gomez 1990: 130–1). Although Hume Industries' bid for Multi-Purpose Holdings was eventually called off, Hong Leong allowed an obscure Bumiputera company, Jaguh Mutiara Sdn Bhd, to obtain a majority 24 per cent stake in Hume Industries by acquiring the rights issues that it had renounced (Gomez 1994: 211–16).

Jaguh Mutiara was owned by Ismail Rashid and Anwar Batcha bin Ibram Ghaney. Ismail Rashid, a former director of UEM, is currently a director of Time Engineering Bhd, a publicly quoted company con-trolled by UEM. Anwar Batcha, once managing director of Time Engineering, was an executive of Peremba Bhd, when UMNO treasurer

Daim Zainuddin was chairman of the company. In April 1990 Fleet Group Sdn Bhd, UMNO's main holding company, acquired the entire equity of Jaguh Mutiara, thus obtaining an indirect stake in Hume Industries (Gomez 1994: 94–9).

The Hume Industries–Fleet Group link was the first major tie-up between companies controlled by Quek Leng Chan and those associated with UMNO. Later, in 1991, a significant portion of Hume Industries' 84.9 per cent interest in the listed Chinese newspaper company Nanyang Press was acquired from companies linked to Wan Azmi Wan Hamzah, chairman of the Malay and National Chambers of Commerce during 1992 to 1995, who had also worked under Daim at Peremba. Wan Azmi had acquired his stake in Nanyang Press in June 1990 through his listed flagship, Land & General Bhd, via a share swap worth RM50 million (*The Star* 6/8/90). Barely eight months later, in February 1991, Land & General sold its Nanyang Press equity for RM52 million to Peninsula Springs Sdn Bhd, whose major shareholder was Ismail Abdul Rashid, also a shareholder of Jaguh Mutiara (*New Straits Times* 9/2/91). A month later, Peninsula Springs divested its interest in Nanyang Press to Hume Industries, a company in which Quek and the UMNO-controlled Fleet Group both had major interests (*New Straits Times* 1/3/91). By April 1992 Hume Industries had reduced its stake in Nanyang Press to 75 per cent. This meant that UMNO indirectly had – via the Fleet Group, Jaguh Mutiara, and Hume Industries – a significant stake in Malaysia's leading Chinese newspaper, *Nanyang Siang Pau*, controlled by Quek.

Apart from Quek's ties to UMNO through Nanyang Press and Hume Industries, it was disclosed in February 1990 that another Hong Leong–related company, its listed brokerage concern, Zalik Bhd, was collaborating with a number of other companies closely connected to UMNO to establish the Kuala Lumpur Options and Financial Futures Exchange (KLOFFE); this financial futures trading exchange was to be owned by KLOFFE Sdn Bhd, a consortium which included three listed companies apart from Zalik: Renong Bhd, reputedly UMNO's main listed company, NSTP, then controlled by Renong, and the leading Malaysian securities firm, Rashid Hussain Bhd, owned by the politically connected Rashid Hussain.

Interestingly, Wan Azmi's Land & General had an 18 per cent stake in Rashid Hussain. Hong Leong Credit owned 38.2 per cent of Zalik's equity which in turn owned a 20 per cent stake in the Ban Hin Lee Bank Bhd. The bank, incorporated in September 1935 by the Penang-based Yeap family, went public in 1990; it then had eighteen branches and was ranked twelfth in terms of asset size. Another major shareholder of Zalik equity, with a 12.5 per cent stake, was Zahari Abdul Wahab, a director of

Fibroceil Manufacturing Sdn Bhd, which owned an interest in Time
Engineering, controlled by UEM and Renong. Apart from Quek Leng
Chan, Mohd Sofi Abdul Ghafar, son of former Deputy Prime Minister
Ghafar Baba, also sits on Zalik's board of directors.

It was, however, only after the management buy-out of TV3 – then
Malaysia's sole private television network – and NSTP was announced on
5 January 1993 that the link between Quek and Anwar became clearer.
It is widely believed that the buy-out of these two important media
companies from the Renong Group was in the interest of Finance
Minister Anwar Ibrahim, who was then preparing to bid for the deputy
presidency of UMNO.

The management buy-out of a controlling 48.01 per cent stake in
NSTP and 43.22 per cent of TV3 equity was valued at a phenomenal
RM800 million, and executed through Realmild Sdn Bhd, a company
owned by four senior editors and executives of NSTP: its managing
director Khalid Haji Ahmad, its Senior Group general manager Mohd
Noor Mutalib, *New Straits Times* Group editor Abdul Kadir Jasin, and
Berita Harian Group editor Ahmad Nazri Abdullah. Since Realmild
had a paid-up capital of just over RM100,000 and hardly any asset
base, it had to include another publicly listed company in the corporate exercise. Two days after Realmild disclosed its bid for NSTP and
TV3, the Malaysian Resources Corporation Bhd (MRCB), a financially
beleaguered but listed property development firm, recently acquired
by the Hong Leong Group, announced that it would acquire Realmild,
thus obtaining control of the two media companies. Part of Realmild's
reverse takeover of MRCB was financed through the creation of 275
million new MRCB shares, which meant that the Hong Leong Group
had to relinquish control of MRCB. On MRCB's board of directors
during this reverse takeover were Wan Azmi (chairman) and Mirzan
Mahathir, son of the Prime Minister, both of whom, along with most
of MRCB's other directors, relinquished their positions in the company after the appointment of the four NSTP executives to the MRCB
board.

In August 1992, just four months before the management buy-out,
the Hong Leong Group had made a general offer for MRCB, securing a
52 per cent majority stake in the company. By November 1992, however,
Hong Leong had reduced its stake in MRCB to a mere 10 per cent. It
is believed that the government-owned HICOM Holdings Bhd picked
up at least 20 per cent of Hong Leong's MRCB equity. Ownership
of HICOM Holdings was then held by the Ministry of Finance Incorporated, the holding company of Anwar's Finance Ministry. These transactions suggest that the Hong Leong Group played a key role in
facilitating the buy-out for the NSTP executives.

Before the management buy-out, the largest to date in Malaysian corporate history, market speculation had been rife that control of NSTP and TV3 would be taken from the UMNO-linked Renong Group; this was reputedly controlled by Daim Zainuddin through Halim Saad, who had been out of favour with Anwar since early 1991 after disagreements over the management and editorial control of NSTP. The buy-out was thus attributed to Anwar's unhappiness with Halim, even though the latter is a protégé of Daim, who backed Anwar's bid for UMNO's deputy presidency. Control over these media companies was expected to be passed to business associates closely linked to Finance Minister Anwar who apparently wanted to ensure more personal, albeit indirect, control of the two profitable and strategic media organisations before the UMNO party election due in November 1993; NSTP not only publishes the leading English and Malay dailies, *New Straits Times* and *Berita Harian*, but also a host of other newspapers and magazines. Anwar's control over these papers and over TV3 and the other Malay language daily, *Utusan Malaysia*, played a crucial role in his successful bid to wrest the UMNO deputy presidency from Ghafar Baba (see Gomez 1994).

To ensure the financial viability of the once ailing MRCB, the company was awarded lucrative projects and contracts despite not having any relevant experience. In August 1993 MRCB announced its acquisition of an 80 per cent stake in Sikap Power Sdn Bhd, an obscure company given a licence to set up a RM3.4 billion power generation plant to supply electricity to the corporatised national electricity generation and distribution company, Tenaga Nasional Bhd (TNB), at a guaranteed purchase price ensuring handsome profits (*The Star* 3/7/93). The licensed independent power producer Sikap Power then also acquired a 35.6 per cent interest in a publicly listed plantation concern, Malakoff Bhd. Later MRCB disclosed that it would be part of a consortium – comprising the government-controlled Sime Darby Bhd and TNB, as well as a subsidiary of the Negeri Sembilan State Economic Development Corporation – to construct and operate a power plant in Negeri Sembilan (*New Straits Times* 25/6/93). In mid-1994 MRCB received a potentially profitable cellular telephone licence from the government despite its lack of experience in the telecommunications industry (*Far Eastern Economic Review* 14/7/94).

In November 1993, just after Anwar became UMNO deputy president, the Hong Leong Group announced – after a protracted attempt since January 1993 – its RM1.1 billion takeover of the MUI Bank Bhd, and its financial subsidiary, MUI Finance Bhd, from Khoo Kay Peng, who apparently 'was railroaded into selling the bank' after falling out of favour with senior UMNO leaders in the late 1980s (see *Asian Wall Street*

Journal 12/11/93); Khoo allegedly had a 'close relationship' with former Finance Minister Tengku Razaleigh Hamzah, who had become leader of the opposition Parti Melayu Semangat 46 (Heng 1992: 137). The Hong Leong Group, which has long sought but failed to secure a bank licence in Singapore, not only got speedy approval from Anwar's Finance Ministry for the takeover but was also exempted from complying with Malaysia's banking rules (the Banking and Financial Institutions Act) which limit the shareholdings of any individual corporate shareholder of a bank to no more than 20 per cent (*Asian Wall Street Journal* 12/11/93). Approval was given although the Hong Leong Group had also developed a significant interest in the Ban Hin Lee Bank, which the group subsequently divested most of. The MUI Bank was a much larger concern than the Ban Hin Lee Bank, which is still controlled by the Penang-based Yeap family despite Hong Leong's protracted attempts to secure majority ownership.

The MUI Bank has since been renamed the Hong Leong Bank, while MUI Finance has been renamed United Merchant Finance Bhd, and injected into a new investment holding company, the United Merchant Group Bhd (UMG), and listed on the KLSE in August 1994; offered for sale at RM2.75 per share, each UMG share yielded a premium of RM3.25 when the shares began trading (*The Star* 19/8/94). A day after listing, 39.2 per cent of UMG's equity was sold by the Hong Leong Group to another publicly listed entity, Advance Synergy Bhd, controlled by Ahmad Sebi Abu Bakar, another reputedly close business associate and contemporary of Anwar Ibrahim at the University of Malaya (*The Star* 20/8/94).

Hong Leong had not been interested in acquiring MUI Finance from Khoo Kay Peng since the Group already had its own well-established finance company, Hong Leong Finance Bhd; Khoo, however, was unwilling to relinquish his stake in the bank unless Hong Leong also agreed to acquire the finance company (*Asian Wall Street Journal* 12/11/93). Advance Synergy acquired the UMG stock via a share swap: its 50.1 per cent stake in a merchant bank, Perdana Merchant Bankers Bhd, was injected into UMG in exchange for UMG shares. UMG also acquired another 20 per cent stake in the merchant bank from Vincent Tan's Berjaya Group. Along with this acquisition, UMG also acquired Hong Leong Credit Bhd's 41.1 per cent stake in the Ban Hin Lee Bank. In exchange for these acquisitions, 141.9 million new UMG shares were issued, which almost doubled UMG's paid-up capital, from RM180 million to RM321.9 million; this meant that although the Hong Leong Group remained a shareholder of UMG, Ahmad Sebi's Advance Synergy has a controlling 39 per cent stake in the company (*The Star* 20/8/94; *The Sun* 5/9/94). Hong Leong's reduced interests in

UMG and the Ban Hin Lee Bank – by allowing Advance Synergy to buy into UMG – has involved developing interlocking interests with yet another politically influential businessman; in fact the UMG acquisition only transpired after Advance Synergy had aborted its attempt to acquire a direct 32.8 per cent stake in the Ban Hin Lee Bank from the Hong Leong Group (*The Star* 20/8/94). Hong Leong Bank was publicly listed in October 1994 at a substantial premium. With this crucial bank acquisition, the Hong Leong Group in Malaysia has managed to further diversify its interests over many key industries in the country, including the media and manufacturing (see Figure 3.3).

In response to allegations of close links between the Hong Leong Group and Finance Minister Anwar, a senior executive of the Group claimed that these ties were 'not political' and that there was 'no harm aligning ourselves to the government' (*The Straits Times* [Singapore] 1/12/93). When queried on the matter, Anwar insisted that he did not 'favour any group. As long as everything is in order and it benefits the economy, business proposals will be approved' (*The Straits Times* [Singapore] 1/12/93; *Malaysian Business* 1/3/94).

This case study, however, reveals how the collaboration between influential Malay politicians and Chinese businessmen has provided mutual benefit to both parties. The fact that MUI was only taken over by Hong Leong after Anwar's ascendancy in November 1993 also suggests that it may not have been politically expedient for Anwar if the transactions had been concluded before the election. Allowing a Chinese,

Figure 3.3   The Hong Leong Co. Group's Malaysian Operations Simplified Corporate Structure, 1993

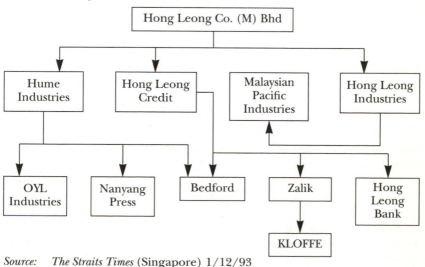

Source: *The Straits Times* (Singapore) 1/12/93

rather than a Malay, to gain control of the previously Chinese-owned MUI, also implies that the Chinese are not being completely shut out of the highly controlled banking sector, which was an important signal before the 1995 general election; such corporate deals subsequently proved to be an important factor in the Barisan Nasional's overwhelming victory in the general election which was primarily attributed to the non-Bumiputera support it secured (see Gomez 1996a). The Hong Leong case study also suggests that Chinese business groups who have co-operated with Malay power-brokers have achieved greater success than other Chinese businessmen and institutions.

Case Study 5: Shamsuddin Abdul Kadir and the Sapura Group

Shamsuddin bin Abdul Kadir, a British-trained electrical engineer, began his career in 1959 with the Telecoms Department. He left the public utility in 1971 to join United Motor Works Bhd (UMW), then controlled by the maverick Chinese entrepreneur Eric Chia. In January 1975 Shamsuddin incorporated Sapura Holdings, using it to buy out (from UMW) its payphone manufacturer, Uniphone Works Sdn Bhd, renaming it Uniphone. The government became the company's main customer, and lucrative contracts from the Telecoms Department were mainly responsible for Uniphone's rapid development. When its ten-year contract to supply and operate payphones in urban areas expired in December 1988, Uniphone obtained a fifteen-year extension. From 1977 until 1989, the company was also the government's sole supplier of telephones to the Telecoms Department. In 1976 Uniphone was also awarded a RM2.5 million cable-laying contract by the government (*Malaysian Business* 1/4/92, 1/7/93; Cheong 1993: 296–305; Mansor 1993: 2–28).

In June 1984 Sapura Holdings acquired a majority stake in the foreign-controlled Malayan Cables Bhd, then the smallest of three cable-manufacturing and distributing companies listed on the stock exchange; the following year Sapura Holdings sold all its equity in Uniphone to Malayan Cables in return for a larger stake in the company. In 1988 Malayan Cables acquired its new name, Uniphone Telecommunications Bhd. By 1992 Shamsuddin's interest in his main publicly listed concern came to 50.62 per cent (KLSE 17 (II) 1991: 213–16).

Apart from Uniphone Telecommunications, Sapura Holdings also has a majority 69.5 per cent stake in another quoted company, Sapura Telecommunications Bhd, publicly listed in December 1990. Incorporated on 23 May 1983 as Rilla Holdings Sdn Bhd, the company initially served as an investment holding company for Sapura Holdings. Among the companies Sapura Holdings injected into Sapura Telecommunications were Uniphone Usahasama Sdn Bhd, a telephone cable network operator, Teledata Sdn Bhd, a telephone manufacturer, and Komtel Sdn Bhd, a paging services operator. By 1992, when Uniphone Telecommunications sold 40 per cent of its equity in Uniphone, the latter was also selling phone cards and distributing Apple computers nationwide, in addition to manufacturing and installing telecommunication equipment. In return, Uniphone Telecommunications obtained a 39 per cent stake in Sapura Telecommunications, thus allowing Sapura Holdings to have cross-holdings between the two listed entities. Shamsuddin is executive chairman of both Uniphone Telecommunications and Sapura Telecommunications (KLSE 17 (I) 1991: 396–9; *Malaysian Business* 1/4/92; Cheong 1993: 300–2). By 1993 the net worth of Shamsuddin and his wife's stakes in Uniphone Telecommunications and Sapura Telecommunications was estimated at RM215 million, while the combined capitalisation of both companies was RM1.2 billion (*Malaysian Business* 1/7/93, 1/8/93).

Shamsuddin acknowledges his close relationship with Prime Minister Mahathir. Rameli Musa, the vice-chairman of both Sapura and Uniphone, who owns a 10 per cent stake in Shamsuddin's holding company, Sapura Holdings, is reportedly 'a confidant' of Deputy Prime Minister Anwar Ibrahim; they were schoolmates at the Malay College in Kuala Kangsar and also active together in Angkatan Belia Islam Malaysia (ABIM, or the Malaysian Islamic Youth Movement), of which Anwar was president for many years (see *Malaysian Business* 1/7/93, 1/8/93).

Shamsuddin has also served as a director of Permodalan Bersatu Bhd, once the holding company for the UMNO co-operative KUB. In July 1987 Uniphone Telecommunications acquired a 20 per cent stake in TV3 from the Fleet Group, then UMNO's most important holding company. In February 1989, however, not long after TV3 was listed on the KLSE, Uniphone Telecommunications divested its entire interest in the company to the Berjaya Corporation Bhd, a listed company controlled by Vincent Tan Chee Yioun, another businessman who has cultivated strong political ties (see Case Study 10, p. 152). Shamsuddin, however, retains a small interest in TV3 and remains a director of the company (Gomez 1990: 74–7).

Despite these close links with UMNO leaders and companies, Sapura Holdings has developed a strong reputation for its entrepreneurial capabilities. After first obtaining government contracts to supply telephones, Sapura Holdings teamed up with reputable international telephone manufacturers, such as German-based Siemens and Belgium's Bell Telephone, to move into manufacturing. Then, after placing much emphasis on research and development, the company began to manufacture its own telecommunication products. Since then Sapura

Holdings has launched the first Malaysian-designed telephone, the first locally manufactured mini-PABX telephone system, and even the world's first voice-activated, hands-free telephone. The company has also developed its own direct paging software program, a supervisory control and data acquisition (scada) system, phone cards, credit card telephones, and intelligent pay phone software (Mansor 1993: 1–28). In 1990 Sapura Holdings even established a subsidiary, Sapura Research Sdn Bhd, specifically to develop new telecommunications equipment (Mansor 1993: 1–28).

Sapura Holdings has also moved beyond relying on government contracts to venture abroad; to date the company has secured infrastructure contracts in Brunei, Vietnam and Indonesia. The company has also established joint ventures with foreign companies, like US-based Hewlett-Packard for marketing purposes, and with Sumitomo Electric Industries Ltd, the largest Japanese manufacturer of wires and cables, to develop its manufacturing base. Sapura Holdings has also formed a joint venture with Sumitomo and another Japanese concern, the Marubeni Corporation, to undertake major cable-laying contracts in Malaysia, and with an Indonesian company, P. T. Catur Yasa, to participate in a cable installation contract on the island of Sumatra (Cheong 1993: 301–4; Mansor 1993: 3–4).

While Shamsuddin greatly benefited from state patronage during the early years of Sapura Holdings' development, he has deployed the rents available to him well to develop an internationally competitive manufacturing capacity for technological innovation. The productive manner in which he has used government-allocated rents makes him an important example of how rents can be used to promote genuine industrial entrepreneurship. Unlike most other NEP rentier beneficiaries, Shamsuddin had had some expertise and experience in the field of telecommunications when he was first awarded the rent opportunities by the state; it does not seem that he has relied heavily on party-political influence to gain access to yet more rents (Mansor 1993: 5–6). In a sense his own success has won him more opportunities. Such performance criteria have become increasingly significant in recent years and helps explain why rentier activity has not undermined Malaysian growth.

Furthermore, Uniphone Telecommunications and Sapura Telecommunications have expanded without becoming involved in the often intricate and extensive mergers and acquisitions (and asset swapping) which have come to characterise the corporate wheeling and dealing of many other newly emerging Bumiputera capitalists since the mid-1980s. Apart from its short- term interest in TV3, the growth of the Sapura Holdings Group is primarily attributable to its focus on the telecommunications industry, where its expertise lies.

4

Privatising State Assets

Promoting Privatisation

In Malaysia the term privatisation is used rather loosely by the government and the media to refer to a broad range of measures from the partial divestment of ownership (of an activity or enterprise) from the public to the private sectors, to the licensing of private competitors in an activity previously dominated by the public sector, or to the private management of a public sector activity. Whichever way the term is used, privatisation generally involves new control of economic activities as well as implications for the economic welfare of consumers and employees. The political dimensions of privatisation can become more pronounced when the welfare impact of the policy is unevenly distributed among the population. In view of the multi-ethnic composition of the Malaysian population, there is keen interest in the ethnicity of ownership, giving privatisation in Malaysia even greater political implications.

In the 1970s and early 1980s, during implementation of the NEP, public sector investment increased substantially. According to official figures:

> In 1981, the value of investments undertaken by the public sector agencies amounted to M$2.527 billion or 27 per cent of the total public sector investments ... In 1982, federal-government equity in government-owned companies amounted to M$1.28 billion, whilst loans advanced were M$7.2 billion and investments in federal statutory bodies were M$13.5 billion. The size of the government investment as at September 15, 1987, amounted to M$5.739 billion or 78 per cent of the total paid-up capital of these agencies. (Malaysia 1989: 216–17)

Despite the government's extensive investments, rapid public sector expansion under the NEP was generally deemed to have led to a bloated bureaucracy, inferior services, economic inefficiency, high costs, low productivity and limited innovation. There were a number of reasons contributing to the poor performance of public enterprises. As in many other countries, the managers of public enterprises in Malaysia are expected to maximise several often conflicting objectives; state-owned enterprises are expected to fulfil certain social (that is, redistributive) goals, usually associated with the NEP, besides efficiency and profit maximisation. Such mixed objectives tend to undermine the efficient and profitable operation of these public enterprises. Moreover, there is usually no proper system or criterion for evaluating and giving priority to these objectives; thus even social priorities are usually vaguely targeted and so rather arbitrarily reflected in the administration and implementation. Furthermore, the ostensible social goals of most public enterprises have often meant that managers and bureaucrats have been expected to follow directives from politicians who use these enterprises for personal economic or political gain (for example to augment support, during both party and general elections) to the detriment of the enterprises themselves. Another factor contributing to the inefficiency of public enterprises has been the serious shortage of competent Bumiputera managerial expertise, especially in the 1970s. Consequently most managers (including seconded and retired civil servants) in these enterprises were often inexperienced and unable to manage efficiently; inevitably, decisions taken were not always in the best interest of the enterprises. Despite the limited experience of those running these public enterprises, very little monitoring, let alone financial discipline, was exercised by their government financiers, especially when funds readily flowed in before the fiscal and debt crises of the mid-1980s. This 'soft budget constraint' was reflected in limited supervision and evaluation of management, with audits seldom undertaken. Although there were many overlapping objectives and functions within the numerous public enterprises established, there was little coordination among them. Finally, since there was limited auditing, transparency and accountability, public sector expansion tended to encourage the emergence of self-aggrandising rentier managers, rather than disciplined, competent and entrepreneurial administrators (Kasper 1974: 87–8; Gomez 1994: 14–21).

Inevitably, most public enterprises in Malaysia lacked a competitive, entrepreneurial ethos, which had the effect of impeding profitability. They were heavily dependent on government funds and preferential access to business opportunities, while remaining immune from financial discipline and competitive market forces. Evidently, while bureaucrats may have been competent in matters of administration, they were neither prepared to tackle the massive intervention exercise that the

NEP actually entailed nor trained for coming up with the kinds of commercial strategies required of them. In spite of this, and in view of the social functions these public enterprises were supposed to serve and the substantial funds invested in them, their managers assumed that there was little likelihood of liquidation even if they performed poorly and losses mounted. These losses or low profits and wastage of investment resources increased the government's fiscal burden and slowed economic growth. In 1984, for instance, the Ministry of Public Enterprise could report the annual returns of only 269 out of a total of 900 public enterprises; their accumulated losses came to RM137.3 million (Supian 1988: 120–3; Kamal and Zainal 1989: 22–3). According to one World Bank report, another disincentive to profit-making by these enterprises was the threat of takeover by trust agencies like PNB, which had a proclivity for searching out 'the most profitable companies for takeover, which are precisely those most coveted by the parent organization. In such an environment, some cross-subsidization, or pro-vision of uneconomic services, then serves to minimize the threat of transfers' (World Bank 1989: 60–1) (see Chapter 3).

While the government was better able to absorb such costs during the 1970s when growth and revenues were high, especially after Malaysia became a net petroleum exporter in the mid-1970s, and as prices of other primary products remained reasonably buoyant, this was no longer possible by the mid-1980s, when the economy slipped into recession, official revenues fell, the yen appreciated, and actual production operations ran into serious problems in the mid-1980s. Falling oil prices between 1982 and 1986, the collapse of the tin market in 1985, as well as the declining prices of Malaysia's other major exports – rubber, cocoa and palm oil (after 1984) – contributed to the economy registering a minus 1 per cent growth rate in 1985.

Exacerbating the recession were declining trading conditions for Malaysia. Besides the growing protectionism in the West, Malaysia experienced declining terms of trade, for instance as much as by 17 per cent between 1981 and 1982, which increased the current account deficit (Adam and Cavendish 1994). Capital flight increased as private investment continued to decline from the mid-1970s, and unemploy-ment rose steadily when the government could no longer afford to raise public spending after 1982.

Another factor contributing to Malaysia's economic malaise in the mid-1980s was the government's heavy industrialisation strategy, actively promoted by Prime Minister Mahathir. In an attempt to diversify the country's industrial sector and to compensate for declining private investments with increased public investments, Mahathir launched his (import-substituting) heavy industrialisation program in the face of widespread criticism and protest, even from within his own cabinet. Understandably there was much reluctance on the part of private capitalists to make massive investments in heavy industries because of the huge capital investment required, the long gestation periods, the lack of relevant technological expertise, and the expected heavy reliance on government protection and subsidies; with the NEP-inspired practice of 'ethnic bypass', the government also seemed reluctant to involve Chinese Malaysians in these projects (Jomo 1994). HICOM was therefore set up to pursue the heavy industrialisation program by collaborating with foreign, mainly Japanese, companies to develop a variety of industries, ranging from steel and cement production to the flagship manufacture of a national car. To finance these initiatives, the government resorted to massive borrowings from abroad, mainly from official Japanese sources (see Malaysia 1986, 1989).

As a result of these investments in heavy industries, average annual public sector investment in commerce and industry leapt from RM0.3 billion in 1978–80 to RM0.9 billion in 1982 and RM1.5 billion in 1984 (Malaysia 1986). Not unexpectedly, the companies established through HICOM at first turned out to be losing concerns. By 1989 even the government's *Mid-Term Review of the Fifth Malaysia Plan* had to concede that although

> the public sector continued to play the leading role in the development of heavy industries ... in general, the performance of heavy industry projects sponsored by the public sector was far from satisfactory. A number of these projects suffered heavy financial losses due to the sluggish domestic market and the inability of the industries concerned to compete in international markets. (Malaysia 1989: 196)

Eventually the government had to bring in Japanese and Chinese Malaysian managers to run most of these industries, though it has to be said that the economic boom from the late 1980s also proved crucial in turning around the financial performance of these heavily protected industries.

From 1980, as the nation turned increasingly to foreign loans to try to spend its way out of the recession, Malaysia's accumulated public sector foreign debt grew from RM4.9 billion in 1980 to RM28.5 billion in 1987. Including loans from domestic agencies, total public sector borrowings increased from RM26.5 billion in 1980 to RM100.6 billion in 1986 (Jomo 1990: 186). In 1983 a massive two-thirds of total government debt expenditure on public enterprises was attributed to only 27 of over 1000 public enterprises (Khoo 1992: 52). By 1987 public enterprises accounted for more than a third of the public sector's outstanding debt and more than 30 per cent of total debt servicing (Jomo 1990: 186).

Poor management and weak financial discipline were not the only factors contributing to the mediocre economic performance of the public enterprises; abuses of power also resulted in great losses. Malaysia's second largest bank (in terms of assets), the government-owned Bank Bumiputra, for example, was involved in the infamous RM2.5 billion BMF scandal, while Pernas was used to buy UMBC from Daim Zainuddin at a high price. After these affairs both enterprises declared phenomenal losses; Bank Bumiputra had to be kept afloat with massive state funds from Petronas, the cash-rich national petroleum agency.

To encourage foreign investment to help revive the economy, an accommodative Investments Promotion Act was enacted in 1986. It provided generous tax holidays and pioneer status for periods of five years, renewable in some cases for up to ten years, for investments in export-oriented manufacturing and agriculture as well as tourism. To promote domestic private investment, the government in 1987 again amended the Industrial Coordination Act's stringent Bumiputera investment and employee exemption limits for licensing of manufacturing enterprises (Koh 1990: 233–4). The government even either suspended or relaxed some NEP requirements to promote investments. These policy moves, coupled with favourable external market conditions, resulted in a resurgence of export-oriented manufacturing, largely under the auspices of foreign – especially East Asian – capital, which reinvigorated the economy enough for it to register over 8 per cent annual growth since 1988 (Jomo and Edwards 1993: 33–8).

Another new policy initiative to tackle Malaysia's domestic economic problems was privatisation, which appeared on the policy agenda as the government came under increasing pressure from multilateral and bilateral institutions to institute economic reforms. The shift towards more private sector–oriented development policies by major multilateral financial agencies, such as the World Bank, the Asian Development Bank, and the International Monetary Fund, was encouraged by the 'counter-revolution' in development economics that followed the resurgence of conservatism. The governments of Britain and the United States in the 1980s were particularly strongly biased in favour of private enterprise, and advocated policies to deregulate economies, reduce government economic intervention and curb government spending. Swayed by this new disposition towards development led by the private sector, these multilateral agencies also argued against extensive government involvement in the economy (Cook and Minogue 1990: 390; McKenzie and Lee 1991: 3; Donahue 1989: 1).

The 1983 announcement of privatisation in Malaysia was a radical move since it involved a reversal of the state's earlier promotion of public enterprises, ostensibly to boost economic growth, redistribute wealth and create opportunities for employment. Apparently Mahathir had long been of the opinion that public enterprises should only serve as a temporary vehicle for creating a Bumiputera property-owning class (Mahathir 1981). Ironically, after his appointment as prime minister in 1981, public enterprise spending increased – mainly to finance his new heavy industries – until the mid-1980s. Mahathir also saw privatisation as a crucial means of sponsoring the emergence and consolidation of Malay rentiers, whom he hoped would somehow transform themselves into an internationally competitive industrial community. So it is quite possible that even without external prompting or the fiscal debt crisis of the mid-1980s, privatisation may have been pursued by Mahathir as a policy tool for the promotion of Bumiputera capitalism.

The Prime Minister and then Finance Minister Daim Zainuddin had both believed that excessive growth in the public sector and state intervention in the economy had resulted in declining private investments and the country's economic slowdown. In introducing it in 1983 Mahathir (1989: 10) said that he saw privatisation as 'the transfer of government services and enterprises to the private sector' because, as he was now ready to concede publicly, 'companies and services owned and managed by [the] government have been less successful or have run at a loss because the government's management methods differ greatly from those of the private sector'. Mahathir's new private sector–oriented prescriptions meant the severe curtailment of public enterprise growth in the economy and promotion of the private sector as the new engine of growth, especially after the mid-1980s.

Thus when the officially stated objectives of privatisation were reiterated with the announcement of the government's Privatisation Master Plan, released in February 1991 (nearly eight years after the policy was first announced), the government, as expected, voiced its hope that implementation of the policy would reduce the number of public sector personnel as well as its own financial and administrative burden. The plan also repeated the Prime Minister's claim that by promoting competition, privatisation would improve efficiency, stimulate private entrepreneurship and encourage investment. Privatisation would, of course, ultimately reduce the size and presence of the public sector in the economy (see Malaysia 1991c: 21).

Since privatisation is, in effect, denationalisation, it was also stressed that the policy would be consistent with the NEP. Anticipating Bumiputera apprehensions that the community would not benefit from privatisation, Mahathir was quick to state that 'it would not negate the objectives of the NEP. The Bumiputeras will get their share, both in terms of equity and in employment' (quoted in Gomez 1991b). In fact, as mentioned, Mahathir was already of the view that privatisation fitted in with his redistributive plans for Bumiputeras as he believed there were now enough people who could acquire privatised entities and manage them profitably if given the chance. Milne (1986: 1374–5) suggests that the Prime Minister also promoted privatisation to undermine the 'subsidy mentality' among Bumiputeras that the NEP had encouraged, hoping that with control of lucrative privatised assets, Malay businessmen would operate their businesses independently of further state patronage.

Given the highly politicised access to business opportunities for Malaysia's corporate sector since the 1980s with UMNO's enhanced political hegemony, the privatisation policy was bound to have an impact on politics. Some claimed that since the private sector – and not public enterprises – now the main vehicle for economic development, political influence on the economy through public enterprises, especially for patronage, would be checked. This argument, however, is flawed. Substantial corporate stock had been captured through political patronage and was controlled by an elite few connected with the UMNO leadership by the late 1980s (see Gomez 1990, 1994); this often also ensured privileged and continued access to patronage, especially with privatisation, thereby reinforcing their positions in the party and in business. Politicians who had exploited their political influence to help businessmen expand their corporate interests and those who had cultivated close ties with members of the business community found that they had an advantage over other aspiring politicians, especially during elections. As Craig (1988: 257) has noted, given its rather unique 'political/bureaucratic/business complex', privatisation in Malaysia is 'unlikely to be more than a rearrangement of economic and political power'.

Forms of Privatisation

As in most other countries, privatisation in Malaysia has primarily entailed divestment of state-owned enterprises, although various other means have been used to implement the policy. Among the most important state-owned companies to have been divested are Sports Toto (M) Bhd in 1985, the Malaysian International Shipping Corporation (MISC) in 1987, Malaysia Airlines Bhd, HICOM Holdings Bhd and Petronas Dagangan Bhd in 1994, and Petronas Gas Bhd in 1995.

In some cases public enterprises had first to be corporatised before divestment through public listing. With corporatisation the status of these public enterprises would be changed to that of a public limited company, with the government still retaining ownership; this has helped to ascertain the public enterprise's financial position, to introduce managerial reforms, and to make the company more 'marketable' for launch in the stock market (Jones 1991). Syarikat Telekom Malaysia Bhd, for example, was incorporated in 1987 to take over the activities of the Telecoms Department, while Tenaga Nasional Bhd was established to take over the National Electricity Board. In both instances, the equity of these corporatised entities was later offered for sale to the public with listing on the Kuala Lumpur Stock Exchange.

The 'contracting out' of services previously provided by the public sector was also initiated by the government. Among the various activities that have been contracted out are parking services and garbage disposal, Port Kelang's container terminal services and the Telecoms Department's RM2.5 billion telecommunications development projects (Kennedy 1995).

Licences were also issued in certain sectors to allow competition where the government had previously enjoyed a monopoly. In 1983 a licence was issued to Sistem Televisyen Malaysia Bhd to run a third television channel, TV3; the other two were government-owned. In 1993 a licence for a fourth television network, Metro Vision, was issued to a company controlled by the Melewar Group, while a licence was also given out to establish a cable television network in 1994. To promote the fledgling Malaysian telecommunications industry, numerous licences have been issued for cellular phones and satellite services to Tajudin Ramli's Celcom Sdn Bhd, T. Ananda Krishnan's Binariang Sdn Bhd, and companies controlled by Shamsuddin Kadir's Sapura Holdings Bhd and Vincent Tan Chee Yioun's Berjaya Group Bhd. Several independent power producer (IPP) licences have also been issued to the government-controlled conglomerate Sime Darby Bhd, the Malaysian Resources Corporation Bhd (through Malakoff Bhd) which is linked to Deputy Prime Minister Anwar Ibrahim, and two politically well-connected Chinese-controlled publicly listed companies, Lim Goh Tong's Genting Bhd and Yeoh Tiong Lay's YTL Corporation Bhd. IPP licences are also expected to be issued to companies linked to Ananda Krishnan and Basir Ismail (see *Far Eastern Economic Review* 1/9/94). In April 1994 a licence was issued to Air Asia Sdn Bhd to operate Malaysia's second national airline for five years; its international destinations, however, were limited to Jakarta, Hanoi, Hong Kong, Osaka and Bombay. Eighty-five per cent of Air Asia's equity was then held by HICOM, while the remaining stake was allocated to Mofaz Air Sdn Bhd (*New Straits Times* 15/4/94).

Management buy-outs were introduced for the first time in 1990 with the privatisation of the public enterprises, Peremba Bhd and Kumpulan Fima Bhd. Although no other privatisations have since been implemented through management buy-outs, it was disclosed in May 1994 that negotiations had begun for the privatisation of MARA Holdings Sdn Bhd, a wholly owned subsidiary of the Majlis Amanah Rakyat, the first Bumiputera trust agency formed by the government; the company is expected to be privatised for RM200 million – the total amount of its capitalisation – to its top management. An investment holding company, MARA Holdings, is involved in the securities and transportation sectors (*The Star* 10/5/94). In October 1993 another MARA subsidiary, KK Industries Sdn Bhd (KKI), was privatised through a partial management buy-out when KKI's top management obtained 45 per cent of the company's equity (*The Edge* 2/1/95). In September 1994 it was reported that the senior management of Pernas had submitted a proposal to implement a takeover of the trust agency. Led by Pernas' long-standing – since 1975 – chief executive officer, Tunku Shariman Tunku Sulaiman, the management team proposes to acquire 20 per cent of its equity for between RM300 and RM400 million, while another 50 per cent is to be taken up by another trust agency, PNB, thus allowing the government to maintain majority ownership of Pernas (see *The Edge* 26/9/94).

During the 1980s the North Port Kelang toll road bypass, the Jalan Kuching–Jalan Kepong flyover and the North–South Highway were privatised through the 'build-operate-transfer (BOT) or 'build-operate' (BO) methods. In 1994 the Sarawak state government privatised the RM15 billion Bakun Dam project to Ekran Bhd using the 'build-operate-own' (BOO) method, while the main terminal building of the RM9 billion Kuala Lumpur International Airport, one of 55 packages, was awarded to a mainly Japanese consortium for RM1.74 billion. Through these methods the government has drawn private financing into construction projects. Table 4.1 gives a breakdown of the privatisation methods used between 1983 and 1993, while a list of the more prominent privatised projects to date is given in Table 4.2.

The main modes of implementing privatisation, according to the Privatisation Master Plan, have been through the sale of assets or equity, lease of assets, management contracts, and BOT or BO private financing of new infrastructure. Although the plan also claims that the valuation of assets for sale or lease is based on net tangible assets or price-earning ratios, while discounted cash flows are also considered, there is no evidence that any of these methods have been strictly adhered to in determining the actual price (or lease rate) of privatised government assets (Malaysia 1991c: 22–5). On the contrary, very substantial discounts (in the case of sales) and premiums (in the case of privatised infrastructure projects) seem to have been the norm, with the proportion apparently related to the political influence of the beneficiary.

Table 4.1   Malaysia: Mode of Privatisation

Method	Year (19—)											Total
	83	*84*	*85*	*86*	*87*	*88*	*89*	*90*	*91*	*92*	*93*	*Total*
Sale of equity			1				1	2	9	8		21
Public listing			1	1		1	1	3				10
Leasing			1					1				2
Management contract				1	3	1						5
Sale of assets and leasing				1				1				2
Sale of assets								3	1	3		7
Management buy-out								2				2
Corporatisation and listing								1		1		2
Build-operate-transfer (BOT)	1		1		2	2	2	1	1			10
Build-operate-own (BOO)	1											1
Build-operate (BO)											2	2
Corporatisation									1	4	3	8
Total	2		4	3	5	4	4	14	12	16	5	72

Source: Economic Planning Unit, cited by Rugayah 1995: 71

Table 4.2   Malaysia: Major Privatised Projects, 1983–95

Project	Year
(I) *Divestment*	
Klang Container Terminal	1986
Malaysian International Shipping Corporation Bhd (MISC)	1986
Syarikat Gula Padang Terap Sdn Bhd	1989
Cement Manufacturers Sarawak Bhd	1989
Cement Industries of Malaysia Bhd (CIMA)	1990
Edaran Otomobil Nasional Bhd (EON)	1990
Syarikat Telekom Malaysia Bhd (STM)	1990
Holiday Villages Sendirian Bhd	1990
Pernas International Hotels and Properties Bhd (PIHP)	1990
Peremba Bhd	1990
Kumpulan FIMA Bhd	1990
Tenaga Nasional Bhd	1990
Heavy Industries Corporation of Malaysia Bhd (HICOM)	1994
Petronas Dagangan Bhd (PDB)	1994
Petronas Gas Bhd	1995

(II) *BO/BOT/BOO*
North Klang Straits Bypass	1983
Jalan Kuching/Jalan Kepong Interchange	1983
Rural Water Supply Project	1986
Labuan Water Supply Project	1987
Kuala Lumpur Interchanges	1987
North–South Highway	1988
Ipoh Water Supply	1989
National Sewerage Project	1993
Light Transit Rail System	1993
Bakun Dam	1994
Singapore–Johore Baru Link Crossway	1994
Main Terminal Building, KL International Building	1994

(III) *Management Contract*
National Park Tourist Facilities	1986
Semenyih Dam	1987
Marketing of Airtime, Radio Malaysia	1987
RISDA Marketing Activities	1987
Maintenance of Tube Wells, Labuan	1988
Kuala Lumpur Mini-bus Services	1993
Inspection of Government Vehicles	1993
Support Services for District and General hospitals	1994

(IV) *Management Buy-Out*
Peremba Bhd	1990
Kumpulan Fima Bhd	1990
KK Industries Sdn Bhd	1993

(V) *Licence*
TV3	1983
Big Sweep Lottery	1988
Telecommunications (Time Engineering Bhd)	1992
Independent Power Producer (Time Engineering Bhd)[a]	1992
Independent Power Producer (YTL Corp.)[a]	1993
Metro Vision (TV4)	1993
Satellite Services Network (cable television)	1994
Satellite/Telecommunications (Binariang Sdn Bhd)	1994
Telecommunications (Malaysian Resources Corp. Bhd)	1994

(VI) *Lease*
RMAF Aircraft Maintenance Depot	1985
Shah Alam Abattoir (Swine section)	1990

(VII) *Corporatisation*
Lumut Dockyard	1991
Postal Services Department	1992
Keretapi Tanah Melayu (KTM)	1992
Johore Port Authority	1992
Bintulu Port	1992
Department of Civil Aviation (DCA)	1993

Sources: *Sixth Malaysia Plan*, p. 73: Table 2.8; Abdul Aziz Abdul Rahman 1993:
103–4
Note: [a] IPP licences are also BOO contracts

Justifying Privatisation

Although the government has not provided detailed figures, it has claimed that through privatisation it annually saves RM4.8 billion in operating expenditure, RM17 billion in development expenditure, and RM37.7 billion in capital expenditure; between 1983 and 1994 it is claimed the government saved RM40.6 billion in operating expenditure through privatisation. In addition, by 1994, the bureaucracy had been trimmed by around 92,700 personnel and the government had raised almost RM10.8 billion in revenue from the sale of equity in privatised companies (*Investors Digest* July 1992; *The Star* 23/9/94; *The Edge* 2/1/95). By implementing projects through the BOT method, more than RM8.2 billion in capital expenditure for infrastructural development has been privately financed, while close to RM7.45 billion of outstanding government debt has been transferred to the private sector (*New Straits Times* 10/8/89). Meanwhile the government's tax burden has also been reduced as privatised companies take over loan refinancing. Recurrent revenues were also expected from taxation and leases from privatised entities like the Kelang Port Container Terminal (KCT).

The government also attributed the increase in variety and quality of television programs to privatisation with the introduction of competition from TV3. In the telecommunications industry, new and improved services were introduced in the market with the issue of numerous licences. At the Kelang Port Container Terminal, the average vessel turnaround time had been reduced from 11.7 hours to 8.9 hours two years after privatisation. After being privatised, the Labuan water supply project was completed not only ahead of schedule but at reduced cost (see *New Straits Times* 10/8/89).

Independent analysis of these government claims attest to the fact that they have not been merely rhetorical. Jones and Fadil (1992c) noted that KCT registered an efficiency gain of 53 per cent, while MAS and Sports Toto recorded a revenue rise of 22 per cent and 11 per cent respectively. KCT's improvements were attributed to internal management changes which also resulted in cost efficiency gains. At MAS, international ticket price competition and wise investment decisions have been credited with improvements. Meanwhile Sports Toto gained market share through improved marketing even before complete divestiture (Jones 1994: 75–84).

The Privatisation Master Plan also claimed that the policy had stimulated economic growth by providing greater opportunities to the private sector. Citing the case of TV3, the plan claimed that there were multiplier effects with the introduction of the private television network which had stimulated the domestic film and advertising industries. This compensated not only for the decline in public expenditure but also encouraged private entrepreneurship. Apart from this, the government contended that the privatisation of TV3, MISC, MAS, STM and TNB apparently increased business opportunities by allowing the private sector to venture into areas previously monopolised by the government, namely broadcasting, shipping, airlines, telecommunications and power generation. The listing of the shares of these privatised companies on the KLSE also substantially increased Malaysia's capital market. By June 1992 the public listing of thirteen privatised entities was worth RM201.1 billion, which accounted for 28 per cent of total market capitalisation (Mohd Sheriff 1991: 188–9; *Investors Digest* November 1992). The privatised government entities listed on the KLSE include MAS, MISC, Proton, TV3, EON, STM, TNB, KCT, Sports Toto, Tradewinds, Kedah Cement, PIHP, Cement Industries of Malaysia (CIMA) and Cement Manufacturer of Sarawak (CMS) (*Investors Digest* November 1992). In 1994 two other major public enterprises, HICOM Holdings and Petronas Dagangan, were also listed on the local bourse; 94.5 million Petronas Dagangan shares worth RM2.80 each and 416.7 million HICOM Holdings shares valued at RM2.10 each were sold to private investors, raking in more than RM1 billion for the government; by the end of 1994 the number of privatised companies listed on the KLSE had risen to nineteen (*Malaysian Business* 1/2/94, 16/2/94; *The Edge* 2/1/95). Through these listings, privatisation helped to make the KLSE the largest stock market in Southeast Asia and the fourth largest in Asia (*Malaysian Business* 16/8/92). The Privatisation Master Plan also stressed that since most privatisations required at least 30 per cent Bumiputera participation, the policy had advanced the NEP's inter-ethnic wealth redistribution objectives. The government also maintained that the benefits accruing from the implementation of privatis-ation were crucial in enabling it to spend more on alleviating poverty, although no evidence of this was provided.

Questioning Privatisation

The merits of privatisation expounded by the government have been refuted on a number of grounds. It is generally agreed that effective use of resources by the public sector, and not its size, is the measure of its performance (Kirkpatrick 1993: 95). The performances of the public sectors in countries such as Singapore, Taiwan and South Korea have been cited as examples of efficiently managed public sectors. Fur-thermore, privatisation does not necessarily provide a universal solution for the inefficiencies associated with the public sector. It has also been questioned whether private enterprises can guarantee that the public interest will be effectively served by private interests taking over public sector activities. It is asserted by some that diverting private sector capital from new investments to buy over public sector assets would retard economic growth rather than stimulate it. It is also indisputable that if there were managerial reforms, greater public accountability and a more transparent public sector, greater efficiency could be achieved by curtailing public sector waste and borrowing.

Since only profitable, or potentially profitable, enterprises and activities are attractive to the private sector, it is only these that the government has been able to privatise. While the revenue generated from the divestment of state assets may reduce fiscal deficits, this entails only temporary reduction of a fiscal deficit since the public sector would lose income from the more profitable privatised public enterprises and would still be burdened with financing the unprofitable ones; hence privatisation undermines the potential for cross-subsidisation within the public sector.

A major obstacle to privatisation in Malaysia is the politics of ethnicity. Since the sale of public enterprises to non-Bumiputeras, particularly Chinese, would prove politically unpopular, especially among influential politically linked Bumiputera businessmen, the range of possible buyers is restricted (Milne 1991). In fact when the government privatised some major projects to non-Bumiputeras in 1992 and 1993, UMNO members were among the most severe critics of such privatisations (see Gomez 1994). For instance, during UMNO's General Assembly in November 1992, members were critical that the government had privatised some of the most lucrative contracts to non-Bumiputera businessmen; among such beneficiaries mentioned were Vincent Tan Chee Yioun and T. Ananda Krishnan. These protests occurred despite the widespread knowledge that non-Bumiputera firms have limited access to opportunities for privatisation; the possibility of their participation in privatisation is usually enhanced by linking up with politically influential Malays, again pointing to the crucial ethnic factor.

It has also been argued that privatisation tends to adversely affect the interests of the public, especially poorer consumers, to whose needs the public sector has been more sensitive. Privatisation gives priority to profit maximisation at the expense of social welfare and the public interest, except on the rare occasions when the two coincide; hence, for example, only profitable new services are likely to be introduced, rather than services needed by the people, especially the poor and those without political influence. Privatisation may also lead to increased costs of living and poorer services and utilities, particularly in remote and rural areas, because of the 'economic costing' of services such as telephones, water supply and electricity. Employees of privatised concerns may also be faced with the possible loss of jobs, increased work load or lower real wages.

The substitution of a private monopoly for a public one through privatisation does not increase competition and hence does not necessarily led to greater efficiency or cheaper and better-quality services. Rather, some adverse consequences of privatisation include the increased 'costs' to the public in the form of reduced, inferior or more costly services. An often-quoted case is the unit charge for local telephone calls, which was increased by 30 per cent just before STM was incorporated; by 1994 STM was suggesting that it would reduce its rates if government approval was given for it to dispense with providing subscribers with 100 free calls which, in effect, meant increased charges for the consumer (see *Aliran Monthly* 1994: 14, 6). Furthermore, through privatisation, two sets of services have emerged: one for those who can afford privatised services and the other for those who cannot and therefore have to continue to rely on public services, for example medical services and education. This has meant that with privatisation of public enterprises, when the priority is increasingly profit maximisation, the quality of service to the public has diminished considerably.

There has also been much criticism that those buying shares of privatised entities have made huge gains from the state selling off its assets too cheaply. Much more controversial has been the government's award of contracts without competitive bidding or the sale of assets without actively seeking the best possible offer. Apart from the fact that such policies avoid competition that may benefit consumers and taxpayers, they have also exacerbated the politicisation of access to lucrative business opportunities controlled by the government (*Investors Digest* August 1989). With the transformation of public sector monopolies into private ones, unless privatisation is supported by strong competition and anti-trust legislation, a new set of allocative inefficiencies may eventually replace existing ones (Jesudason 1989: 188–9). In fact even regulation has sometimes proved to be inadequate in controlling privately owned monopolies (see White 1988).

Reduced government ownership of certain monopolies as a result of privatisation has not necessarily led to increased competition or significant changes in operations, for the government still owns the 'golden share' that gives it veto powers over all major management decisions. The golden share concept is a compromise mechanism between the political concerns of the government and the commercial goals of a privatised entity's management. The golden share ascribes certain rights and privileges to a single government-held share in privatised public enterprises. The share is held by the government, while other shares may be sold to the private sector (*The Star* 18/9/90). But despite the device of the golden share, there have been few changes in the management of some public enterprises; the management of MAS, for example, was left largely intact even after its supposed privatisation in 1985 (*Malaysian Business* 1/5/88).

Furthermore, despite the Malaysian government's active implementation of privatisation and its golden share clause, its ownership of various sectors of the economy is still extensive. Even after a decade of divestments, the government in 1995 still owned 77 per cent of TNB, 75 per cent of STM, 75 per cent of Petronas Dagangan – all of which operate as monopolies – and 49 per cent of HICOM Holdings. Although Bank Negara had divested its 52 per cent stake in MAS and 29 per cent interest in MISC by 1994, 11.5 per cent of the airline's equity and 23 per cent of the shipping corporation's stock was channelled to the government's Pensions Trust Fund (*Malaysian Business* 1/2/94, 16/2/94; *New Straits Times* 1/6/94). HICOM Holdings, however, was totally divested in late 1995 in a controversial deal to the politically well-connected Yahya Ahmad (see *Far Eastern Economic Review* 2/5/96).

In addition, through privatisation the government has transferred majority control of monopolies such as HICOM Holdings, MAS and Sports Toto and companies like Peremba to businessmen with strong political ties. This has helped to enlarge their control of the economy, particularly in the property development, heavy industry, construction and gaming sectors. In the process, the promotion of Bumiputera entrepreneurship was affected as political favouritism limited access to such privatisations. The development of Bumiputera entrepreneurship was also hampered as contracts awarded to Bumiputeras were, in turn, sub-contracted to foreigners and non-Bumiputeras (see Gomez 1990, 1991b, 1994). Apart from this, the minimal investments by private contractors concerned only with short-term profits has long-term implications for the nature of economic growth.

Many privatisation exercises in Malaysia do not even pretend to achieve other alleged advantages and benefits of the policy by invoking NEP restructuring considerations, which are supposedly to increase Bumiputera ownership of wealth and business opportunities. With increased Bumiputera competition, political influence and connections have become increasingly decisive. In fact for top government decision-makers, who have the power to shape the privatisation process and select its beneficiaries, there are considerable prospects of long-term gains as well as the possibility of short-term pay-offs (Milne 1992).

Extensive political nepotism and patronage have grown with privatisation in the absence of an independent, accountable monitoring body to ensure proper implementation of the policy. The possibilities for massive gains have therefore been high. For example, the policy's commitment to achieving the NEP objectives as well as the 'first-come, first-served' policy have provided opportunities for political leaders and politically connected businessmen to gain tremendous advantage. In fact, since privatisation in Malaysia in most cases has not even involved the formality of an open tender or auction system, many beneficiaries have been chosen solely on the basis of their political and personal connections.

Privatised Patronage

Numerous cases can be cited as evidence of political patronage in the implementation of privatisation. In 1986 RM1.4 billion worth of water supply projects involving 174 schemes was awarded without open tender to Antah Biwater Sdn Bhd, a company in which the Negeri Sembilan royal family had 51 per cent equity through Antah Holdings Bhd, which had no relevant record in engineering; the remaining 49 per cent equity, however, was held by a company which possessed the expertise to implement the project – Biwater Ltd, a British water supply and treatment group, with strong political connections to the Thatcher government. Despite the privatised status of the water supply project, the government remained responsible for the operation and maintenance of the schemes. Antah Biwater had, in fact, secured a turnkey contract, with a British government financing arrangement thrown in as an aid package. It was anticipated that all of the design and engineering work would be handled by Biwater at the expense of Malaysian engineers and consultants who had previously handled such projects. When disgruntled Malaysian civil engineering firms claimed that Antah Biwater was charging much more than they would have, government officials pointed to the British aid package inducement, which had secured the deal for Biwater.

In 1983, despite competition from other established companies, a licence was issued to a newly incorporated joint venture, STMB, to operate its private third broadcasting network, TV3. The major shareholders of STMB included UMNO's holding company, the Fleet Group (the leading partner with a 40 per cent stake, which also had the prerogative to determine the remaining shareholders); Maika Holdings, the MIC-controlled investment holding company which obtained a 10 per cent stake; and Daim Zainuddin, soon to be appointed Finance minister, whose holding companies were given 10 per cent of the equity. The Syed Kechik Foundation, controlled by Syed Kechik, was given a 20 per cent stake in TV3 (Gomez 1990: 72–8). As the only private television station, TV3 proved to be very profitable. Although it incurred a loss of RM1 million in 1984, the first year of operation, the company has not failed to record handsome profits since. In fact, despite a severe recession, TV3 declared a pre-tax profit of RM2.16 million in 1985 (see Gomez 1994: 80–3); five years later, in 1990, the company's pre-tax profits had risen almost fifteenfold to RM31.59 million (*Investors Digest* April 1991). In view of this, since 1983, the shareholding structure of TV3 has been rapidly changing (see Gomez 1994: 80–3). By 1994 the majority shareholder of the company was Malaysian Resources Corporation Bhd (MRCB), a listed company controlled by businessmen closely associated with Deputy Prime Minister Anwar Ibrahim.

By 1994 TV3 had emerged as the largest shareholder in the privatised television cable network Satellite Network Services (SNS), with a majority 40 per cent stake; the government, with a 35 per cent interest, is the second largest shareholder. Another SNS shareholder, with a 12.5 per cent stake, is Eurocrest Sdn Bhd, controlled by Samsudin Abu Hassan, a protégé of Daim (*New Straits Times* 16/8/94). Since the cable network will offer subscribers access to five television channels, it is expected to generate much revenue (see *Malaysian Business* 15/8/94).

The highly profitable gaming entity Sports Toto was sold in 1985 to companies controlled by Vincent Tan Chee Yioun and Tunku Abdullah of the Negeri Sembilan royal house. Through his holding company, B&B Enterprise Sdn Bhd, Tan was awarded the right to acquire 70 per cent of the lucrative gaming concern, then controlled by the Ministry of Finance Incorporated, a holding company under the jurisdiction of Finance Minister Daim. B&B Enterprise later sold 10 per cent of its stake in Sports Toto to Tunku Abdullah's Melewar Group for RM4 million. Tunku Abdullah is a longtime close associate of Prime Minister Mahathir, while Tan has been involved in companies in which Daim has had an interest.

In 1986, through another holding company, Nautilus Corporation Sdn Bhd, Vincent Tan was given a licence to operate another gaming entity, Ascot Sports, which commenced operations in 1988 (*Asiaweek* 23/9/88). Ascot Sports, the only off-course betting operator in Malaysia for English and Australian horse races, ceased operations in June 1990 (*The Star* 9/6/90). In 1993 Tan was also given a licence to publish an English language tabloid daily, *The Sun*.

In early 1993 Indah Water Konsortium Sdn Bhd, led by Vincent Tan's main listed company, the Berjaya Group Bhd, was awarded, without tender, the RM6 billion national sewage disposal project (*The Star* 18/5/93). Berjaya owned a 20 per cent stake in the consortium, while its main partner was Northwest Water (M) Sdn Bhd, a subsidiary of the major British utilities company, Northwest Water Ltd. The contract involved the privatisation of around 143 local water authorities through-out Malaysia. Indah Konsortium is to manage, operate and maintain the urban sewerage systems for 28 years (*Malaysian Business* 16/12/93). Protests against the award of this contract came from many quarters, including UMNO Youth members, over, as one regional magazine pointed out, 'Berjaya's relative lack of experience in public works. Although Berjaya is involved in small road-building projects in Malaysia, it has never built anything the size of the national sewerage project' (*Far Eastern Economic Review* 1/4/93) (see also Case Study 10, p. 152).

In 1987 the RM86 million Jalan Kuching–Jalan Kepong interchange project was contracted to a RM2 Bumiputera company, Seri Angkasa Sdn Bhd, which had previously never transacted any business but was owned by a brother of Daim, another of his business protégés, Hassan Abas, and T. K. Lim and his family. Seri Angkasa promptly subcontracted the project to a Japanese construction company (*Asian Wall Street Journal* 31/5/88). Seri Angkasa was later acquired by publicly listed Kamunting Bhd via a share swap which gave the company a controlling interest in Kamunting. In 1989 T. K. Lim used Kamunting to take over publicly listed Multi-Purpose Holdings Bhd, a conglomerate five times its size in terms of paid-up capital which had been built and controlled by the MCA (Gomez 1994: 211–15).

In September 1988 Pan Malaysian Sweeps Sdn Bhd, the holding company of T. Ananda Krishnan, another close associate of Prime Minister Mahathir, was awarded the privatised Big Sweep lottery licence, originally held by the Selangor, Perak and Penang Turf Clubs, which could sell the tickets only to their members. Pan Malaysian Sweeps, however, was given the right to sell tickets to the public from 1 February 1989 (*New Straits Times* 16/2/89). In another development in January 1989, Ananda Krishnan's Pan Malaysian Pools Sdn Bhd secured from the Totalisator Board of Malaysia the contract to manage the Numbers Forecast Totalisator Operation (NFO), then also under the manage-ment of the turf clubs (*Malaysian Business* 16/11/91). Besides benefiting from the privatised gaming sector, Ananda Krishnan has also moved into the telecommunications industry, another rapidly developing sector in Malaysia. Through Binariang Sdn Bhd, a consortium which he leads, Ananda Krishnan obtained licences not only to launch a satellite, Measat I, in 1995, but also to develop various telephone and broad-casting services (see Case Study 11, p. 159).

In 1993 the government disclosed that the publicly listed Diversified Resources Bhd would head a consortium that would have a virtual monopoly of the privatised minibus services in Kuala Lumpur (Cheong 1993: 89–97). The following year, through its subsidiary, Pusat Pem-eriksaan Kenderaan Berkomputer Sdn Bhd (Puspakom), Diversified

Resources also obtained a privatised fifteen-year commercial vehicles inspection concession, which is expected to involve a yearly turnover of between RM45 and RM55 million (*The Star* 5/8/94). One director of Diversified Resources is Nasaruddin Jalil, a former political secretary of Deputy Prime Minister and Finance Minister Anwar Ibrahim. The company's executive chairman, Yahya Ahmad, a former schoolmate of Anwar, is believed to be strongly favoured by Prime Minister Mahathir (*Asiaweek* 17/11/93; *Malaysian Business* 1/7/93). Yahya Ahmad and Nasaruddin Jalil are also directors of another listed company, Gadek Bhd, while the latter is also an executive with the MBf Group, led by Loy Hean Heong and Tunku Abdullah.

Together with Perusahaan Otomobil Nasional Bhd (Proton), the government-controlled, publicly listed car manufacturer, Diversified Resources also formed a joint venture, Usahasama Proton-DRB Sdn Bhd, to develop, manufacture and distribute various new Proton models. Despite the involvement of government-controlled Proton in the project, Diversified Resources was given a majority 51 per cent stake in the joint venture, while Proton's interest amounted to only 30 per cent. In 1994, following Prime Minister Mahathir's initiative, this joint-venture company teamed up with France's Automobile Citroen to manufacture and market Citroen-type cars under the Proton trademark (Cheong 1993: 89–97; *Asiaweek* 17/11/93; *Malaysian Business* 1/12/93; *New Straits Times* 19/7/94). In October 1995 the government announced its intention to sell its 32 per cent stake in its largest public enterprise, HICOM Holdings, which also owns majority stakes in Proton and the publicly listed Proton distributor EON, to Yahya Ahmad. Despite his relatively recent involvement in Malaysia's corporate sector, by the end of 1993 Yahya Ahmad was listed as the sixteenth largest owner of publicly listed stock, and was then worth RM1.95 billion; he was listed above established Chinese entrepreneurs such as banker Teh Hong Piow of the Public Bank and industrialist William Cheng of the Lion Group, and major foreign concerns including Nestlé SA and Shell Overseas Holdings Ltd (see *Malaysian Business* 1/12/93).

In December 1993 it was announced that Malaysian Helicopter Services Bhd (MHS), a publicly quoted company controlled by Tajudin Ramli, another protégé of Daim Zainuddin, would acquire a 32 per cent stake in MAS from Bank Negara for RM1.79 billion, or RM8 per MAS share. The MAS acquisition involved a share swap, with Bank Negara obtaining 112 million new RM1 MHS shares, issued at a price of RM16 each. The Finance Ministry described the MAS divestment as a 'further privatisation of the national airline' (*Malaysian Business* 16/1/94). There was no open bidding for the airline shares. This was the second time such a transaction had taken place. Some MAS equity had been sold to the public and the Brunei government in September 1985 for RM180 million, but the government still retained a significant interest in the airline. On 31 December 1993, Bank Negara sold its remaining 11.5 per cent stake in MAS to another government-controlled agency, the Pensions Trust Fund, while the government retained a golden share in MAS (*The Star* 1/6/94). Later, after the fall in share prices in early 1994, the share swap involving MAS and MHS was rescinded; instead, in June 1994, RZ Equities Sdn Bhd, in which Tajudin Ramli has a 99.9 per cent stake, agreed to acquire the 32 per cent MAS equity at the same price of RM1.79 billion; MHS, however, was given a one-year option to acquire RZ Equities from Tajudin, an option which it took up in August 1994 (*The Star* 16/6/94 and 19/8/94; *New Straits Times*, 12/8/94). After the sale of the MAS equity, it is believed that the government's plan to develop a second airline, Air Asia Sdn Bhd, has been suspended indefinitely. Although Air Asia, which is majority-owned by HICOM (then controlled by the government), was issued a licence in April 1994, there has been a delay in starting operations. According to HICOM's chairman, Jamil Mohamed Jan, this is probably because 'the high price paid for the MAS shares must have caused the private sector company to approach the government to be cautious towards us' (*The Star* 26/8/94).

Although it was privatised in 1985, MAS had been in the black in some years in the early 1990s mainly because of the sale of some of its aircraft. For the financial year 1992/93, for example, although the airline company recorded an operating loss of RM179.6 million, it was able to declare a pre-tax profit of RM157.5 million only after taking into account the RM337.1 million revenue it received from the sale of aircraft (*Malaysian Business* 16/1/94). Interestingly, just before the (further) privatisation of MAS to Tajudin's MHS, a company one-fifth the size of MAS in terms of paid-up capital, it was apparent that MAS was beginning to show a profit without having to resort to the sale of its assets (*New Straits Times* 28/2/94).

Tajudin Ramli has also benefited substantially from his involvement in the telecommunications industry through Celcom Sdn Bhd. Celcom, which got the first licence to operate a cellular telephone network, was originally a joint venture between UMNO's Fleet Group and the government-owned STM. In 1992 Tajudin gained total ownership of Celcom, which had a virtual monopoly of the cellular telephone net-work sector. Through this highly lucrative company, Tajudin managed to consolidate his majority ownership of the publicly listed TRI via a reverse takeover (see Case Study 9, p. 148).

Although it was disclosed that even MARA, the main Bumiputera trust-holding company, would be privatised, a number of the company's main investments were divested before the privatisation was implemented. For example, ostensibly through a partial management buy-out, MARA's wholly owned subsidiary, KK Industries Sdn Bhd (KKI), was sold to three parties: 45 per cent of KKI's equity of RM50 million was allotted to its senior management; of the remaining equity, 10 per cent was awarded to the Yayasan Bumiputera Pulau Pinang, reputedly a political flagship of UMNO deputy president Anwar Ibrahim, and then under the chairmanship of his protégé, Ibrahim Saad, a federal deputy minister who also served one term as the deputy chief minister of Pulau Pinang from 1990 to 1995. The remaining 45 per cent of KKI was taken up by Au Metalvest Sdn Bhd, owned by an UMNO State Assemblyman in Pulau Pinang, Ahmad Saad, who is also the deputy chairman of the Permatang Pauh division, headed by Anwar (*The Edge* 2/1/95).

Of the three companies appointed by the Health Ministry for the privatisation of support services to district and general hospitals in April 1994, one of them was the UMNO-linked hotel and property concern, the Faber Group. Another was a tripartite consortium which includes Konsortium Tongkah, owned by Tongkah Holdings Bhd; a major shareholder of Tongkah Holdings is Prime Minister Mahathir's son, Mokhzani Mahathir. The third recipient of the contract, Asia Lab Sdn Bhd, is expected to be injected into MRCB, a company led by associates of Anwar Ibrahim; one of the two shareholders of Asia Lab is Azmi Jaafar, a director of Malakoff Bhd, controlled by MRCB (*New Straits Times* 28/4/94; *Malaysian Business* 16/5/94; Cheong 1993: 283–8). This project involves the privatisation of clinical waste management, laundry, and facility engineering and biomedical engineering services, and is expected to generate an annual revenue of at least RM600 million, yielding a profit of at least RM50 million (*New Straits Times* 28/4/94).

The majority shareholders of Metro Vision, Malaysia's second licensed private television network – with a combined stake of 75 per cent – are Melewar Corporation Bhd and Utusan Melayu (M) Bhd. Melewar is controlled by Tunku Abdullah, a close associate of Mahathir, while UMNO was disclosed as having a direct majority stake in Utusan Melayu when the company was publicly listed on the KLSE in August 1994. Among the other shareholders of the new television network are Vincent Tan's Berjaya Group Bhd and Quek Leng Chan's Nanyang Press Bhd (*The Star* 22/7/94).

One of the most controversial privatisation cases so far has involved the multi-billion ringgit North–South Highway project contracted in 1986 to United Engineers (M) Bhd, then an ailing publicly listed company with a dismal record in the construction industry and no experience in highway-building. But UEM was by then majority-owned by Hatibudi, an UMNO holding company (*Asian Wall Street Journal* 28/1/88). The privatisation of the highway contract to a company owned by UMNO was justified by Mahathir on the grounds that the party needed funds to pay off expenses incurred in building its massive RM360 million headquarters in Kuala Lumpur (see *The Star* 29/8/87).

Since UMNO gained control of UEM, the company has been the beneficiary of a number of other privatised government contracts despite the controversy surrounding the privatisation of the highway contract to UEM. In 1985 the company was awarded a RM250 million contract to design the National Sports Complex in Sungei Besi, on the outskirts of Kuala Lumpur; UEM is also expected to get the contract to build this complex (*Business Times* 5/1/87; *New Straits Times* 20/5/93). Two years later UEM obtained the RM47.5 million project management consultancy for the expansion of the gas-processing plant and the export terminal in Terengganu under the Peninsular Gas Utilization (PGU) Phase II project (Lim Kit Siang 1990). In February 1990 UEM secured a contract from the Penang government to undertake a land reclamation project involving about 392 hectares of foreshore land (*The Star* 12/2/90). In December 1990 the company was also assigned the construction of the first phase of the RM1.671 billion second causeway between Malaysia and Singapore; as usual, there was no open bidding for the contract because the government had awarded it on a 'first come, first served' basis (*New Straits Times* 14/12/90). In August 1990 UEM also submitted a RM2.4 billion proposal for the development of the west Johore port near Gelang Patah. The four-phase project, to be completed in twenty years, covers over 600 hectares of reclaimed land (*The Star* 25/4/91). In May 1994 the Health Ministry awarded the privatisation of its pharmaceutical laboratories and stores to Southern Task (M) Sdn Bhd, a company wholly owned by UEM; the award involved a fifteen-year concession to manufacture and distribute drugs to government hospitals. During this period the government's annual expenditure for drug acquisition was estimated at RM150 million (*New Straits Times* 19/5/94; *The Star* 19/5/94); the government hand-picked UEM for the project although the company had no previous experience in the pharmaceutical industry. UEM later divested 30 per cent of its stake in Southern Task to the publicly listed Kuala Lumpur Industries Holdings Bhd for RM13.2 million (*The Sun* 9/6/94).

Apart from this, other publicly listed companies owned or controlled by UEM have also benefited substantially from privatisation. In February 1992 Time Engineering Bhd received a RM41.44 billion combined cycle power station contract from the Perlis State Economic Development Corporation (*The Star* 26/2/92). In November 1992 Time Engineering was also awarded a twenty-year licence for various telecommunications services; in June 1994 it obtained another telecommunications licence for more sophisticated services (see *Malaysian Business* 16/8/94). After the 1993 announcement by Prime Minister Mahathir of the government's decision to construct a new multi-billion ringgit international airport, Kinta Kellas plc, another listed company owned by UEM, disclosed that at the invitation of the government it had submitted a proposal to provide project management services for construction of the airport (*New Straits Times* 12/5/93). In late 1991 Ho Hup Construction Bhd, a listed construction firm that had just been acquired by UEM, obtained a RM118 million contract, part of the RM830 million Sungei Selangor Water Supply Scheme, soon after its takeover by UEM (*New Straits Times* 10/9/91). In April 1994 the government appointed UEM as the contractor for the RM1 billion highway leading to the country's proposed new international airport in Sepang, outside Kuala Lumpur (*New Straits Times* 27/4/94). UEM's main shareholder, Renong Bhd, also benefited from privatisation when it was earmarked to obtain the second phase of Kuala Lumpur's light rail transit project (*The Star* 13/5/94).

Detailed studies of the privatised management buy-out of Kumpulan Fima and Peremba and the RM15 billion BOO construction of the Bakun Dam in Sarawak help highlight the manner in which patronage has been abused through the privatisation policy (see Case Studies 6 and 7, pp. 100–16).

The Politics of Privatisation

The case of privatisation in Malaysia is intriguing in that despite the extent to which patronage has figured prominently in the award of Malaysia's privatised projects, implementation of the policy in the nation has been deemed quite successful and is being used as a model for other, especially developing, countries (see Malaysia 1991a). Yet since privatisation in Malaysia is centrally directed, and there is overwhelming evidence that centralisation of power in the executive arm of government, particularly in the hands of Mahathir's UMNO, has contributed to the extensive practice of patronage in the execution of the policy, an independent monitoring agency is urgently needed. This will help to eliminate rent-seeking activities which have probably undermined the effectiveness of privatisation and allowed questionable executive decisions that have enabled greater control over resources to pass into the hands of a corporate sector dominated by politically linked companies. This form of power centralisation and political involvement in the companies which have obtained privatised rents has meant that there is little protection of investments, sometimes even through the judicial process, from arbitrary executive decisions. Judicial review is seldom seen as a viable alternative that can be undertaken by companies operating in Malaysia for fear that this might jeopardise access to other privatised rents. Since the removal of the Lord President from office in 1988 under rather suspect circumstances – five other Supreme Court judges were also subsequently charged with 'gross misbehaviour' – it is credible to argue that many suspect the capacity of the judicial system to provide a decision that will antagonise the ruling elite (see Lee 1995).

Another drawback of political patronage is that privatisation has provided not only a relatively few cronies with very lucrative opportunities, but also political interference in the private sector continues despite, or rather through, privatisation. With such companies under the control of politically influential businessmen, it is inevitable that these political ties will continue to affect business operations. Although this change of ownership appears to have advanced the interests of new, more sophisticated, politically well-connected Bumiputera rentiers, they are nevertheless far from being entrepreneurs of the Schumpeterian type. The fact that the most influential and wealthy Malaysian businessmen by the early 1990s were also those most closely associated with Prime Minister Mahathir Mohamad – Deputy Prime Minister Anwar Ibrahim and government economic adviser Daim Zainuddin – suggests that the creation and disbursement or allocation of these rents have been crucial for continued political hegemony as rent-financed patron–client relations continue to be important in Malaysian politics.

Even though some non-Bumiputera interests may have benefited from privatisation, this does not mean that implementation of the policy has been of much benefit to most Chinese and Indians, or for that matter, Malay businesses. In fact, despite much evidence that deregulation has had a greater impact on Chinese investor confidence, Chinese business access to state rents still depends largely on their capacity to establish mutually beneficial links with powerful UMNO leaders who appear to be in control of Malaysia's privatisation process and are able to determine the prime beneficiaries of privatisation.

This would suggest that, given the manner in which privatisation is being implemented, the rents created by the state do not enhance competition nor do they provide substantial improvements in managerial efficiency. Since the political associations of those benefiting from privatisation also cloud assessments of whether the funds provided were due to the confidence of financial institutions in the managements of the companies, this also raises some doubts about the extent to which these managers are subject to the discipline of the financial market. With the threat of takeover and bankruptcy remote, managerial performance can hardly be said to have been affected by market discipline, which could enhance the efficiency of these companies. In the long run privatisation may not necessarily, therefore, lead to greater efficiency and promote investor confidence unless the government takes more active steps to ensure that the market is more carefully structured, devoid of extensive political interference, and subject to close scrutiny by regulatory agencies.

Assessments of privatised projects (see, for example, Case Studies 6 and 7, pp. 100–16) have also indicated that there is little evidence to support suggestions that with privatisation, improved managerial efficiency, extended research and development, and new market opportunities have emerged which have promoted economic development with increased participation by the private sector (see also Jomo 1994; Abdul Aziz 1994; Toh 1989). Moreover, in view of the close links between politicians and those securing privatised rents, the question that needs to be asked, and answered, is not just how effective privatisation has been or can be, but whether new control of economic activities as well as the economic welfare of consumers and employees warrant the active implementation of the policy. What is obvious is the evidence of further concentration of wealth, which in turn exacerbates economic inequality. Thus despite the changed nature of government intervention in the economy under privatisation as compared to the NEP period, there appears to be a similarity between the two policies in at least one sense: the efforts to centralise corporate ownership in the hands of new Bumiputera rentiers who enjoy close ties with influential politicians.

Case Study 6: The MBO of Kumpulan Fima and Peremba

A management buy-out (MBO) involves some or all of a company's management negotiating the acquisition of the company from its previous owners and would entail organising the finances to fund the purchase. When ownership changes, the former owners normally have no further interest in the company (Coyne and Wright 1985: 1). Gains in efficiency are expected from such transactions by eliminating the principal/agent dichotomy. Such MBOs reduce the likelihood of managers acting in their own interest at the expense of the company they do not own and may also relieve the management from previous owner-imposed constraints; this, in effect, 'remarries ownership and control within industry, and encourages independent, entrepreneurial decision-making' (Coyne and Wright 1985: 3).

Such buy-outs are not limited to the sale of government-owned enterprises to their managements. Coyne and Wright (1985: 11) list five major circumstances in which MBOs generally arise:

1 receivership of an independent company, where the buy-out may be the only means of continuing the company;
2 receivership of the parent company, where a viable subsidiary (or subsidiaries) is bought out while the remainder of the parent company is liquidated;
3 retirement or death of the current owners;
4 divestment of a subsidiary by a still active parent company;
5 privatisation of all or part of a nationalised industry, where an MBO is a more attractive or feasible proposition than immediate flotation on the Stock Exchange.

Generally, it is not the owners but the management – particularly in the case of large or government-owned companies – who know more about the assets of a company and are thus better able to influence the value of these assets (von Thadden 1990: 642). This presumption strengthens arguments favouring the MBO of public enterprises because managers who are also owners will be more motivated to generate greater profits, which would help increase efficiency.

As noted above, the theoretical case for the promotion of MBOs is based mainly on the principal/agent theory which maintains that the divorce of ownership from management in state-owned enterprises provides little incentive for the management (that is, agents) to perform in a manner that maximises the benefits to the owners, that is, the government (or principal) (White 1988: 19). In line with rational choice theory, agents are presumed to be primarily interested in maximising their own interests rather than those of their principals; owners of large private companies are usually not in a position to effectively control the decisions made by their managers as well (Vining and Poulin 1989). In line with asymmetric or incomplete information arguments, agents are presumed to be only privy to partial information about the principal's interests, while the principal tends to be inadequately informed about the agent's behaviour; the agent may also have his own priorities which are at variance with the interests of the principal (Donahue 1989: 38–9).

According to the principal/agent theory, these drawbacks can be reduced by privatisation because managerial behaviour is disciplined by shareholders through the share market. Managers are disciplined by the need to meet shareholders' interests to ensure their continued support for the company, thus retaining, if not enhancing, the value of the stock. The confidence of stockholders in a company's management provides managers with a means for further generation of funds; this reduces the probability of bankruptcy, hostile takeovers and, most importantly, attempts to replace the management (White 1988: 19).

Kumpulan Fima Bhd

Kumpulan Fima, a product of Malaysia's NEP, was incorporated on 23 February 1972 and had a paid-up capital of RM190 million. Its equity was once almost wholly owned (99.95 per cent) by the Ministry of Finance Incorporated, the Finance Ministry's holding company. The Sabah State Development Economic Corporation owned the remaining 0.05 per cent of Kumpulan Fima's equity (*Malaysian Business* 1/10/90). Although food-processing is the company's main activity, the Kumpulan Fima Group is also involved in trading, manufacturing, plantation agriculture and general services. In fact Kumpulan Fima functions primarily as a holding company for its sixteen subsidiaries, seven associate companies, and three publicly listed companies (*Malaysian Business* 1/10/90; *New Straits Times* 25/3/91).

Among Kumpulan Fima's former directors were Mahathir (who resigned in 1981, when he assumed office as prime minister), Razaleigh Hamzah, a former Finance minister who left UMNO in 1988 to form the opposition Parti Melayu Semangat 46 (he rejoined UMNO in 1996), Lorrain Esme Osman, who was involved in the BMF scandal, and Eric Chia, a prominent Chinese businessman with long-standing ties with Mahathir (Gomez 1990: 32–4).

Kumpulan Fima's most important asset was its stake in the publicly listed Fima Metal Box Bhd. Formerly known as Metal Box, and under British control until 1981, Kumpulan Fima successfully gained majority ownership of the company through a share-for-asset swap by injecting a major subsidiary into Fima Metal Box (Gomez 1990: 33–4). In December 1989, just before it was involved in the MBO exercise, Fima Metal Box took over the government's security printing operations despite limited relevant experience (*The Star* 2/12/89). Under this privatisation exercise, Fima Metal Box took over the Security Printing Branch of the National Printing Department for RM7 million. It thus became responsible for the printing of all government security documents, except currency (*The Star* 2/12/89). In September 1990 the MBO of Kumpulan Fima was announced on the eve of the October general election when Mahathir's political future was more effectively challenged than ever before. Apart from Kumpulan Fima's controlling 33 per cent stake in Fima Metal Box, two other publicly listed companies were associated with Kumpulan Fima: United Plantations Bhd and Nestlé (M) Bhd, in which Kumpulan Fima had 19.08 per cent and 3.4 per cent stakes respectively. After the buy-out, Kumpulan Fima divested its stake in United Plantations for RM125 million (*Malaysian Business* 15/10/90, 1/12/92), almost two-thirds the price of Kumpulan Fima's MBO, valued at RM190 million.

Kumpulan Fima's MBO was led by Basir Ismail, who had replaced Mahathir as director in 1981 and had become chairman in 1986. After making his reputation in the Johore State Economic Development Corporation, Basir became director and chairman of other government-owned entities established under the NEP, most notably the government-owned Bank Bumiputra from 1985 to 1990, and Petronas, the national petroleum company. Basir is also chairman of Malaysian Airports, another corporatised entity, and of a number of publicly listed companies: United Plantations, Cold Storage (M) Bhd, Cycle & Carriage Ltd, and Cycle & Carriage Bintang Bhd. Even though he emerged from the mid-1980s as a major corporate player, Basir was appointed to head the Capital Issues Committee, a government regulatory body, which was responsible for monitoring and approving corporate exercises until 1993 (*The Star* 13/7/91; *Malaysian Business* 1/12/92).

Basir also acquired a minor stake in the publicly listed TRI, controlled by Tajudin Ramli, who is also closely linked to Daim Zainuddin. Interestingly, both Cold Storage and TRI were once majority-owned by Daim. In fact, Daim's equity in Cold Storage had been acquired from Kumpulan Fima (Gomez 1991a: 25–6). Through his main holding company, Kegiatan Makmur Sdn Bhd, Basir also owned a stockbroking firm, Capitalcorp Securities Sdn Bhd. In 1991 Basir bought into Jernih Insurance Corporation Sdn Bhd, a company controlled by the Hong Kong–based Kuok Group (*New Straits Times* 11/10/91).

Under the terms of Kumpulan Fima's MBO, the company was sold to Basir's holding company, Kegiatan Makmur, whose major shareholders included Basir and Mohamed Noor Ismail, the managing director of Kumpulan Fima. The RM200 million loan for the MBO was arranged by Bumiputra Merchant Bankers Bhd, a subsidiary of Bank Bumiputra, of which Basir had been chairman until earlier that year (1990). The loan was provided by the government-controlled UMBC (then owned by the government trust agency, Pernas), Bank of Commerce Bhd (an UMNO-controlled bank), Public Bank Bhd and Pacific Bank Bhd. Collateral for the loan was the entire Kumpulan Fima equity and 2.8 million TRI shares in which Basir then had a minor stake (*Malaysian Business* 1/12/92).

Basir later divested part of his 80 per cent equity in Kegiatan Makmur to Subur Rahmat Sdn Bhd, a company controlled by Mohamad Azlan Hashim, a former merchant banker, probably to reduce the debt taken to acquire Kumpulan Fima. Kegiatan Makmur later disclosed its intention to divest part of its Kumpulan Fima equity to the company's employees, ostensibly to promote their ownership and participation in the development of the company (*New Straits Times* 25/3/91; *The Star* 13/7/91; *Malaysian Business* 1/12/92).

Although it was speculated that the takeover of Kumpulan Fima would be worth at least RM300 million, since the company then had investments worth almost RM232 million – Kumpulan Fima's stake in its listed entities alone amounted to RM226 million at the time – and was registering sales totalling more than RM150 million a year (see *Malaysian Business* 1/10/90), the MBO was surprisingly priced at a mere RM190 million. Even though the MBO meant that Kegiatan Makmur would take over Kumpulan Fima's liabilities totalling RM138 million (*New Straits Times* 25/3/91), the buy-out was severely censured by various quarters. Allegations of favouritism were made by the opposition Democratic Action Party (DAP), while other critics alleged that profitable government-owned entities were being privatised to businessmen with close connections to top UMNO leaders (see *Malaysian Business* 1/12/90; Gomez 1991a: 23–7).

Since the MBO of Kumpulan Fima in 1990, the group has continued to register increases in turnover and profits (see Table 4.3). However, despite these increases, a breakdown of Kumpulan Fima's major activities in 1991 indicates that there have been no major changes in the breakdown of its turnover (see Table 4.4).

Although Kumpulan Fima's MBO privatisation was supposed to improve efficiency in the face of competition, by 1993 the company was

Table 4.3   Kumpulan Fima Group Performance, 1989–91 (RM million)

	1989	*1990*	*1991*
Turnover	205.7	251.7	281.5
Profit before tax	8.9	6.3	6.5
Profit after tax	4.5	6.5	2.9

Source: *Malaysian Business* 1/12/92

Table 4.4   Turnover of Kumpulan Fima, 1989–91 (percentages)

	Turnover		
	1989	*1990*	*1991*
Agriculture	1.3	1.4	1.6
Manufacturing and trading	89.9	90.3	88.9
Bulk handling	2.9	3.5	3.6
Investment holding	6.2	4.8	6.0

Source: *Malaysian Business* 1/12/92

forced to divest its investments in tin-manufacturing and packaging as it began to lose much of its market to its main competitor, Kian Joo Can Factory Bhd, which only began operations in 1985. With profits plunging, Kumpulan Fima eventually had to divest its entire interest in Metal Box (M) Bhd, Malaysian Can Company Sdn Bhd, and Plasticon (M) Sdn Bhd, to a foreign-owned company, CarnaudMetalbox Overseas Ltd, a merged entity including the English-based Metalbox Overseas Ltd (Cheong 1993: 83–5). Ironically, when Kumpulan Fima first participated in the industry in 1976, it had Malaysianised the tin-canning operations then owned by Britain's Metalbox Overseas Ltd; the wheel had, embarrassingly, come full circle (see Gomez 1990: 32–4). Kumpulan Fima, meanwhile, renamed itself the Fima Corporation, and announced that its primary involvement would be in the security-printing industry, an assured source of government rents (Cheong 1993: 83–5).

Peremba Bhd

Peremba was incorporated on 3 May 1979 as the commercial and construction arm of the government-owned Urban Development Authority. Another product of the NEP, the UDA was established to help Bumiputeras expand their businesses in small manufacturing, retailing and services by providing them with suitable premises in urban commercial areas (Gale 1981: 141). Soon after its incorporation, more than 30 UDA subsidiaries, involved in land and development ventures, were put into Peremba, making it one of Malaysia's leading property development concerns within a span of less than two years. In fact just eighteen months after its establishment, Peremba's founding chairman, Daim Zainuddin, was publicly describing the company as 'one of the largest property companies in South East Asia' (*Asian Wall Street Journal* 8/11/80).

Besides Daim, another founder-director of Peremba was Mohd Desa Pachi; both men were then also directors of the Fleet Group, then UMNO's main holding company. Daim remained a director of Peremba until 1984, when he was appointed Finance Minister. In 1985 Fleet Group was used to attempt a takeover of the lucrative, asset-rich Peremba; the acquisition, however, eventually fell through after a downturn of the property market, precipitated by the mid-1980s economic recession, which badly affected Peremba (Gomez 1991a: 24–5). During Daim's tenure as Peremba chairman, a number of now prominent Bumiputera businessmen were in the employ of the company. Among them were Wan Azmi Wan Hamzah of the publicly listed R. J. Reynolds Bhd and Land & General Bhd; Halim Saad, the executive chairman of UMNO's main listed company, Renong Bhd; Mohd Razali

Mohd Rahman, a shareholder of Hatibudi Sdn Bhd (another UMNO holding company which bought into UEM); and Samsudin Abu Hassan, who owns a major interest in Granite Industries Bhd, Cold Storage Bhd and Aokam Perdana Bhd, all listed companies once controlled by Waspavest Sdn Bhd, another UMNO holding company (see Gomez 1990).

The Peremba MBO was ostensibly spearheaded by its chairman, Mohd Razali, its chief executive, Abu Bakar Noor, and Hassan bin Chik Abas, the managing director of Landmarks Bhd, Peremba's main publicly quoted company, in which it had a controlling 40 per cent stake. Apart from having been a director of UMNO's Hatibudi, Mohd Razali had also served as a director of a number of private holding companies owned by Daim including Sykt Maluri Sdn Bhd, Taman Bukit Maluri Sdn Bhd, Pradaz Sdn Bhd, Daza Sdn Bhd and Baktimu Sdn Bhd. Mohd Razali had also served in an executive capacity in the Malaysian French Bank Bhd and was appointed a director of UMBC when Daim's companies owned a majority stake in these banks (Gomez 1990: 108). Hassan Abas was also involved as director and shareholder of some companies linked to Daim, most prominently Sri Alu Sdn Bhd. Sri Alu had a 35 per cent stake in Seri Angkasa Sdn Bhd, which was awarded the privatised Jalan Kuching–Jalan Kepong interchange project though it had no previous experience in construction.

Peremba's MBO was estimated at RM350 million, with all the company's equity used as collateral for the buy-out (*Malaysian Business* 16/5/92). Not having recovered completely from the mid-1980s real property slump, Peremba did not appear as profitable as Kumpulan Fima and also had fewer corporate assets. Peremba's future potential, however, lay in its underused real property assets. By the late 1980s, apart from its majority stake in Landmarks and its extensive land banks, including properties in Kuala Lumpur's Golden Triangle area, Peremba had interests in Saujana Resort (golf course and hotel) and UBN Holdings (hotel, office and apartments), and was also involved in the Wangsa Maju township project, a major development venture on the outskirts of Kuala Lumpur (*Malaysian Business* 16/5/92).

Before the 1990 MBO, Peremba's total assets were worth RM374 million, while its liabilities amounted to RM65.4 million. Like the property market more generally, Peremba was clearly on the road to recovery, with its turnover increasing from RM139 million in 1989 to RM208 million in 1990. In 1990 it declared a pre-tax profit of RM4.7 million in contrast to its RM28 million loss the previous year (*Malaysian Business* 16/5/92).

Landmarks had been controlled by prominent Chinese property developer Chong Kok Lim and his family before Peremba obtained a

43 per cent stake in 1989, after a restructuring scheme to save the afflicted listed company from liquidation. To revive Landmarks, Peremba sold some of its better subsidiaries to the ailing company, including Saujana Resort, Golf Associates Sdn Bhd, and part of its equity in the highly lucrative UBN Holdings (Cheong 1990b: 137–9). Apart from these companies, Landmarks also owned the Parkroyal Hotels in Kuala Lumpur and Penang, and the Sungai Wang Plaza, a huge shopping mall in the heart of the capital. Buoyed by these new assets, and with the recovery of the property sector by the end of the 1980s, Landmarks' performance improved appreciably. By 1991, just a year after Peremba's MBO, Landmarks' turnover and pre-tax profits had almost doubled (*Malaysian Business* 16/5/92).

Most of the Peremba assets taken over by Landmarks were paid for with the issue of new Landmarks shares, increasing Peremba's stake in the company to more than 60 per cent. Around a fifth of these Landmarks shares were then sold to the listed company's minority shareholders, reducing Peremba's stake in the company to around 42 per cent. Despite this divestment, which helped broaden ownership of Landmarks, Peremba maintained control of the listed company and raised almost RM152 million, which helped ease its own debts and improve its financial standing (*Malaysian Business* 16/5/92).

Since the MBO in 1990, Landmarks has obtained a 60 per cent stake in Teluk Datai Resorts Sdn Bhd – the remaining 40 per cent equity is held by the Kedah State Economic Development Corporation – which has built an attractive holiday resort in Pulau Langkawi, a major tourist location in Kedah. Through another wholly owned subsidiary, Landmarks Engineering & Development Sdn Bhd, Landmarks benefited from a number of minor privatised projects and was, in the words of its managing director, Hassan Abas, 'still trying for bigger privatisation projects' (*Malaysian Business* 16/5/92).

Although the property development sector recovered significantly in the late 1980s, deft manoeuvring of shares and assets by Peremba, rather than new property developments, appears to have been primarily responsible for the revival of both the ailing company and its once almost moribund flagship, Landmarks. Furthermore, most of the restructuring to revive Peremba and its subsidiaries seems to have transpired before the MBO, a strong indication that the company was only sold after its dire financial position had already been overcome while still owned by the government. Hence the recovery of Landmarks and Peremba cannot be attributed to improved management after privatisation.

Despite the remarkable recovery that Landmarks achieved after the MBO, Peremba's entire 40 per cent equity in the listed company was sold in October 1993 to Samsudin Abu Hassan, another ex-Peremba protégé of Daim (*Malaysian Business* 16/10/93). Under the terms of the sale, after acquiring Landmarks, Samsudin would relinquish the listed company's ownership of three companies (Saujana Resort (M) Sdn Bhd, Saujana Hotel Sdn Bhd, and Gracom Sdn Bhd) to Peremba for RM124 million; this would give Peremba control of two important businesses, the Hyatt Saujana Hotel and the Saujana Golf and Country Club (Cheong 1993: 24–5). The terms of the transaction suggest that the sale of the lucrative Landmarks, Peremba's only listed vehicle, was to provide Samsuddin with another listed vehicle for corporate expansion. In fact, by early 1994, it was believed that Landmarks would be used to acquire the government-owned Bank Bumiputra, which was also expected to be privatised (see *Malaysian Business* 16/3/94). Although this deal did not materialise, Landmarks' huge capital base was used to acquire an interest in another minor listed tin mining concern, Austral Amalgamated Bhd, in August 1994 (*New Straits Times* 31/8/94). This suggests that the MBO of Peremba was an interim measure to concentrate lucrative government-owned assets in the hands of a favoured crony, later to be shifted around for other business deals.

In fact Samsuddin had also acquired almost 30 per cent of the equity in the publicly listed Perstima Bhd from Kumpulan Fima, only to sell it a month later for a profit of more than RM27 million (*Malaysian Business* 16/10/93). In August 1994 Samsuddin's private company, Eurocrest Sdn Bhd, in which he has a 70 per cent stake, was also awarded a 12.5 per stake in the privatised television network Satellite Network Services (*New Straits Times* 16/8/94). Samsuddin also owns more than 24 per cent of the equity in the publicly listed Cold Storage Bhd, probably in trust for Daim; another 43 per cent stake in Cold Storage is owned by Cycle & Carriage Ltd, linked to Basir Ismail of Kumpulan Fima (Cheong 1993: 19–22).

From these case studies, there appears to be little evidence that the MBO privatisation of Kumpulan Fima and Peremba improved their management; rather, the divestitures of these two public enterprises provide examples of how privatisation has been abused to benefit the politically powerful. Apart from evidence of apparently preferential treatment in the selection of MBO privatisation beneficiaries, both these companies appear to have returned to profitability before the buy-outs by their managements, thus undermining claims that privatisation, or more specifically the MBOs, improved management. Furthermore, even though both Peremba and Kumpulan Fima registered increased profits after the MBOs, there does not appear to be any evidence of substantial improvements in managerial efficiency. The improved performances seem to have reflected the generally improved economic environments of the early 1990s rather than any major managerial improvements following the MBOs. In fact, as Kumpulan Fima's divestment of its tin-packaging companies suggests, it has not been able to improve efficiency and increase profitability in the face of competition despite private management by the owners.

In both cases the MBOs were financed with loans secured from financial institutions, with the shares of the companies involved pledged as collateral. Despite the signs of recovery shown by Kumpulan Fima and Peremba before the MBOs, their management's access to such financing seems to have been due more to their political links, particularly with former Finance Minister Daim.

If the government incurred high costs in propping up inefficient and loss-making public enterprises under the NEP, these problems do not seem to have been eradicated with privatisation. While tougher budget constraints since the fiscal crisis of the mid-1980s have imposed a new discipline, this policy is quite distinct and should be distinguished from privatisation. Instead the new form of patronage seems to involve selling profitable government-owned enterprises, at generous discounts, to businessmen who appear to be proxies of the top political leaders. Both Kumpulan Fima and Peremba have benefited from other privatisations before and immediately after the MBOs. Thus the MBO privatisation of profitable companies, while allowing them to have the benefit of preferential access to finance and business opportunities, is hardly testimony to improved management through privatisation. Meanwhile the mode of state patronage prevalent during the NEP period appears to be giving way to new, more sophisticated modes of political patronage of private business.

The fact that Kumpulan Fima and Peremba both displayed signs of recovery before the MBOs suggests that public enterprises can be profitable despite or even because of government ownership. In fact the case studies demonstrate that in spite of the change of ownership from the public to the private sector, competition does not appear to have increased because of or even just with privatisation. There is also little evidence to support suggestions that with these MBOs new market opportunities have emerged, which have promoted economic development with increased participation by the private sector. The case studies suggest that private ownership in itself has not significantly enhanced efficiency or improved productivity, thus supporting the contention that it is enhanced competition and not ownership change that is likely to promote efficiency. This then also suggests that the government's immediate revenue from divestiture of such profitable enterprises does not merit the loss of long-term, future revenues if ownership had been retained.

Case Study 7: The Bakun Dam BOO

In January 1994 Malaysia's largest privatised contract, the construction of the massive RM15 billion Bakun Dam project in Sarawak was awarded, without tender, to the publicly listed Ekran Bhd, controlled by Ting Pek Khiing, a Sarawakian Chinese timber tycoon closely associated with Sarawak Chief Minister Abdul Taib Mahmud, economic adviser Daim Zainuddin, and Prime Minister Mahathir. The Bakun Dam project, touted as the largest hydro-electric dam project in Southeast Asia, involves the construction of a dam 190 metres high and 300 metres wide and the underwater installation of two 648 kilometre-long electricity transmission lines between Sarawak and Peninsular Malaysia, which will be the longest in the world. On completion in the year 2004, the dam is expected to supply at least a quarter of Malaysia's power requirements, generating an annual revenue of at least RM3.5 billion. Apart from this, the timber revenue from the massive Bakun Dam site should generate at least RM2 billion in the first few years of the project (*Far Eastern Economic Review* 10/3/94; *Malaysian Business* 16/3/94; *Asian Wall Street Journal* 2/2/94).

The Sarawak state government originally intended to maintain a stake in the Bakun Dam project by privatising the contract to the Sarawak Electricity Supply Corporation (SESCO), the state's power utility. SESCO was then to be involved in a reverse takeover of the publicly listed Dunlop Estates Bhd, controlled by T. K. Lim through Multi-Purpose Holdings Bhd, thus also giving the Sarawak government control over a quoted entity. Ting's Ekran, however, apparently managed to get the dam contract at the eleventh hour through the intervention of Daim (see *Asian Wall Street Journal* 2/2/94).

To pacify a reportedly fuming T. K. Lim, Dunlop Estates was compensated for losing the potentially lucrative Bakun Dam project when the federal government approved a partial privatisation of SESCO; Dunlop Estates' reverse takeover of 45 per cent of SESCO's equity would enable the Sarawak state government to hold a 45 per stake in Dunlop Estates, while Multi-Purpose Holdings' interest in the company would diminish to 37 per cent. The Sarawak state government would retain a direct interest in the remaining 55 per cent of SESCO's equity (*The Edge* 19/6/95). SESCO is proposing to build a smaller dam in Sarawak, the Muram Dam (*Malaysian Business* 16/3/94).

It is generally doubted that Ekran even submitted a full-fledged proposal for the construction of the dam to the state government before the company was awarded the privatised contract. In early 1994 Ting himself acknowledged that his environmental impact assessment (EIA) report on the Bakun Dam would only be ready in June, almost six months after the project was awarded to Ekran (see *New Straits Times* 24/2/94); when the first part of the report was finally released at the end of March 1995, the document was only available in Sarawak at a cost of RM150 per copy. After protests from environmentalists, two copies of a 318-page report – basically a summary of the assessment, without the crucial appendices – were made available to the public in Kuala Lumpur in July 1995 (*The Star* 30/7/95).

There were criticisms that the Bakun Dam contract was overpriced by at least RM6 billion, that Ekran had no relevant experience in dam construction, and that the company would have much difficulty raising the massive funding required for the project on its own (see *Far Eastern Economic Review* 10/3/94). Although Ting disclosed that Ekran would have to 'borrow about RM12 billion to complete the job', from sources that were 'all local', he insisted that Ekran would 'not be getting a government grant'; the company, however, had 'earmarked at least 50.1 per cent equity [of the project] for the Sarawak state government' (*Malaysian Business* 16/3/94).

So it was not surprising when the government announced in April 1995, a year later, that 51 per cent of the Bakun Dam was to be allocated to Ekran and the Sarawak state government, while the remaining 49 per cent was to be divided between the government-controlled but publicly listed HICOM Holdings Bhd and TNB – among the most heavily capitalised companies on the local stock exchange – and the government's Employees' Provident Fund (EPF). While this would enable these government entities to have an interest in the Bakun Dam, Ekran remained responsible for its construction. Despite this announcement by the government, the manner and extent of involvement of these entities has not been finalised; for example, even four months after the announcement, the EPF was still undecided about participating in the project by taking up equity participation or merely by acting as financier (see *Business Times* 10/7/95). This suggests that although these major government-controlled companies and the EPF would largely finance and eventually own the dam, whose profitability is uncertain, Ekran's own profits were guaranteed by the high price tag as well as logging concession rights for the area to be flooded.

After disclosure of the EPF's involvement in the project, opposition to the controversial project increased. In one joint statement to the government, for example, nine non-government organisations (NGOs) protested against the possibility that 'the bulk of the funds (for the project) [would] come from the EPF' and queried how 'the EPF Board [could] justify sinking so much of the funds belonging to ordinary Malaysians into such a controversial project which is almost devoid of any meaningful public accountability' (*Aliran Monthly* 15 (5) 1995).

Despite vocal opposition to the project, since NGOs have very limited or no access to the controlled local press, the protest campaign has been muted.

The Bakun Dam project had previously been proposed and then shelved by the government. It had been on the government's drawing board for some time; government-appointed foreign consultants completed a feasibility study for a hydroelectric project in Bakun as early as July 1982, and by March 1986 the Ministry of Energy, Telecommunications and Posts had issued its own report on the dam project. After sustained protests by both Malaysian and foreign environmentalists, however, Mahathir announced in 1990 that the government was abandoning the project; 'Malaysia', he said, was 'making a big sacrifice for the environment' (*Hak* 1/3/94).

The protests by environmentalists were on the grounds that since the dam would cover almost 200,000 acres (an area larger than the size of Singapore), dislocate almost 5,000 people from five of Sarawak's numerous tribal communities (Kenyah, Ukit, Kayan, Kajang and Penan), and submerge around 173,000 acres of forest, it would cause irreparable damage to the state's ecosystem (*Hak* 1/3/94). But unlike the previous occasion, the protests in 1994 were not only by government critics. Criticisms have also surfaced from within UMNO ranks, particularly from its Youth division. It is doubtful that protests by such politicians have been solely due to the desire to protect the interests of the larger Bumiputera community, let alone those of the tribal communities of Sarawak, or even the environment. The UMNO Youth protest against the Bakun Dam appears to reflect discontent within UMNO over the allocation of rents in the process of privatisation. After all, during the 1992 UMNO General Assembly, objections had been raised by UMNO Youth members that non-Malay businessmen were obtaining lucrative privatised contracts.

By May 1994 there appeared to have been mounting tension between Deputy Prime Minister Anwar Ibrahim and Daim Zainuddin over the manner in which those close to Daim – some of whom, like Ting Pik Khiing, were non-Bumiputeras – had been securing the most lucrative privatisations; this had upset Bumiputera businessmen closely associated with Anwar which put the Finance Minister under some pressure. Anwar was also believed to have been upset over reports that at least 60 per cent of the government-owned Bank Bumiputra's equity was to be bought over, without his consent, by Samsudin Hassan, a protégé of Daim (see *Malaysian Business* 16/3/94); this appeared to challenge Anwar's power over his own domain, the Finance Ministry. Not long after, in an unexpected turn of events, the *New Straits Times*, controlled by Anwar associates, began to carry less than fully favourable reports on the Bakun

Dam project (see May 1994 issues). There was thus growing evidence of Daim's associates gaining extensive control over the most lucrative business opportunities awarded by the government to the corporate sector, with Ekran providing only the latest instance of this.

Incorporated as Wiradaya Sdn Bhd on 10 September 1991, Ekran's name-change was effected in March 1992 after a reverse takeover of the publicly listed Federal Cables, Wires and Metal Manufacturing Bhd (FCW), then a suspended, ailing telephone and electric cable manufacturer and supplier. Ting had managed to get a controlling stake in FCW after a protracted tussle with two other companies, one of which was the influential Sapura Holdings Bhd, controlled by Shamsuddin Kadir. After acquiring FCW, Ekran took over FCW's listed status, while the latter was renamed FCW Industries Sdn Bhd. Ting then also injected into Ekran his main private company, Woodhouse Sdn Bhd, a timber and housing construction concern (*New Straits Times* 6/4/94). By this time Ting had also acquired a stake in another listed company, Pacific Chemicals Bhd.

Ting is Ekran's major shareholder with a 25.25 per cent stake; his wife holds another 5 per cent of Ekran's equity. Two minority shareholders of the company with approximately one per cent each are Mahmud Abu Bekir Taib and Sulaiman Abdul Rahman bin Abdul Taib, both sons of Sarawak Chief Minister Taib Mahmud; both men are also minority shareholders of Pacific Chemicals (*Asian Wall Street Journal* 2/2/94). By the end of 1993, at least 43 per cent of Ekran's remaining equity was held by nominee companies, making it impossible to identify the other shareholders of the company (KLSE 19 (II) 1993: 171–4). Two other minority shareholders of Ekran were Shuaib Lazim (0.66 per cent equity) and Abdul Rasip Haron (0.99 per cent equity).

Shuaib Lazim is a former UMNO senator and State Assemblyman from Kedah. A close associate of Prime Minister Mahathir, Shuaib was also secretary of UMNO's Merbok division in Kedah, of which Daim was then chairman. Shuaib Lazim gained some prominence in the late 1980s, when he was awarded the privatised contract to develop a commercial centre under Merdeka Square (the former Selangor Club field) in Kuala Lumpur. His company, however, had no construction experience and eventually went bankrupt. The project was eventually completed by a company controlled by Wan Azmi Wan Hamzah, another Daim protégé.

Rasip Haron is also a director of another quoted company, Jasa Kita Bhd, which is listed on the KLSE's Second Board; the majority shareholder of Jasa Kita is Robert Tan Hua Choon, reportedly a close business associate of both Daim and Ting. Robert Tan gained prominence – and notoriety – when he was implicated in the infamous scandal involving the sale of nine million privatised STM shares, which were allocated to the MIC's public holding company, Maika Holdings, but were instead channelled to three obscure private companies apparently connected to MIC president S. Samy Vellu. Daim, then Finance Minister, was responsible for the award of the privatised STM shares to these companies. One of the three companies linked to Samy Vellu which received the STM shares was Clearway Sdn Bhd; Jasa Kita had reportedly been instrumental in helping Clearway dispose of the STM shares for a profit. A shareholder and director of Clearway was Robert Tan's driver, Baharuddin Mohd Arip, who also served as a director of Jasa Kita (*The Star* 17/7/92; Gomez 1994: 274; *Malaysian Business* 16/7/92).

Popularly known as the 'Casio King', after he managed to secure the franchise to distribute Casio brand watches and calculators, together with Ting, Tan got control of Pacific Chemicals in 1992; not long afterwards, Tan divested a major portion of his stake in Pacific Chemicals to Ting, but remained a minority shareholder and deputy chairman of the company (*Malaysian Business* 16/7/92, 16/8/93, 1/4/94). Tan also has an interest in another listed company, the UCM Corporation Bhd.

In 1993 another of Tan's companies, Spanco Sdn Bhd, obtained a lucrative privatised contract from the government to service all publicly owned vehicles. Rasip Haron is also a director and shareholder of Spanco. Under this scheme, Spanco would acquire all government-owned vehicles and then lease them to the government; it would thus become responsible for their maintenance. Since the project involves leasing at least 60,000 vehicles to the government at market rates, Spanco is expected to generate an annual turnover of around RM1.5 billion (*Malaysian Business* 16/8/93, 1/4/94).

In December 1993 FCW Industries was sold by Ekran to Robert Tan, Rasip Haron, and Mohd Noordin Daud for RM202 million; thus Ekran made an extraordinarily large gain of RM78 million by divesting its interest in FCW (*Malaysian Business* 16/3/94). This was a surprising divestment since FCW's involvement in cable manufacturing was expected to be crucial for Ekran's implementation of the Bakun Dam project. But in March 1994, within a few months of the FCW acquisition, the Canadian-controlled listed shoe manufacturer Bata (M) Bhd announced its takeover of FCW for RM202 million, the same amount paid by Tan and his associates to acquire the cable company; in the process, Tan obtained control of yet another listed company (*Malaysian Business* 1/4/94).

In this takeover Bata's major shareholders relinquished their 62.1 per cent stake in the company to FCW's shareholders; in return they obtained the entire shoe-manufacturing business and RM58 million cash, leaving Bata a shell company; the new shareholders would then inject FCW into Bata. After the takeover Bata's new shareholders announced that the company's name would be changed to FCW Holdings Bhd and that its main activity would be the manufacture of fibre optic and submarine cables. The company was also confident of being awarded the undersea cabling portion of the Bakun Dam project by Ekran (*The Star* 8/9/94).

Through this reverse takeover, FCW Holdings obtained an indirect listing on the KLSE. The RM202 million paid by Tan and his associates to Ekran for FCW Holdings was apparently 'very cheap' (*Business Times* 18/3/94). This was confirmed when in mid-1995 – after a two-for-one bonus issue and a one-for-five rights issue were declared – 30 per cent of FCW Holdings' equity was sold by Tan to another Daim protégé, Halim Saad of the Renong Group, for RM304.78 million, giving Tan handsome returns for his investment in FCW Holdings; despite this divestment of a major stake in the company, Tan still owned 21.58 per cent of FCW Holdings' equity (*The Star* 25/7/95).

Ting has also had business dealings with other Bumiputera businessmen closely linked to Daim. In November 1994, through a share swap, Ting took over the ailing, publicly listed Granite Industries Bhd, controlled by Samsudin Abu Hassan. Diamond League Sdn Bhd, a holding company for a few of Ting's unlisted companies, was to be injected into Granite in return for a majority stake in the company (Cheong 1995: 65–7). It appears that though Ting had managed to get control over another publicly listed company, he was asked to help bail out Granite after the latter's ventures into China's gaming industry failed to take off, leaving the company stuck with mounting losses. Considering the manner in which control of companies linked to Ting and Daim's other business associates have been shifted around, Ting's control of Granite could well be a stop-gap measure.

Plans are under way to ensure that most of the lucrative contracts from the Bakun Dam project are awarded to companies associated with Ekran. Pacific Chemicals has been offered the land-clearing contract by Ekran involving 17,750 hectares of forests located in the dam area, while FCW Holdings is expected to be awarded the multi-billion ringgit contract to lay 2,700 kilometres of submarine and high-voltage transmission cables (see *The Edge* 2/7/95). Since such potentially profitable contracts can help increase the value of the companies receiving them, significant profits can be made through further share manoeuvrings involving closely associated companies; thus lucrative control of the Bakun Dam project and profitable access to its contracts has been retained despite Ekran's relative small eventual stake in the dam.

The manner in which Ekran managed to get the Bakun Dam contract reflects the capacity of senior government leaders to make decisions favouring associated interests. Although Ting quickly established a strong reputation for himself in construction, the Sarawak state government's original decision to award the massive Bakun Dam contract to a single company that had no relevant construction experience suggests favouritism and may have several implications, one of which was the embarrassing need to change the terms of the award of the contract. The fact that the directors and shareholders of Ekran and the companies associated with it (for example, FCW Holdings and Pacific Chemicals) seem to be closely linked with Daim appears to confirm that numerous new business figures, including non-Bumiputeras, have been involved in the extension of his corporate influence. This trend also suggests that inter-ethnic business co-operation has been endorsed at the highest level and has grown since the mid-1980s, and that state patronage in Malaysia is, once again (as before the 1970s), available to politically connected non-Bumiputeras. However, the co-operation of non-Bumiputera capitalists mainly involves only a few politically powerful corporate players. Considering the manner in which these new non-Bumiputera corporate figures have emerged, it is unclear to what extent they serve as business proxies as well as the extent of government support they can consistently count on and the degree of freedom and initiative they enjoy and can develop in furthering their own business interests.

5

The 'New Rich'

Mahathir and the Promotion of Malay Capitalists

Despite the growth of a Malay middle class and marked changes in the country's ownership patterns as a result of the NEP, differences had emerged by the end of the 1980s over the inequitable distribution of wealth among Bumiputeras. While UMNO hegemony over the state has been primarily responsible for this, other factors have contributed to the rapid concentration of wealth in the hands of a few.

Mahathir Mohamad's appointment as prime minister in July 1981 has been another major reason for the rapid change in ownership patterns since the 1980s. A strong and consistent advocate of the development of Malay capitalism through political patronage, Mahathir's fixation with the creation of Bumiputera capitalists has been evident since the publication of his 1970 'treatise' on the problems of the indigenous community, *The Malay Dilemma*. His views on the failure of the state to help promote Bumiputera capitalism were deemed controversial and promptly banned. So Mahathir probably welcomed the NEP, particularly its objective of using government-owned enterprises, especially so-called trust agencies, to acquire assets on behalf of the Bumiputeras. He has also, however, strongly believed that the best way to develop Malay capitalists is to privilege those most capable of generating further wealth. In *The Malay Dilemma* he criticised agencies such as RIDA (now MARA) because,

> run on the lines of a welfare department, RIDA denied money to capable Malay businessmen but gave hand-outs to poor people with vague notions of going into business. Anyone with any indication at all of succeeding in business was denied aid on the grounds that RIDA was not meant to help rich people become richer. (Mahathir 1981: 40)

A number of problems and contradictions, however, arose as the government intensified its efforts to develop Bumiputera businessmen. Many Malay businessmen began to complain that government enterprises were becoming obstacles to the development of Malay businesses. As mentioned, in the construction sector, since public agencies like the UDA and Pernas were given preference for most public infrastructure projects, private Malay contractors and developers either had difficulty getting contracts or were awarded small-scale jobs, thus limiting profits and growth. Small and medium-sized Malay contractors, in particular, argued that when public enterprises were involved in major buy-outs and acquired majority equity interests in commercial property and residential housing estates, they had limited access to financial resources. Since the rents were captured by these enterprises, although this constituted an increase in the Malay share of the economy, it also meant lost opportunities for small-scale Malay entrepreneurs, inhibiting their growth (Tan 1993: 76).

But it was undeniable that the UMNO-led government had for political reasons encouraged the development of a 'subsidy mentality' among the Bumiputeras with the implementation of the NEP. While accumulation through ethnic affirmative action was being portrayed by some UMNO politicians as a historically justified birthright, Mahathir was also reminding the Malays that the NEP was only a temporary boost to compensate for past injustices. Thus by the 1980s, as Khoo (1994: 150) has pointed out, Mahathir had become increasingly aware and disappointed that although

> Malay businessmen had been nurtured on easy credit, business licences, government contracts, and other forms of preferential treatment ... they did not fulfil NEP's vision of a class of competitive Malay entrepreneurs. Malay professionals were raised in 'MARA colleges' and trained abroad on state scholarships to form a 'permanent middle class' but clung to the state for employment. NEP's restructuring appeared to have removed the racial imbalances only in form because in reality NEP fostered a 'dole', 'subsidy' or 'get-rich-quick' mentality among the Malays. State protection had perpetuated Malay dependence on the state.

Upset with excessive Malay mass reliance on the state, Mahathir sought to pull the Malays out of this dependency before the NEP's expiration in 1990 to ensure that when assets acquired by the state were passed on to Bumiputeras, they would also have the knowledge and expertise to maintain and develop these assets. To quote Mahathir on this point: 'The best way to keep the shares between the Bumiputera hands is to hand them over to the Bumiputera most capable of retaining them, which means the well-to-do' (*Far Eastern Economic Review* 13/4/79). Otherwise Mahathir feared that the Malays, with their 'get-rich-quick' mentality, would only pass on their new-found wealth to non-Bumiputeras, particularly the Chinese. Even in the early 1980s, although a considerable number of Malays had obtained top positions in major companies, their contributions to these businesses were often nominal; most of the Malays who were 'active' in the corporate sector were merely playing high-profile roles in their companies, with their Chinese partners often running the actual operations behind the scenes (Hing 1984: 312). Mahathir was also distressed that many Malay businessmen who had emerged as major corporate players and remained active in business continued to do so only because of substantial government patronage.

In line with Mahathir's explicit desire for the development of Bumiputera capitalists through government patronage via policies such as the NEP and privatisation, a number of major conglomerates controlled by Bumiputeras with close links to the political elite emerged and developed rapidly during the 1980s. The ostensible reason for the award of government contracts to such businessmen was that these Bumiputeras had acquired the 'expertise' to build on these rents, although this was not usually the case. In most cases these Bumiputera businessmen formed joint ventures or subcontracted their operations to foreign or local enterprises which had the expertise to get the job done. Notable examples of those who have benefited from such government patronage are the Antah Holdings Group and the Melewar Group, both controlled by Negeri Sembilan royalty; the Arab Malaysian Group controlled by Azman Hashim; the R. J. Reynolds and Land & General Groups controlled by Wan Azmi Wan Hamzah; the Uniphoenix Corporation Bhd led by Ibrahim Mohamed, who was once also involved in Promet Bhd; and more recently, Basir Ismail, who leads Cycle & Carriage Ltd and Cold Storage Bhd; Tajudin Ramli who controls TRI, MHS and MAS; Halim Saad who controls Renong Bhd and UEM; Yahya Ahmad who controls HICOM Holdings Bhd, Diversified Resources Bhd and Gadek Bhd; Mohd Razali Mohd Rahman who owns Peremba Bhd; and Samsudin Abu Hassan who is the chairman of Aokam Perdana Bhd and Landmarks Bhd, owns a major stake in Cold Storage Bhd and has an interest in Austral Amalgamated Bhd and Dataprep Holdings Bhd (of which Mahathir's son, Mirzan, is a major shareholder). Before their ministerial appointments, former Finance Minister Daim Zainuddin and former Deputy Prime Minister Ghafar Baba were also prominent businessmen leading their own publicly listed companies. In all instances, these conglomerates were seldom initiated and developed as active manufacturers for export. Case studies of Wan Azmi Wan Hamzah and Tajudin Ramli will help show how Bumiputera capitalists have rapidly developed through government deployment of rents (see Case Studies 8 and 9, pp. 138–52).

It would not, however, be fair to say that all these Bumiputeras have not contributed to productive investments. For example, while Wan Azmi's contribution to the turnaround and growth of his main property development concern Land & General Bhd has been favourably acknowledged, he has also deployed some of these rents productively in other sectors. Through his private holding company, Rohas Sdn Bhd, he owns a majority interest in Syarikat Sepatu Timur Sdn Bhd, a shoe company originally established by Chinese and Malay businessmen. Wan Azmi's involvement in the company was crucial for obtaining supply contracts from both the government or government-controlled companies like MAS and Proton; with majority control of Syarikat Sepatu Timur, Wan Azmi's involvement has facilitated the expansion and diversification of the company's products (see Rugayah 1994: 81–8). Wan Azmi has also collaborated with the Chinese-owned listed plantation conglomerate, KL Kepong Bhd, to venture into major property development projects on the outskirts of the federal capital, in which his involvement has been substantial. Interestingly, these examples not only suggest that close co-operation between Chinese and Malay businesses can have favourable and productive results, but also that there is increasing collaboration between major established Chinese companies and those controlled by influential Bumiputera businessmen.

'Money Politics' and the 'New Rich'

One of the most widespread and controversial aspects of the continued practice of political patronage has been the growing influence of money on politics, most apparent during party and general elections. As controversial as the manner in which funds are spent during electoral contests are the ways in which most ruling coalition political parties and politicians get funds to finance their activities, particularly since the mid-1980s, when contests for powerful political posts have become increasingly expensive. The impact of money as well as business and economic favours on election outcomes has become extremely significant.

Despite the desirability of curbing 'unfairness' in the electoral process (the disproportionate amounts of money spent during election campaigns greatly distort Malaysia's system of representative democracy) and despite recent calls by leaders for greater accountability and transparency in government there have been no attempts to make new laws or enforce existing ones to curb such activity. This has led to increasing use of the term 'money politics', which refers to a number of related issues, including political party involvement in business, abuses of power for corrupt purposes, and political patronage.

With the centralisation of power within a hegemonic UMNO, and the declining independence and influence of the bureaucracy, legislature, judiciary and monarchy, the balance of power within the state has shifted in favour of an increasingly centralised executive. As the powers of the various branches of the state have been progressively diminished, the close links of the more powerful executive with an emergent breed of mainly, but not exclusively, Bumiputera rentiers have become increasingly pronounced; the prominent new capitalists linked to UMNO leaders include Halim Saad, Tajudin Ramli, Samsudin Abu Hassan, Wan Azmi Wan Hamzah, Yahya Ahmad, Ahmad Sebi Abu Bakar, Vincent Tan Chee Yioun, T. Ananda Krishnan, T. K. Lim, and Ting Pek Khiing.

The development, through political patronage, of this 'new rich' in Malaysia has also been reflected in the change in UMNO's grass-roots leadership, which is increasingly dominated by businessmen. Although this reflects the significant class changes in Malay society generally and the party hierarchy in particular, UMNO's political hegemony is still sensitive to the demographic distribution of ethnic groups and a gerry-mandered electoral system favouring rural areas where Malays continue to predominate. In spite of overreliance on rural constituencies to ensure its continued hegemony in the legislature and the Barisan Nasional, UMNO's leadership at divisional and branch levels has been taken over by urban-based businessmen-cum-'weekend politicians'. This widening economic gap between party leaders and members has also been reflected socially.

One of the main reasons for growing intra-ethnic economic in-equalities, associated with the rise of a Malay business and middle class, has been the extensive development and capture of rentier activities by Malay politicians through the spread of political patronage involving the party (see Gomez 1994). Malay politicians are aware that given UMNO's political dominance, patronage through allocation of government resources or privatisation can be secured by building a strong base in the party. After all, NEP implementation often meant that state inter-vention in the economy most favoured those best able to exercise political influence, and facilitated their access to rentier opportunities. Since their close ties with influential politicians had given them access to business opportunities to develop their corporate holdings, such businessmen are, in turn, expected to financially support their political patrons. This has led to increased spending to capture positions in UMNO, usually involving wasteful cliental deployment of economic resources. In the process, the active involvement of Malay politicians in business, and the growth of politically connected business groups, also led to new rivalries and resentments.

The increasing practice of patronage in UMNO also exacerbated the problem of limited accountability, particularly since ties between politics and business have become increasingly personal since the mid-1980s. There have been several reasons for this change, which has transpired as the government began to transfer control of its assets to individual businessmen. The mid-1980s economic recession and fiscal crisis severely curtailed the number of business opportunities that could be disbursed through the government, leaving UMNO deeply divided. In 1987 a new opposition faction – led by former UMNO Treasurer and Finance Minister Tengku Razaleigh Hamzah, who left the party to establish the opposition Parti Melayu Semangat 46 – alleged that UMNO President Mahathir had formed a kitchen cabinet which had centralised decision-making powers and that most government contracts and business opportunities were being distributed to members of this inner circle. Furthermore, his faction also alleged that Daim – who, as UMNO treasurer, had control of Fleet Holdings, then UMNO's main holding company – had abused his position as party trustee to channel most of UMNO's assets to holding entities controlled by his family (see *New Straits Times* 23/4/87). Opposition leaders of the DAP also publicly embarrassed the Prime Minister by almost winning a lawsuit in which they charged the government leadership with a conflict of interest in privatising the multi-billion ringgit North–South Highway project to UEM, which as we have seen is closely linked to UMNO.

UMNO seemed to control, through its treasurer, vast interests in the private sector before its deregistration in 1988. The party was deregistered when twelve Razaleigh supporters, after Razaleigh's narrow defeat by Mahathir for UMNO's presidency in 1987, filed a suit claiming that the election should be nullified on the grounds that delegates from 30 unregistered branches had attended the UMNO General Assembly. In February 1988 the court ruled UMNO an illegal organisation because of the presence of these unregistered branches. Mahathir subsequently formed UMNO Baru (New UMNO) and used the opportunity to deny his critics membership of the new party. In the process, although UMNO lost control of its vast corporate assets, which were taken over by the official assignee as required under the Societies Act, an opportunity arose for party leaders to reconstitute the manner in which its assets were held. The party's assets were channelled to private businessmen, apparently to ensure that the party dissidents, who had been left out of the new UMNO and had then formed Semangat 46, could not make any claim on these corporate entities. By 1992 UMNO would claim that it no longer had legal control over its assets; some leaders even went so far as to say that the party was no longer involved in business. Meanwhile, however, UMNO's co-operative, KUB, was emerging as a major corporate player, having obtained stakes in two publicly listed companies, Datuk Keramat Holdings Bhd (which has a controlling interest in the United Malayan Banking Corporation) and Damansara Realty Bhd; UMNO was also disclosed as having a controlling stake in Utusan Melayu Bhd, when the company was listed on the KLSE in 1994. More importantly, UMNO leaders had manoeuvred themselves into a position where they were no longer accountable to party members for the manner in which UMNO's assets were deployed. Furthermore, this has also meant that UMNO *per se* would not be the object of criticism regarding contentious ties between politics and business; instead attention has now shifted to individual leaders, particularly those at the top of the party hierarchy.

In fact, despite denials by senior UMNO leaders, it is widely acknowledged that these men still control the party's dispersed corporate assets since these companies are now run by businessmen who had previously held UMNO's corporate assets in trust. Halim Saad, for example, gained control of Renong Bhd, where most of Fleet Holdings' main listed and private companies, including UEM, have been situated. Tajudin Ramli and Samsudin Abu Hassan obtained control of the publicly listed companies that had been owned by Waspavest Sdn Bhd, another of UMNO's holding companies; Tajudin gained control of TRI, while Samsudin had control of Granite and Cold Storage. Wan Azmi Wan Hamzah has an indirect stake in the D&C Bank, which had also been part of the Waspavest Group (see Gomez 1990, 1994). But since these links are now mainly based on personal ties between party leaders and businessmen, it is not clear whether the party actually effectively controls these assets; for example, would a new UMNO leadership hostile to the present party leaders be able to wrest control of these assets from the current trustees, who may see themselves as personally beholden to those responsible for the elevation in the first place?

All this suggests that relations between politics and business have become more complex, with reciprocity becoming increasingly sophisticated. The development of various patron–client relationships and structures within the party has, in turn, increased competition, factionalism and the cost of rising up the party hierarchy. The contest for the UMNO deputy presidency between Deputy Prime Minister Musa Hitam and Finance Minister Tengku Razaleigh Hamzah in 1981 and 1984 involved much funds and patronage to secure support. When Razaleigh later allied himself with Musa to challenge Mahathir for the UMNO presidency in 1987, the stakes involved in the contest probably increased significantly, with Mahathir apparently depending heavily on

Daim to stave off the challenge that almost toppled him. With political campaigns becoming more expensive and the economy increasingly privatised, it is believed that funds are increasingly being raised through the stock market by manipulating the trading and prices of shares of politically controlled corporations (see Gomez 1996b).

UMNO Factionalism and Money Politics

The importance of effective patronage and the forging of links between political leaders and influential businessmen in climbing the political hierarchy was confirmed in 1993, when the then UMNO vice-president Anwar Ibrahim decided to contest the party's deputy presidency; the incumbent, Ghafar Baba, a long-serving vice-president until 1987 owing to his popular grass-roots support, had been a prominent figure in the corporate sector between 1976 and 1986 before he was wooed back into government by Mahathir to replace Musa Hitam as deputy prime minister to block Razaleigh's ascendance.

Anwar, who had been a vocal critic of politicians who abused money and power to get support in UMNO, had rapidly climbed the party ranks with the support of Mahathir and Daim. An outspoken critic of the Barisan Nasional government in the 1970s, Anwar had been courted by Razaleigh and Mahathir to join UMNO in 1982. Soon after winning a parliamentary seat in Penang in the 1982 general election, Anwar contested and narrowly won the UMNO Youth leadership, thus also becoming an *ex officio* vice-president of the party. In the severely factionalised 1987 party election, Anwar was voted in as one of UMNO's three directly elected vice-presidents. By late 1993, almost three years after taking over the powerful Finance Ministry, Anwar had managed to displace Ghafar as deputy president, and also became deputy prime minister.

Almost a year before Anwar secured the deputy presidency, rumours were rife that the party was being divided by the impending contest between the two UMNO leaders. While Anwar managed to secure the support of upcoming, younger politicians, Ghafar's more loosely based faction enjoyed the tacit support of some more senior politicians, who were concerned that their positions and prospects in the party were being undermined by Anwar's meteoric rise in the party.

Anwar had been a strong critic of political ties with business; according to him, 'UMNO should have no business in dealing with business. It should remain a political party ... But it is accepted that the relationship between political leaders and business leaders are [*sic*] often close' (*Far Eastern Economic Review* 6/6/91). Thus by 1993 it was not surprising that a new group of influential, mainly Bumiputera, corporate leaders was increasingly closely identified with him. Many of these ambitious new corporate figures had long been frustrated by the dominance of the Malay corporate world by those who had emerged with Mahathir's and Daim's patronage, such as Wan Azmi Wan Hamzah, Halim Saad, Tajudin Ramli, and Samsudin Abu Hassan. The support that Anwar enjoyed from this generally younger generation of corporate-cum-political figures was crucial in overwhelmingly displacing Ghafar as UMNO deputy president and consolidating Anwar's claim to succession of the party leadership.

Some of the main political-cum-business figures that Anwar has been linked with include Ishak bin Ismail and Mohamad Sarit Haji Yusoh. During the 1990s, Ishak Ismail rapidly gained control of a number of publicly listed companies, including Idris Hydraulic Bhd, Wembley Industries Holdings Bhd, Golden Plus Holdings Bhd, Benta Bhd, and KFC Holdings (M) Bhd. Ishak Ismail once served as secretary of UMNO's Permatang Pauh division, headed by Anwar. One of Ismail's business partners, Mohamed Sarit, served as Anwar's political secretary and has held shares and directorships in Golden Plus, Wembley Industries, and KFC Holdings (Gomez 1994: 143–6).

Idris Hydraulic (M) Bhd, then a minor listed company controlled by UMNO's co-operative KUB, was acquired in January 1991 by Ishak Ismail's RM2 investment holding company, Tanjung Layang (M) Sdn Bhd. In September 1992 Ishak Ismail obtained control of Wembley Industries through another obscure holding company, Grand Care Sdn Bhd. His partner in Grand Care was Mohamed Sarit Yusoh. A month later, in October 1992, Ishak Ismail and Mohamed Sarit acquired a 32 per cent stake in Golden Plus which was used to acquire a substantial stake in the country's leading fast-food operator, KFC Holdings, in December 1992 (Gomez 1994: 143–6).

Other prominent businessmen who appear to have close links with Anwar include Kamaruddin Jaffar, Kamaruddin Mohamad Nor, Nasaruddin Jalil, and Ahmad Sebi Abu Bakar. Anwar's schoolmate Yahya Ahmad and Nasaruddin Jalil are both directors of the publicly listed Gadek Bhd, which obtained a 90 per cent stake in Credit Corporation (M) Bhd in 1994, and Diversified Resources Bhd, which has obtained two major privatised contracts from the government for the operation of Kuala Lumpur's minibus services and the inspection of private vehicles on behalf of the Road Transport Department; the company is also involved with government-owned Proton Bhd to produce new variants of the Malaysian car in collaboration with Citroen of France (*New Straits Times* 26/4/94; Cheong 1993: 93–5). In late 1995 the government also sold its majority interest in HICOM Holdings to Yahya. Like Mohamad Sarit, Nasaruddin Jalil is a former political secretary of the Finance Minister, while the two Kamaruddins, like Yahya Ahmad, were Anwar's schoolmates at the Malay College in Kuala Kangsar; Ahmad Sebi was Anwar's contemporary at the University of Malaya. From 1981 to 1985 Kamaruddin Jaafar, a former academic, was the secretary-general of ABIM, of which Anwar had long been the president before his induction into UMNO in 1982; Kamaruddin is currently a director of Setron Bhd and Sabah Shipyard. Setron, one of the first companies linked to Anwar, is controlled by the Yayasan Bumiputera Pulau Pinang (Penang Bumiputera Foundation), of which the Finance Minister had been chairman since 1988. Anwar resigned as its chairman after his appointment to the Finance Ministry in 1991. Anwar's replacement as chairman was his protégé, Ibrahim Saad, a deputy minister. A former academic, Ibrahim had served as Anwar's political secretary between 1982 and 1986. Kamaruddin Mohamad Nor, a former vice-president of ABIM, succeeded Anwar as regional representative of WAMY, the World Assembly of Muslim Youth. Anwar's father, Ibrahim Abdul Rahman, a former UMNO member of parliament, is chairman of Industrial Oxygen Incorporated Bhd, a publicly listed plantation concern, which was part of a consortium awarded a RM391 million contract for the redevelopment of the government's psychiatric facility in Johore (*Asiaweek* 17/11/93). There is, however, some indication that Anwar has been embarrassed by the business involvement of his family members.

The management buy-out in January 1993 of the influential media companies NSTP and TV3 is widely believed to be preparatory to Anwar's successful challenge later that year for UMNO's deputy presidency – and hence the deputy prime ministership (see Case Study 4, p. 66). In the run-up to the election, although TV3 and the NSTP newspapers were not blatantly supportive of Anwar, they gave him prominent and favourable coverage, while ignoring Ghafar and his camp. A number of candidates in Ghafar's faction – including party vice-presidents Abdullah Ahmad Badawi, the Foreign Minister, and Sanusi Junid, the Agriculture Minister – accused the press of not only ignoring them but also of distorting and misquoting their statements. Even Prime Minister Mahathir complained that his statements had been taken out of context or misquoted, especially when he voiced support for Ghafar or when he said that the top posts in the party should not be contested for the sake of party unity. In the contest, Anwar's 'Wawasan' (Vision) team members were elected as vice-presidents, even displacing the popular Abdullah Badawi, while many of the Finance Minister's supporters were inducted into the party's Supreme Council, thus further consolidating his position in the party. In fact, although Mahathir has not been challenged for the presidency, it is widely believed that Anwar has gained control of UMNO and has emerged as the most powerful politician in the country, subtly laying siege to the Prime Minister; it is now widely suggested that Mahathir, unlike Anwar, has not spent much time cultivating his grass-roots base, leaving a vacuum that has been filled by the energetic Anwar and his ambitious younger men. Anwar, however, has wisely denied allegations that he intends to accelerate the succession process.

The management buy-out of the two media companies was not the only business controversy associated with the November 1993 UMNO election. Numerous rumours and allegations were made about insider trading, involving companies listed on the KLSE, as a way of raising funds for Anwar's campaign and of buying support. Between 4 January and 9 June 1993, the average daily trading volume on both the first and second boards of the KLSE amounted to 356 million units valued at RM892.3 million. The average daily trading volume on both boards for the whole of 1992, however, only amounted to 77.7 million units valued at RM207 million, while for 1991 it was only 49.6 million units worth RM120.9 million (*New Straits Times* 15/6/93). Speculation that this dramatic rise in trading activity was linked to the impending UMNO elections was supported by the particularly high trading of company stocks linked to UMNO, such as Idris Hydraulic, Granite and Renong. The value of the shares of these three companies appreciated almost threefold over little more than a month. The KLSE even queried Granite over the rapid rise in the price of its shares, which leapt from RM3.68 to RM8.50 within a week in early June (*New Straits Times* 17/6/93). The Registrar of Companies also began its own investigations into suspected insider trading involving UMNO-linked companies such as TV3, NSTP, Renong and the Malaysian Resources Corporation Bhd – which had acquired TV3 and NSTP – after surges in their share prices in early 1993 (*The Star* 27/2/93); the results of the probe have still not been disclosed and are unlikely to lead anywhere, especially given the outcome of the challenge. In fact one UMNO faction is said to have raised approximately RM300 million, mainly through the stock exchange, to fund the campaign (see Gomez 1994; *Far Eastern Economic Review* 15/7/93).

Speculation that the stock market was being abused to raise funds appears to have been confirmed when share prices began to plunge just as the UMNO Assembly commenced in early November. Interestingly, this downward trend occurred even after the Finance Minister had announced another pro-business budget for 1994, one week before the UMNO General Assembly, which carried numerous benefits for corporations, including generous tax cuts. Although this should have improved company balances, which should, in turn, have pushed up stock prices, the KLSE Composite Index began to fall just before and soon after the UMNO General Assembly.

Ironically, during the 1993 UMNO General Assembly, the resurgence of money politics in UMNO was clearly acknowledged – and denounced. Almost every delegate who took to the rostrum used it to denounce the extensive use of money and gifts by aspiring politicians to buy support. One delegate claimed that he was given RM1,000 for his vote, while an analyst contended that 'never has money been spent on such a scale before in an UMNO election' (*Far Eastern Economic Review* 18/11/93). While money had been used before to buy the support of delegates to the party's assemblies, now it was also being extensively used to buy support at the divisional level to ensure that candidates for the top two leadership positions received sufficient nominations to 'reflect' their supposed popularity. Some delegates even alleged that strongarm tactics were used to deal with the recalcitrants among them. So intense was the call to curb money politics that UMNO president Mahathir received unanimous support from the delegates when he suggested that amendments be made to the party constitution to curb such activities.

However, in the unlikely event that money politics in the party is curbed, it is even less likely that the use of money to obtain support during general elections will cease. Furthermore, since Anwar's faction has demonstrated the success with which money can be used to usurp positions once thought unassailable, such amendments are likely to help preserve Mahathir's position and to protect Anwar against challenges by other senior party leaders. For example, when UMNO Baru was formed, the party's constitution was amended, allowing nominees for the post of UMNO president and deputy president to be awarded ten bonus votes for each divisional nomination they receive. It was then presumed that this amendment virtually consolidated the position of the top two leaders in the party. Since this was not proving to be the case, Mahathir again attempted to amend the constitution to delete the bonus votes, claiming that it contributed to the escalation of money politics.

In any case, patronage networks are still being developed by aspiring politicians. Privatised contracts are still being given out to businessmen with close political ties. In fact it seems that Finance Minister Anwar now has control over a vast patronage apparatus, which his supporters deem crucial to his maintaining political support and undermining the influence of opponents and defectors. While some business groups are clearly aligned with particular political factions or faction leaders, not all businesses or politicians neatly fit into clearly defined, mutually exclusive camps. Political and business realities are much more complicated and constantly shifting to boot. This element of uncertainty exacerbates the short-termism which dominates, or at least influences, many business decisions. Since business links with politicians are rarely institutionalised but rather personalised, further uncertainty is common. Faction leaders are particularly hard-pressed to deal with either political or business rivalries in their own factions.

By early 1994, in fact, it appeared that a dispute had arisen between Anwar and Daim over the manner in which privatisations were being decided and distributed. The dispute appears to have been precipitated by the claim that businessmen close to Daim were benefiting most from privatisation. In June 1994, for example, the government finalised the sale of its 32 per cent stake in the national airlines, MAS, to RZ Equities Sdn Bhd, a minor unlisted company owned by Tajudin Ramli, a business associate of Daim. Robert Tan Hua Choon, reportedly a close associate of Daim, obtained a lucrative privatised contract through his company, Spanco Sdn Bhd, in 1993 to service government-owned vehicles. In January 1994 the RM15 billion Bakun Dam project, which had been earmarked for privatisation to a company in which the Sarawak state government would have had a stake, was awarded *in toto* to Ting Pek Khiing at the eleventh hour after Daim's intervention (see *Asian Wall Street Journal* 2/2/94). In 1994 UEM, controlled by Halim Saad through Renong, obtained the privatised contract to construct the second link causeway between Malaysia and Singapore. During this period there was also strong speculation that a majority 60 per cent stake in Bank Bumiputra, Malaysia's second largest bank, would be sold by the government to Landmarks Bhd, controlled by another close Daim protégé, Samsudin Abu Hassan, who has no previous banking experience (see *Malaysian Business* 16/3/94).

Apart from this, it is likely that big businesses controlled by Chinese interests have been funding particular UMNO leaders: Hong Leong Group's Quek Leng Chan and the MBf (Malayan Borneo Finance Bhd) Group's Loy Hean Heong, for example, are reported to have supported Finance Minister Anwar's successful 1993 bid for the UMNO deputy presidency (see Case Study 4, p. 66). Since UMNO-linked companies have managed to get significant control of important sectors of the economy, such as the construction, media and banking industries, most of these non-Bumiputera interests hope to benefit from business opportunities accruing from UMNO companies. Furthermore, since UMNO leaders also control the most important cabinet portfolios, particularly finance, there are numerous other economic benefits for politically well-connected non-Bumiputera interests.

After the November 1993 UMNO elections, the Barisan Nasional had to face a state election in Sabah, then controlled by the opposition Parti Bersatu Sabah (PBS). It is quite clear that the Barisan Nasional was eager to wrest control of the state from the opposition for a number of reasons; victory would also augur well for the Barisan Nasional in the forthcoming general election. Furthermore, this was to be the PBS's first electoral contest with the Barisan Nasional after its pull-out from the ruling coalition on the eve of the 1990 general election; a visibly shocked and angry Mahathir had then described PBS's defection – after nominations were over – as a 'stab in the back' (Khong 1991). Midway through the campaign period for the 1990 general election, PBS president Joseph Pairin Kitingan joined the Gagasan Rakyat coalition which was led by Semangat 46, committing his party to the opposition's joint manifesto. The Barisan Nasional had little time to counter the defection, and during the election the PBS swept all twenty of the parliamentary seats it contested in Sabah. The PBS's defection also meant that, for the first time since 1969, the Barisan Nasional was under severe threat of losing not only its two-thirds parliamentary majority, but also its control of the government. By stepping up its campaign along racial and religious lines, however, the Barisan Nasional managed to discredit Semangat 46 enough to secure its two-thirds majority in parliament (Khong 1991).

The Politics of Money: the 1994 Sabah State Elections

Situated in the north of Borneo island, Sabah was included in the Federation of Malaysia in 1963. It has a population of approximately 1.7 million, and a high proportion of recent immigrants from the Philippines and Indonesia. Almost 40 per cent of Sabahans are Muslims, 20 per cent are Chinese, while the remaining 40 per cent are indigenous non-Muslims, mainly Christians, the largest community of whom are Kadazans. Ruled since 1985 by the PBS, a multi-racial party dominated by Christian Kadazans, the party came to power just a year after its inception, when it narrowly defeated the then ruling Barisan Nasional coalition member Berjaya, with the support of the Kadazan and Chinese communities. Hence the PBS – led by a Christian Kadazan, Joseph Pairin Kitingan – had an uneasy relationship with other member parties of the Barisan Nasional, especially UMNO, after it was admitted to the ruling coalition in 1986 until it left abruptly in 1990.

Despite the Barisan Nasional's overwhelming influence over the media, especially the television and radio networks, and its access to vastly greater funds, most pre-election analyses of the Sabah situation predicted a victory, albeit a narrower one, for the ruling PBS in the state election scheduled for February 1994. After nine years of rule, the PBS had a well-oiled party machine. The state government's machine, including its numerous agencies and the influential Sabah Foundation, had also been deployed to buttress its position. Kadazan nationalism had been strongly propounded to cement the community's support for the PBS.

In addition, the PBS also appeared to have overcome its problems with the Muslims when it forged a coalition just before the election with the United Sabah National Organisation (USNO), once led by Pairin's erstwhile political foe, Mustapha Harun, who had first joined UMNO when it came into Sabah in 1991. When Mustapha resigned from Mahathir's cabinet and UMNO, citing irreconcilable differences with 'opportunistic local leaders', to team up with PBS on 19 January, only weeks before the state election, it appeared that UMNO's hopes of wresting Sabah from the PBS were quite remote (*Aliran Monthly* 14 (1) 1994). Since USNO's support had primarily come from the Muslims, the coalition between the PBS and USNO could have pooled, for the first time, the support of the two largest and indigenous communal groups in the state electorate: the indigenous Christians and Muslims.

In its electoral campaign the Barisan Nasional did not hesitate to use its control over the federal government to channel money to current and future projects in Sabah. For example, it offered RM700 million for low-cost housing over the next seven years; it also pledged to raise the per capita income of Sabahans from RM3,600, one of the lowest in Malaysia, to RM10,000 by the end of the decade. The Barisan Nasional government also promised to set up a new university in Sabah and more than 100 new schools, to upgrade infrastructure and to improve health care. In all, it was estimated that the Barisan Nasional had promised to invest close to RM1 billion in Sabah over the next few years (*Asian Wall Street Journal* 17/2/94, 21/2/94). And, as if to drive home the point, Deputy Prime Minister Anwar Ibrahim warned Sabahans that none of this would materialise if the PBS were re-elected to office (*Asian Wall Street Journal* 23/2/94).

The PBS's main issues were grievances against federal control, particularly the marginalisation of Sabah by the Barisan Nasional federal government, seen for example in reduced federal fund allocations for Sabah's development. The victimisation by the federal government of PBS leaders was another issue; Jeffrey Kitingan, the younger brother of the chief minister, had been detained without trial under the Internal Security Act for almost three years. The PBS also repeated its old demands for a new university and its own television network, and reiterated the need for more autonomy to safeguard state rights (*Asian Wall Street Journal* 19/2/94). Handicapped by Sabah's declining timber revenues and meagre industrial base, the PBS was not in a position to match the promises made by the Barisan Nasional. The fact was that the state government had been selling assets to pay its debt.

To undermine the coalition between the PBS and USNO, UMNO leaders claimed for themselves the role of protector of the Muslim community. Drawing explicit analogies with the dominance of a primarily Christian West over the Muslim third world, UMNO managed to galvanise effective support. Mahathir even brought up the issue of ethnic strife in Bosnia-Herzegovina to evoke fear among Sabahans that Malaysian Muslims would be oppressed by a predominantly Christian leadership if the PBS were re-elected.

The Barisan Nasional also actively courted the support of the Chinese who, in view of their 20 per cent proportion of the Sabah electorate, had the ability to swing the final outcome decisively. The PBS itself was rocked by the exodus of Chinese leaders such as Yong Teck Lee, its influential deputy president and deputy chief minister, who resigned on 20 January, two weeks before nominations and a month before the elections were due (*Aliran Monthly* 14 (1) 1994). Yong quickly formed the Sabah Progressive Party (SAPP) with the help of a prominent Chinese businessman, Joseph Ambrose Lee, who was instrumental in organising and funding the party; Lee is widely believed to be a business associate of UMNO leaders (see *Asian Wall Street Journal* 14/3/94, 17/3/94). The SAPP, which was immediately admitted into the Barisan Nasional, was mainly responsible for splitting the Chinese vote during the state election.

Joseph Ambrose Lee controls Suniwang Sdn Bhd, which is the largest private landowner in the Federal Territory of Labuan, once a part of Sabah. Lee's partner in Suniwang is the UMNO member of parliament for Labuan, Abdul Mulok Awang Damit, who claims 'access' to Daim Zainuddin (see *Malaysian Business* 1/8/93). Using Suniwang, Lee and Mulok gained control in 1993 of two publicly listed companies, Construction and Supplies House Bhd and Pengkalan Industrial Holdings Bhd. Both men had been upset that the lucrative Sabah Forest Industries had not been privatised to Suniwang in 1993 (*Malaysian Business* 1/8/93).

To marshal Chinese support, the Barisan Nasional argued that it was the Chinese community who stood to gain the most from the development projects that would emerge with federal funding. The Barisan Nasional, however, did not only use economic inducements to win Chinese support; it also played another card important to the Chinese – education. It promised an allocation of RM30 million for the development of Chinese-medium schools. As much as RM2 million in aid was immediately allocated to 30 Chinese schools at an elaborate and well-publicised ceremony just before the election.

During the campaign period the PBS alleged that millions of ringgit were used to buy votes and to ferry in 'phantom voters', including illegal Filipino and Indonesian immigrants with forged documents, to enable them to cast votes for the Barisan Nasional (*Asian Wall Street Journal* 21/2/94). One PBS leader claimed that 'Sabah's almost 1 million-strong illegal immigrant population was less than legally employed by the National Front (Barisan Nasional)' (*Far Eastern Economic Review* 3/3/94); another estimated that 'there were at least 1,000 illegal voters per constituency' (*Asiaweek* 20/4/94). Some PBS State Assemblymen claimed that they were offered a few million ringgit each to defect to the Barisan Nasional (see *Hua Daily* 12/3/94). According to then Sabah Chief Minister Kitingan, 'money was virtually being thrown from helicopters and distributed freely in coffee shops' by the Barisan Nasional in its efforts to secure victory (*Borneo Post* 21/2/94).

Observers alleged that these funds had been raised through the manipulation of the stock market. In the run-up to the state election, between early January and early February 1994, there were heavy fluctuations in share prices on the KLSE. On 10 January 1994, the day Kitingan announced dissolution of the State Assembly to hold the state election, the KLSE composite index rose by 16.02 points; this rise was significant as the stock market had been slipping after reaching an all-time high of 1314.66 on 5 January (*Malaysian Business* 1/2/94). On the same day (10 January), Daim Zainuddin, the government's economic adviser, was quoted as cautioning investors to divest their equity in the stock market because the stock market was overvalued and minority shareholders would be the most adversely affected if the market plunged (*Malaysian Business* 1/2/94).

After Daim's announcement, the KLSE composite index fell 67.2 points, which, according to one report, 'was the biggest one-day fall in absolute terms the KLSE has seen. It marked the beginning of the first real panic selling seen on the KLSE in six years' (*Malaysian Business* 1/2/94). Exacerbating the problem was the announcement the following day by Bank Negara that severe restrictions would be imposed 'to curb the inflow of foreign speculative funds' (*Malaysian Business* 1/2/94); this announcement led to another massive round of divestment, causing the KLSE composite index to fall even more sharply, by 73.33 points (*Malaysian Business* 1/2/94). It has been alleged that Daim's statement was made after equity held by UMNO proxies had been sold at high prices during the bull run up to early January; after the fall the same stock could again be picked up at much reduced prices. Some observers say it had become easier to manipulate the stock market since the new middle class, especially Bumiputeras, had moved into the market in a big way in 1993, particularly after its protracted bull run began. In fact it is believed that at one stage at least 70 per cent of the KLSE's trading volume was due to retail, rather than institutional, interest (*Malaysian Business* 1/2/94). Interestingly, Bank Negara lifted the restriction on foreign inflows of short-term funds in early August 1994, a mere seven months after it was imposed; there is little doubt that the move was intended to increase liquidity to boost the rather lacklustre stock market (*The Star* 12/8/94). Since a general election was expected, Bank Negara's reversal of its earlier policy was seen as an attempt either to raise funds through the stock market or to muster the support of the Malay middle class, badly affected by the KLSE's slump from early 1994.

Before the Sabah state election, price fluctuations on the KLSE were so great that small investors complained to the local press and the authorities, especially the Securities Commission, that the market was being manipulated by leading government figures to raise funds to enable UMNO to wrest control of Sabah. Eventually even Prime Minister Mahathir had to issue a strong denial that his government had abused the stock market to raise funds for the Sabah election. Later, even members of the Barisan Nasional admitted that the election was 'highly monetized', though they did not disclose the sources of their funds (*Far Eastern Economic Review* 3/3/94).

Ironically, despite such 'money politics' involving UMNO, one of the key campaign issues raised by the Barisan Nasional in Sabah was that corruption had been rampant during the nine years when the PBS ruled the state. Chief Minister Joseph Pairin Kitingan had been charged and found guilty of abusing his power to channel a RM1.4 million construction contract to members of his family; Pairin, however, was fined only RM1,800 for the offence, just RM200 short of the amount which would have disqualified him from running for office (see *Far Eastern Economic Review* 27/1/94; *Aliran Monthly* 14 (1) 1994). It is highly probable that there were other cases of abuses of power by Pairin's government. Pairin faces two more criminal charges, while his younger brother Jeffrey Kitingan had been charged for non-disclosure of assets during a federal investigation. Jeffrey, however, was discharged of the offence soon after his defection to the Barisan Nasional after the election; he was subsequently appointed deputy minister in Mahathir's cabinet before he lost his seat in the April 1995 general election.

Although even UMNO ministers had made private predictions that the Barisan Nasional's electoral chances were slim, the coalition managed to secure 23 of the 48 seats. The PBS only won the state election with a narrow majority of two seats as the PBS's share of the popular vote dropped from 53.9 to 48.7 per cent (*Far Eastern Economic Review* 3/3/94). In the election, nineteen of the 24 Muslim-majority constituencies were won by Barisan Nasional candidates (from UMNO), while all Kadazan-majority areas continued to be won by the PBS; two mixed constituencies were also won by the PBS. Although the PBS had expected to win most of the Chinese-majority constituencies, despite Yong Teck Lee's defection, support was almost even between the PBS (which won four seats) and the Barisan Nasional (which won three). Chinese unhappiness with the PBS, the new SAPP and Mahathir's promises drew a lot of Chinese votes away from the PBS. The results also reflected the declining support for Mustapha Harun's USNO in the face of the UMNO juggernaut. Although it had failed to win, the Barisan Nasional had made significant inroads with its greater use of money, media, and (almost contradictory) racial as well as religious sentiments, which probably compelled the PBS campaign to be more ethnically oriented as well.

With the inroads made by the Barisan Nasional, especially UMNO, into Sabah, some PBS leaders immediately began to advocate closer ties with the federal government, ostensibly to get more federal funds for development, but probably also to ensure that they remained in power in view of their slim electoral majority. After all, the relatively slower pace of economic development in the state was largely due to lack of federal funding. Government statistics released in the *Mid-Term Review of the Sixth Malaysia Plan, 1991–1995* showed that funds allocated by the federal government to Sabah for development was among the lowest among the states per capita. These figures clearly show that the federal government cut funding to Sabah after the PBS pulled out from the Barisan Nasional in 1990 (*Aliran Monthly* 14 (1) 1994). But the possibility of a PBS reconciliation with the Barisan Nasional was virtually impossible as long as Pairin remained leader, owing to Mahathir's personal antipathy towards him.

There were, of course, other personal survival considerations in the subsequent defections of most PBS elected State Assemblymen to the Barisan Nasional fold; since the Barisan Nasional government had begun charging PBS leaders with corruption, there must have been concern among these leaders that they too might soon be challenged or otherwise pressured if they did not get Barisan Nasional protection. So it was not altogether surprising when, a few weeks after the PBS victory, three party members defected to the Barisan Nasional, which precipitated a string of further defections by elected PBS representatives. Three new parties were formed: Parti Bersatu Rakyat Sabah, Parti Demokratik Sabah, and Parti Demokratik Sabah Bersatu, all Kadazan-based and led by defecting senior PBS leaders seeking to maximise their leverage in joining the Barisan Nasional (see *New Straits Times* 20/3/94). Pairin's brother Jeffrey, whose three-year detention under the Internal Security Act had symbolised federal government persecution of the PBS, left the PBS to form the last of these new parties with former PBS secretary-general Joseph Kurup, before abandoning the new party to join another Kadazan-based party, Angkatan Keadilan Rakyat (Akar), an established Barisan Nasional component member which he now heads by getting the incumbent president, Mark Koding, to appoint him against the wishes of the existing party leadership. Since the early defectors to UMNO had enabled the Barisan Nasional to wrest control of Sabah, the three new parties faced problems gaining admission into the Barisan Nasional, apparently because Akar – with Jeffrey Kitingan now part of its top leadership – was opposed to their admission. There have been persistent allegations that some of the early PBS defectors had been paid substantial amounts and promised senior positions in the federal government or in a Sabah state government led by the Barisan Nasional (see *Aliran Monthly* 14 (2), 1994).

Despite the magnitude of the funds used and distributed during this state election – and other federal and state elections – by the Barisan Nasional, and by UMNO in particular, there have been no disclosures of how its campaigns were financed. While there have been instances of UMNO-owned shares held by proxies disappearing, and admissions by party leaders that UMNO went into business to raise campaign funds and achieve financial independence, there has not yet been any public disclosure of financial transfers to the party by any of its alleged corporate holdings.

This suggests that each party within the ruling coalition is required to raise funds independently to finance its own electoral campaigns. Compared to the situation during the 1950s until the late 1960s, UMNO now seems to have achieved independence of the MCA in funding the ruling coalition's electoral campaigns, thus further diminishing the MCA's leverage in the Barisan Nasional. However, although the MCA does not seem to be as involved as UMNO is in business, the party appears still to enjoy financial support from the Chinese business community (see Gomez 1994: 175–239). With its even more limited corporate assets and business influence, the MIC is probably quite dependent on UMNO for funds, despite some funding from Indian-owned businesses, including those connected to top party leaders. But since the MIC generally contests less than ten parliamentary seats – compared to UMNO's almost 100 – the amount of funds it requires for campaigning is more modest, with some funding for the UMNO campaign machines in seats contested by MIC candidates coming directly from party headquarters. UMNO's financial independence, despite the significant increase in the amount of funds spent during elections, can probably be attributed to the party's ability to elicit substantial contributions from most businessmen who have benefited from state patronage. Although most Barisan Nasional parties may also be benefiting from corporate funding, because of the unequal distribution of power in the ruling coalition, UMNO's access to funds is probably much greater than that of the MCA. For example, before the 1990 general elections, when UMNO was expecting keen competition from Semangat 46, the amount of funds raised by UMNO was quite substantial. The *Far Eastern Economic Review* (5/7/90) reported that even before the elections were held, UMNO had raised at least RM1 billion for its campaign and was prepared to spend between RM300 million and RM1.5 billion to win the elections. The study of the Sabah state elections also revealed cogently the role played by Chinese businessmen and the stock market in raising funds, and the abuse of the government apparatus and funds to secure electoral victory.

Politically Linked Non-Bumiputera Capitalists

The emergence of an elite, politically influential group of businessmen since the mid-1980s has not been limited to Bumiputeras, despite the official ethnic bias of political patronage and the ethnic nature of national politics. There has since then been greater inter-ethnic elite co-operation in business matters. It appears that these links were not established just because they were seen as mutually beneficial; the implementation of the NEP, the greater role of the state in the economy, the conglomeratisation of Bumiputera companies, the increasing control of the corporate sector by the UMNO leadership, and the clear domination of certain economic sectors by government agencies and Bumiputeras are other reasons why co-operation is seen as imperative for the development of Chinese business interests.

Another factor affecting the business aspirations of the Chinese elite, whose interests were once better protected and advanced by the MCA, was the party's diminishing influence in the Barisan Nasional and the government. Despite the MCA's position as UMNO's most senior partner in the coalition, it has become rather obvious that MCA leaders have hardly been able to influence policy decisions in favour of Chinese business interests since the 1970s. With diminishing relative control of the Chinese in some key sectors of the economy and with no party-political patron to safeguard their interests, interpersonal inter-ethnic elite business co-operation is therefore seen as imperative.

Furthermore, since the mid-1980s, it appears that even non-Bumiputeras have been used as business proxies for Malay politicians. Such businessmen should be distinguished from those acting to protect their own economic interests. Among the prominent non-Bumiputera businessmen who are seen as business partners of the executive are

Vincent Tan Chee Yioun of the Berjaya Group Bhd, T. K. Lim of Kamunting Bhd, Dick Chan of Metroplex Bhd, and T. Ananda Krishnan of Tanjong Bhd, all of whom have become leading Malaysian corporate figures. The case studies on Vincent Tan and T. Ananda Krishnan (pp. 152–65) help to show how political patronage has been beneficial for the growth of companies under their control.

Vincent Tan and Ananda Krishnan became major corporate figures by building on rents they have captured with the government's privatisation of gaming operations. By injecting these rents into publicly listed companies to get majority control, they have effectively used these quoted companies for corporate expansion. Their relations with top UMNO leaders and their involvement with companies controlled by the party and the government also serve to highlight their close links with the ruling elite. While this does not necessarily mean that they are proxies of UMNO leaders, as in the case of some of the new Malay business elite, the extent of their business independence is difficult to determine.

Moreover, there is little networking between Chinese companies controlled by the politically well connected like Tan, though the situation is similar for more independent but also well-connected Chinese such as Quek Leng Chan of the Hong Leong Group (see Case Study 4, p. 66), In fact the manner of corporate expansion of companies controlled by Chinese businessmen with ties to the UMNO elite appears to have created some animosity among other Chinese businessmen who have not benefited as much from state allotted rents.

This development of inter-ethnic business co-operation suggests that the Chinese have been compelled to expand their business partnerships beyond ethnic boundaries to enhance their business operations and profits. Furthermore, in view of the patron–client ties between the UMNO-led government and the new rentier capitalists, political leaders are inclined to protect the interests of their clients by channelling more rents to expand their business operations as well as economic and political returns. With an increasingly authoritarian and centralised Malaysian government, in which public accountability and transparency have been deliberately diminished by those in power, the strengthening of private business interests, especially of those who are politically well connected, is very likely to consolidate, even increase, rent appropriation in the future rather than eliminate it.

Case Study 8: Wan Azmi Wan Hamzah

Wan Azmi Wan Hamzah, the son of a former Supreme Court judge, was born in 1950 in Kota Bharu, Kelantan, and qualified as a chartered accountant in England. In 1974 he was employed by the Guthrie Corporation, which had earlier given him a scholarship to study in England. In 1977 he joined the then UMNO-owned media giant NSTP as an accountant; he left NSTP in 1979 as its financial controller. His next appointment was with the government-owned property development concern Peremba, then headed by Daim Zainuddin with whom he forged close ties. In 1983 he became managing director of the publicly listed Sime UEP, in which both Daim and Peremba then had an interest, and then a director of the Malaysian French Bank Bhd, in which Daim's family companies held a majority stake (*Malaysian Business* 16/3/91).

In March 1985 Finance Minister Daim appointed Wan Azmi chief executive officer of the government-controlled Malayan Banking Bhd, Malaysia's largest bank; it was an appointment which surprised the financial community because Wan Azmi was then only 35 years old and was replacing the highly regarded Jaffar Hussein, who had been appointed governor of the central bank, Bank Negara. Wan Azmi's tenure at Malayan Banking, however, was short – a mere nineteen months – after which he left, reportedly to take a break. But within six months he was back again in the corporate limelight when he acquired his first publicly listed company, the ailing General Lumber Bhd, which he subsequently renamed Land & General Bhd (*The Star* 7/6/90; *Malaysian Business* 16/3/91; Gomez 1990: 44).

Acquisition of Land & General

In June 1987, Raleigh (later renamed the Berjaya Group) – a company which had been Daim's first flagship and was later controlled by his business associates after his ministerial appointment – sold its 5.01 per cent stake in Land & General to Wan Azmi, who had earlier acquired an 8.13 per cent stake in the company; he subsequently raised his interests in Land & General to 14.5 per cent. Wan Azmi then assumed chairmanship of the company and appointed his brother-in-law, Nik Mahmood Nik Hassan, as its managing director (*The Star* 7/6/90).

Land & General, incorporated in May 1964, was at the time involved in logging and timber-manufacturing; by 1981 it had diversified into trading and furniture production. From 1981 until 1987, the company registered consistent losses (see KLSE 14 1988: 203–6). Land & General was reorganised in 1988, when it declared a nine-for-ten rights issue to help reduce its debt, divested some unprofitable subsidiaries, and acquired a few minor but profit-generating companies, most of which were also involved in the timber industry. Its most important deal was in 1989, when it obtained a contract to log a 200,000 hectare timber tract in Papua New Guinea over a period of 25 years (*New Straits Times* 9/10/89; *Business Times* 8/12/89).

Land & General was Wan Azmi's most important listed vehicle for his forays into the corporate sector, usually involving share swaps. At the end of 1989, Land & General paid RM9.26 million to acquire a 20.9 per cent stake in SPPPB from Permodalan Bersatu Bhd (PBB), the holding company for UMNO's ailing co-operative, KUB (*The Star* 11/12/89). SPPPB's most important asset was its 26 per cent stake in Gadek Bhd, a publicly listed plantation concern; Gadek is currently controlled by Yahya Ahmad, who is closely associated with Prime Minister Mahathir.

Another interesting acquisition by Land & General in December 1989 was of KM Properties Sdn Bhd, which was the lease-holder of an underground car-park and complex at the Selangor Club Padang, now known as Dataran Merdeka (Merdeka Square). The company, then controlled by an UMNO senator from Kedah, Shuaib Lazim, was acquired for RM30 million; the deal in part involved a share swap (*The Star* 27/12/89).

By the end of 1991, in terms of profitability, one local business publication ranked Land & General a very impressive 36 out of more than 350 companies then listed on the KLSE. The company was also ranked 53 by the same publication in terms of market capitalisation and sales, and 50 in terms of total assets (see *Corporate World* July 1992).

Acquisition of Nanyang Press

In June 1990, through a share swap worth RM50 million, Land & General acquired a 30.23 per cent stake in the publicly listed Nanyang Press (M) Bhd, publisher of the influential Chinese newspaper, *Nanyang Siang Pau*. Nanyang Press was incorporated in Singapore on 23 July 1958. In 1962 it began publication of the *Nanyang Siang Pau* in Kuala Lumpur. The company was listed on the KLSE on 17 April 1991. In 1991 the daily average net circulation of the *Nanyang Siang Pau* was 185,000 (KLSE 17 (I) 1991: 326–9). The paper's market share in 1993 was 30 per cent, just 1 per cent short of *Sin Chiew Jit Poh*, the most widely circulated Chinese newspaper in recent years (*Malaysian Business* 16/2/94).

Among the vendors of the Nanyang Press stake was Wan Azmi's brother, Wan Ariff Wan Hamzah (*The Star* 6/8/90). Just three months earlier, in March 1990, Wan Ariff had acquired a 20.26 per cent stake in Nanyang Press through his Hong Kong–based company, Oriental Highland Ltd, making him the single largest shareholder in the listed company (*New Straits Times* 29/3/90); part of Oriental Highland's stake in Nanyang Press was believed to have been bought from the government-owned Pernas Bhd, which obtained a 30 per cent stake in the company when it was restructured in the mid-1980s. It was then speculated that Wan Ariff may have been acting for Wan Azmi, a prospect that did not go down well with the Chinese community, who were fearful that these men were proxies through whom the Nanyang Press stake would eventually end up being controlled by UMNO, particularly since the spectre of a general election was then hovering in the air (see *Far Eastern Economic Review* 28/2/91).

In February 1991, only eight months later, Land & General sold its Nanyang Press equity to Peninsula Springs Sdn Bhd for RM52 million (*New Straits Times* 9/2/91). A month later, Peninsula Springs divested its stake in the publishing company to the publicly listed Hume Industries (M) Bhd, controlled by the Hong Leong Group, which had by then picked up 45 per cent of Nanyang Press' equity (*New Straits Times* 1/3/91).

Company records indicate that Peninsula Springs was incorporated on 10 January 1991, a month before it acquired the Nanyang Press equity. Peninsula Springs' authorised share capital was increased to RM1 million on 4 February; one of its major shareholders was Ismail Abdul Rashid who had served as director of some UMNO companies, notably UEM, Time Engineering Bhd and Jaguh Mutiara Sdn Bhd, which also owned a 23.8 per cent stake in Hume Industries (*The Star* 6/4/91). Jaguh Mutiara was 100 per cent owned by the Fleet Group, which was in turn wholly owned by Renong Bhd, the UMNO-linked company. This appeared to confirm market speculation that Wan Azmi was acting in UMNO's interests. In the process, according to the *Far Eastern Economic Review* (28/2/91), Land & General made a profit of RM12.75 million from its sale of Nanyang Press.

In July 1992, Nanyang Press enhanced its dominance over the Chinese publishing sector by acquiring China Press Bhd, which publishes the Chinese daily *The China Press*. The acquisition by Nanyang Press of a 95 per cent stake in China Press for RM19.7 million (*New Straits Times* 20/7/92) meant that the Hong Leong Group had managed to consolidate its interests in the Chinese media industry.

Acquisition of Sri Damansara

Another of Land & General's important, and controversial, acquisitions in 1990 involved Sri Damansara Sdn Bhd, also through a share swap. Sri Damansara was acquired from the publicly listed Magnum Corporation Bhd for RM200 million, paid for through the issue of 80 million new Land & General shares valued at RM2.50 each. After the deal, Magnum obtained a 28.7 per cent stake of Land & General's enlarged paid-up capital but had to grant Wan Azmi an option, to be taken up within a year, to acquire all its equity exceeding 20 per cent in Land & General

(*The Star* 6/6/90). By the end of 1991, Magnum's stake in Land & General was 21.5 per cent (*Business Times* 14/10/91).

The Sri Damansara deal, however, was objected to by Vincent Tan Chee Yioun, chairman of Berjaya Leisure Bhd (formerly Sports Toto, which then had a 32.9 per cent stake in Magnum, on the grounds that it was apparently unfavourable to Magnum. In November 1991, in what appeared to be a conciliatory gesture, Land & General sold 25 per cent of its 100 per cent stake in Sri Damansara to Sports Toto for RM59.5 million cash, for capital gains of RM9.5 million (*The Star* 6/11/91).

Sri Damansara is the developer of a billion-ringgit housing project in Kepong, on the outskirts of Kuala Lumpur. The land had originally been owned by Multi-Purpose Holdings in the 1980s, when the company was controlled by the MCA. Attempts to develop the land had failed because government approval was not given despite repeated requests over seven years. The approval only came from the Selangor state government after Multi-Purpose Holdings formed a joint venture with the UMNO-owned PBB to develop the land. The joint-venture company was then called Multi-Purpose Bersatu Development Sdn Bhd, in which Multi-Purpose Holdings held a 51 per cent stake. By May 1987 Magnum had bought 100 per cent of Multi-Purpose Bersatu Development's equity for RM50.6 million, and renamed the company Sri Damansara. Although Magnum had made a profit by selling Sri Damansara, most critics of this deal felt that the potential long-term gains from Sri Damansara did not merit its sale to Land & General for such a low price (see Gomez 1990: 157–9).

Most of the objections to the sale of Sri Damansara were raised by MCA leaders. The Magnum Corporation was controlled by Multi-Purpose Holdings, the company incorporated by the MCA to mobilise Chinese capital. In fact the property owned by Sri Damansara had originally been held by Multi-Purpose Holdings, and negotiations for the project had been handled by former MCA president Tan Koon Swan, while he was still managing director of Multi-Purpose Holdings (see Gomez 1993).

Acquisition of Rashid Hussain Bhd

Wan Azmi first obtained a direct interest in Rashid Hussain Bhd, the largest local stockbroking group, in November 1988, when he was allotted the entire Bumiputera allocation of 5.5 million shares when the company went public. In early 1990 Wan Azmi divested his stake in the company, reportedly at a profit of RM20.6 million (*Malaysian Business* 1/11/90).

By December 1990, however, Wan Azmi started reacquiring an interest in Rashid Hussain through Land & General. After an initial purchase of 5.9 per cent of equity, Land & General's interest in Rashid Hussain tripled to 16.7 per cent by February 1991; by March 1992, Land & General's stake in Rashid Hussain amounted to a massive 24.8 per cent (*New Straits Times* 2/3/91; *Business Times* 6/3/92). In February 1992 Bank Negara gave Land & General the approval to increase its stake in Rashid Hussain to 30 per cent, which would have made Land & General the single largest shareholder of the stockbroking company (*New Straits Times* 1/5/92). One of Rashid Hussain's most important assets was its associate company, the D&C Bank, in which it has a 20 per cent stake. This bank, which had been acquired in July 1990 from Singapore-based United Industrial Corporation for RM224 million (see p. 62), was then involved in discussions to merge with Malaysia's third largest bank, UMBC; the negotiations, however, fell through. Rashid Hussain had to stave off bids from Amalgamated Steel Mills Bhd, the Hong Leong Group, and the MBf Group to acquire the 20 per cent stake in the D&C Bank. The final decision on who should acquire the D&C Bank's equity came from the Finance Minister and Bank Negara, as stipulated under Malaysia's banking regulations (*The Star* 19/7/90). Wan Azmi was then also the chairman and 30 per cent owner of the Kuala Lumpur Mutual Fund Bhd, in which the D&C Bank owns a 21 per cent stake (*Malaysian Business* 1/11/90).

Acquisition of R. J. Reynolds

When Wan Azmi divested his stake in the highly lucrative Rashid Hussain Bhd in January 1990, it was seen as a surprising divestiture since he was using the funds – through his family holding company, Rohas Sdn Bhd – to obtain a controlling 51 per cent stake in the ailing publicly listed investment holding company Juara Perkasa Corporation Bhd (JPC). JPC was then so debt-ridden that its shares had been suspended from trading on the KLSE since December 1987 (*New Straits Times* 31/8/90). Despite the company's moribund state, each JPC share was bought for a hefty RM2.53; within four months Wan Azmi had increased his stake in JPC to 55 per cent (*Malaysian Business* 16/9/90).

At the end of August 1990, the American-controlled R. J. Reynolds Tobacco Company announced the reverse takeover of JPC by injecting its highly profitable Malaysian subsidiary, R. J. Reynolds Sdn Bhd into JPC. R. J. Reynolds had been under increasing pressure from the government to indigenise its equity, as required under the NEP, by the end of 1990. The takeover was paid for with the issue of 250 million new JPC shares. Soon after the reverse takeover of JPC by R.J.R. Tobacco, the company's entire 49 per cent stake in J. & P. Coats (Manufacturing) Sdn Bhd was sold to help reduce JPC's debt. Wan Azmi, who had promised to find a buyer for J. & P. Coats during the negotiations for the reverse takeover, eventually bought the company himself (*Business Times* 7/9/90). JPC was relisted on the KLSE on 1 March 1991.

After the takeover and a restructuring of JPC, the American stake in the company was reduced to 70 per cent, while Wan Azmi had 14.5 per cent of equity through his direct and indirect stakes (see *New Straits Times* 7/9/90). Figure 5.1 indicates the shareholding structure of JPC before and after the takeover by R.J.R. Tobacco.

JPC was renamed R. J. Reynolds Bhd, and by the end of 1991 the turnover of the restructured company increased from a mere RM156,000 to a massive RM315.875 million, while its pre-tax profit registered a phenomenal 17,106 per cent increase! By 1991, according to one study, compared to the 350-odd companies then quoted on the

Figure 5.1   Shareholding Structure of JPC Before and After the Reverse
                 Takeover of R.J.R. Tobacco Co. (US)

Before the Deal

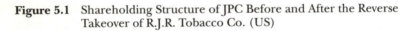

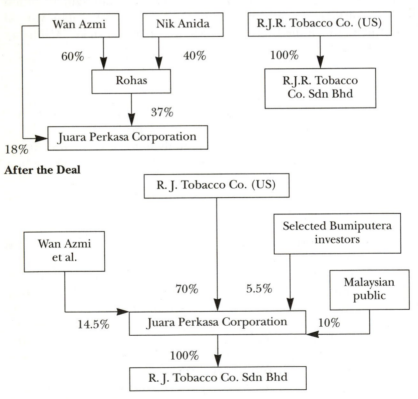

After the Deal

Source: *Malaysian Business* 16/9/90

local stock exchange, R. J. Reynolds was ranked 71 in terms of sales (see *Corporate World* July 1992).

Although Wan Azmi strongly insisted that it was the American party that approached him with the takeover and restructuring proposal, which helped convert the ailing JPC into the highly profitable R. J. Reynolds, it was generally viewed as more than 'just a happy accident', in the words of one analyst (*Malaysian Business* 16/9/90). In 1992 of the ten cigarette manufacturers in the country, R. J. Reynolds was listed as the third largest, with its capture of 19 per cent of the market (*New Straits Times* 4/5/92).

The Acquisition of Cycle & Carriage and Cold Storage

In 1989 Wan Azmi used his Hong Kong–based Yung Pui Company Ltd, which he controlled together with Basir Ismail and Ong Beng Seng, a prominent Singaporean businessman, to acquire a stake in the publicly listed Cycle & Carriage Ltd from the government-controlled PNB. Later Cycle & Carriage Ltd was used to buy a stake in another publicly listed company, Cold Storage Bhd, a company in which Daim Zainuddin had a majority stake in the early 1980s (Gomez 1991a: 23–7). Cycle & Carriage Ltd also owns a 49 per cent stake in another publicly listed company, Cycle & Carriage Bintang Bhd (*The Star* 7/6/90).

Another major acquisition by Cycle & Carriage Ltd involved Ampang Investments Pte Ltd, a joint-venture company in which it had a 40 per cent stake. Ampang Investments in turn, owned Ampang Hotel Sdn Bhd, which was used to acquire the Kuala Lumpur Merlin from the Faber Group, an UMNO-controlled company then in need of funds to fend off liquidation (*The Star* 5/8/89). Ong Beng Seng was also involved in the acquisition of the Kuala Lumpur Merlin, now renamed the Concorde Hotel. In 1989 Cycle & Carriage Ltd's wholly owned subsidiary, Cycle & Carriage Industries (1986) Pte Ltd, was appointed sole distributor for the import and distribution of the Malaysian-made Proton Saga car in Singapore (*The Star* 2/5/89).

Although Yung Pui's stake in Cycle & Carriage was sold to EON, a publicly listed concern then controlled by the government through HICOM Holdings Bhd, Basir Ismail remained as chairman of Cycle & Carriage Ltd, Cycle & Carriage Bintang and Cold Storage. Apart from this, in mid-1992, Cycle & Carriage Ltd, along with a Singapore-based listed company, Hotel Properties Ltd, also bought into another Singapore-based quoted company, Malayan Credit Ltd, controlled by the Teo family of the See Hoy Chan Group; interestingly, Ong Beng Seng controls Hotel Properties (*Corporate World* July 1992). While it appears that Wan Azmi is no longer linked with the Cycle & Carriage Ltd Group, Basir remains a shareholder of the company.

These myriad acquisitions, conducted within the short span of around four years, have now left Wan Azmi with an enormous interest in some of Malaysia's most important companies (see Figure 5.2). According to a tabulation of the direct interests of directors in publicly listed companies undertaken by *Malaysian Business* (16/4/92) in 1992, Wan Azmi was listed number 11 with a total of RM53.544 million; this figure, it should be stressed, was only for his direct interests in two companies, Land & General and Kretam Holdings Bhd, a minor listed oil palm company, in which Wan Azmi then had a 20 per cent stake. By 1993 the Yayasan Gerakbakti Kebangsaan, a foundation owned by UMNO Youth, had gained a stake in Kretam Holdings; the foundation's chief executive officer, Ahmad Zahid Hamidi, is also the deputy chairman of Kretam Holdings (*Malaysian Business* 1/12/93). Ahmad Zahid Hamidi, the UMNO Youth information head, was formerly a senator and had served as the political secretary of Najib Razak, an UMNO vice-president and the Education Minister (*Malaysian Business* 1/12/93). Zahid contested and won a parliamentary seat in the 1995 general elections. He is also the chairman of government-owned Bank Simpanan Nasional Bhd.

According to another tabulation, the estimated value of Wan Azmi's corporate assets, both in Malaysia and in foreign countries, was RM800 million in early 1992 (see *The Star* 19/5/92). It is evident that Wan Azmi has gained greatly from the NEP, which helped him get into Rashid Hussain and to benefit substantially from the indigenisation of R. J. Reynolds. His relationship with Daim and other well-connected businessmen also appears to have been crucial in the development of the Land & General conglomerate. The manner in which some of Wan Azmi's major corporate deals have been undertaken, particularly those involving Nanyang Press and Cycle & Carriage Ltd, also suggests that his companies may have been a conduit for important corporate assets to UMNO-linked companies or to other influential Malay businessmen; interestingly, too, Kretam Holdings is now controlled by UMNO Youth, though it is uncertain if Wan Azmi divested his stake in the company to the political organisation; by 1993 almost 47 per cent of the company's shares were held by nominee companies (KLSE 19 (I) 1993: 784–7). In addition, Wan Azmi has also helped bail out some ailing companies under UMNO's control, such as the Faber Group. Furthermore, like those of many other well-connected Bumiputera businessmen, Wan Azmi's major corporate deals, which have helped fund much of his corporate expansion, have evolved out of his involvement in the property development sector.

As Figure 5.2 indicates, Wan Azmi's corporate holdings are much more extensive than those covered by this case study. However, as a result of his close ties with UMNO leaders and his apparent role in channelling assets to other companies, it is becoming increasingly difficult to distinguish between what he may hold in trust for UMNO or others and his own assets.

Figure 5.2   Wan Azmi Wan Hamzah's Control of the Corporate Sector

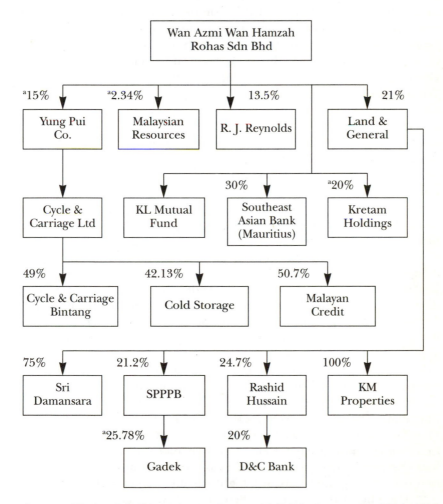

Sources: *The Star* 6/7/90; *Malaysian Business* 16/3/91; *Corporate World* July 1992.
Notes: This shareholding structure was before the sale of Cycle & Carriage Ltd to EON by Yung Pui.
             [a] Wan Azmi had divested his interests in these companies by 1994.

Case Study 9: Tajudin Ramli

Tajudin Ramli, another close associate of Daim Zainuddin, has also become a major business figure. Although his corporate holdings are not as extensive as those of Wan Azmi, since 1992 he appears to have benefited much from government patronage, rapidly emerging as one of Malaysia's more influential businessmen. As in the case of Wan Azmi, Tajudin was once a director of the government-owned Peremba and also of one of UMNO's holding companies, the Fleet Group. He also served as director of Taman Bukit Maluri, a company owned by Daim.

Tajudin first gained prominence in 1983, when he emerged as Daim's partner in a private company, Seri Iras, which acquired a 33 per cent stake in the publicly listed Raleigh (now renamed the Berjaya Group); Tajudin was appointed chairman of the listed company. After Daim's ministerial appointment in 1984, their interest in the Berjaya Group was divested by 1987, with a majority stake of the company eventually coming under the control of Vincent Tan Chee Yioun, reputedly a close ally of some of UMNO's top leaders. After leaving the Berjaya Group, Tajudin remained very much in the background, establishing a few private companies such as Arnah Murni Sdn Bhd, RZ Equities Sdn Bhd, and Alpine Resources Sdn Bhd, his main holding company.

Tajudin's ownership of some of these companies suggests his indirect links with UMNO leaders. For example, records filed at the Registrar of Companies indicate that Alpine Resources was incorporated on 8 September 1987 and that the company's first directors were Abdul Rashid Abdul Manaff and Zaki Azmi. Abdul Rashid had also served as director of Seri Iras and Pradaz Sdn Bhd, one of Daim's more important family holding companies; Pradaz had been used to hold Daim's stake in Cold Storage. Zaki Azmi is a noted UMNO lawyer who has also appeared as a director of a few UMNO-related companies.

In 1989 Tajudin acquired a 51 per cent stake in Celcom Sdn Bhd from Syarikat Telekom (M) Bhd, although the latter was then being prepared for privatisation (*Malaysian Business* 1/4/92). Celcom was incorporated in January 1988 as a joint venture between STM and the UMNO-owned Fleet Group; STM owned 51 per cent of Celcom while the Fleet Group held the remaining stake. Celcom, which had the rights to a highly lucrative cellular telephone network, was only the country's second such network, making the company a highly profitable entity (Gomez 1990: 97). The sale of the government-controlled STM stake in Celcom to Tajudin was thus quite controversial, and not viewed favourably by executives at STM who had set up the company (see *Malaysian Business* 1/4/92).

Acquisition of TRI

Despite Tajudin's control of Alpine Resources and Celcom, both unlisted entities, it was only in June 1990 that he re-emerged as a major corporate player when he was disclosed as a director of Arnah Murni, then a RM2 company, which had acquired a controlling 25.06 per cent stake in the publicly listed Technology Resources Industries Bhd (TRI, formerly Roxy Electric Industries); another buyer into TRI in the same period was Basir Ismail. Daim had also once owned a major stake in this listed company. Arnah Murni's interest in TRI was believed to have been bought from companies linked to Alex Lee, a close ally of Daim and a former deputy minister of the government. Alex Lee, then believed to be experiencing a severe financial crisis, was seeking to dispose of his stake in his flagship company, Roxy, to settle his debts. Tajudin, who also acquired a direct 2.96 per cent stake in Roxy, was appointed executive chairman of the company, which he renamed TRI, and which was to become his main vehicle for corporate expansion (see Gomez 1991a: 42–3).

Although a well-diversified group involved in manufacturing, property development and trading, TRI's most important asset was its stake in the D&C Bank, Malaysia's fifth largest bank established by Alex Lee's father, Henry H. S. Lee, the country's first Finance minister. At its peak in the early 1980s, TRI had a 33 per cent interest in the D&C Bank. But as TRI became enmeshed in debts and losses during the mid-1980 recession, the company began reducing its equity in the bank as a means to settle its outstanding loans (see Gomez 1991a: 31–43). By the time Tajudin obtained control of TRI, its interest in the D&C Bank only amounted to 8.9 per cent. Surprisingly, this stake in the bank was sold off immediately by TRI for RM89.5 million, with the proceeds used to reduce the company's gearing ratio and to venture into new business activities, namely transportation (*Investors Digest* March 1991); this stake in the D&C Bank eventually came under the control of Rashid Hussain Bhd, the listed Malaysian stockbroking conglomerate.

Acquisition of MHS and MAS

TRI's first acquisition under Tajudin, in December 1990, with part of the proceeds from the sale of the D&C Bank, was a 9.8 per cent stake in Malaysian Helicopter Services Bhd, a publicly listed helicopter and air services company in which Tajudin had already acquired a 6.6 per cent stake the year before. A month later, in January 1991, TRI raised its stake in MHS to 11.14 per cent, and in February bought another 12 per cent stake in the company. By March TRI's stake in MHS was 30.6 per cent, while Tajudin's personal stake in MHS was 17.5 per cent (*The Star*

14/1/91, 4/2/91, 12/2/91). The MHS acquisition continued until the trigger point was passed and a general offer had to be made for the company; by April 1992 TRI's stake in MHS was a massive 62 per cent (*Malaysian Business* 1/4/92). It appears that TRI's stake in MHS includes that personally owned by Tajudin Ramli. By December 1993 Tajudin's indirect stake in MHS – through TRI – had been reduced to 51.74 per cent (KLSE 19 (I) 1993: 377–9).

During this same period, MHS was in turn used to acquire a 40 per cent stake in Perbadanan Nasional Shipping Line Bhd from the government-owned Pernas. MHS also had a 9 per cent stake in Pelangi Air Sdn Bhd, a local airline services company; it later increased its stake in Pelangi Air when it acquired another 9 per cent stake in the company from the government-controlled Malaysia Airlines. These acquisitions gave TRI an important foothold in two important areas of the transportation sector: air and sea services (*Investors Digest* March 1991).

In December 1993 MHS announced its intention to acquire a 32 per cent stake in MAS from Bank Negara, the central bank. The MAS acquisition, valued at RM1.79 billion, involved a share swap; in return for the MAS equity, valued at RM8 per share, Bank Negara obtained 112 million new RM1 MHS shares, issued at a price of RM16 each. By June 1994 the terms of the sale of the MAS shares were revised; through his holding company, RZ Equities, Tajudin acquired the 32 per cent MAS equity directly; MHS was, however, given an option to acquire the MAS shares within one year, an option which was subsequently exercised (*New Straits Times* 12/8/94). The Bank Negara MAS divestment was part of the government's ongoing privatisation exercise; as usual, there was no open bid for the airline shares (*Malaysian Business* 16/1/94). After this divestment, although Bank Negara still retained a major stake in MAS, this was eventually divested to the Pensions Trust Fund. It appears that government patronage was crucial in helping Tajudin get control of MAS and consolidate his niche in the transportation sector.

Acquisition of Celcom

Tajudin was also gaining influence in the telecommunications industry. In November 1991 TRI proposed to acquire a 49 per cent stake in Celcom from Arnah Murni, Tajudin's holding company, which had 51 per cent of the Celcom equity. Under the share swap-cum-cash deal, TRI offered Arnah Murni RM259.4 million for its stake in Celcom and also obtained a two-year option to acquire Arnah Murni's remaining 2 per cent stake in the company (*New Straits Times* 11/11/91). The RM259.4 million was to be paid for with the issue of 195.7 million new TRI shares and RM4.99 million cash (*Investors Digest* December 1991).

After the transaction, Tajudin's stake in TRI was increased to 48.2 per cent. The deal, however, fell through when Celcom's other major shareholder, Time Engineering Bhd, a listed entity in the Renong group of companies, objected to the sale. Time Engineering's 51 per cent equity in Celcom was in fact acquired from the Fleet Group, UMNO's holding company. Time Engineering's objection to the acquisition of Celcom by TRI was because the company had 'a "pre-emptive" right to buy any Celcom shares up for sale' (*Malaysian Business* 1/7/92).

Figure 5.3   Tajudin Ramli's Control of the Corporate Sector

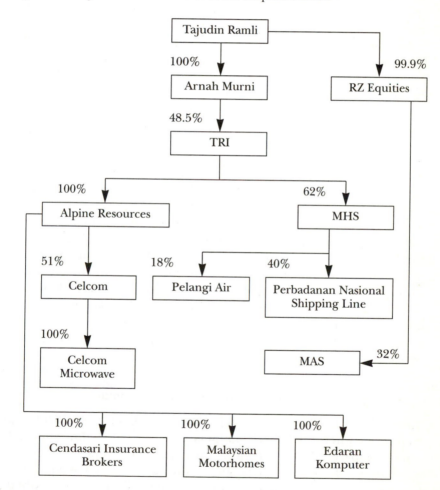

Sources: *The Star* 25/1/91; *Malaysian Business* 1/4/92

In order to circumvent Time Engineering's opposition, in June 1992 TRI proposed to acquire 100 per cent of Alpine Resources – the Celcom equity was held by Alpine Resources, which was wholly owned by Arnah Murni – for RM259.2 million; the figure was slightly lower, by RM0.2 million, than the earlier one proposed by TRI although the company was now gaining an additional 2 per cent stake in Celcom, not to mention the other companies owned by Alpine Resources. With the deal, Tajudin obtained a 48.5 per cent stake in TRI (*Malaysian Business* 1/7/92). In October 1992, in a surprising turn of events, Time Engineering agreed to sell its 51 per cent stake in Celcom to TRI, giving the latter 100 per cent control of the telecommunications company and enabling TRI to enhance its participation in this lucrative industry (*The Star* 2/10/92).

Apart from Tajudin, who is TRI's chairman, Mokhzani Mahathir, the son of the Prime Minister, also sits on the company's board of directors. Tajudin Ramli's ownership of the corporate sector – through TRI (see Figure 5.3) – was estimated to be worth almost RM500 million in 1992. This included his stake in TRI and Celcom, besides property in England (see *The Star* 19/5/92). By December 1993, however, *Malaysian Business* (1/12/93) estimated that Tajudin's locally listed stock alone was worth RM2.641 billion.

As in the case of Daim Zainuddin and Wan Azmi Wan Hamzah, the development of Tajudin Ramli's corporate base is primarily attributable to state patronage. The development of TRI is another example of the creation of Bumiputera conglomerates through changes in ownership, rather than through accumulation and expansion of a company's productive investment activities. Aided by the NEP and privatisation, Tajudin enjoyed favourable government treatment, which gained him control of two enterprises developed by the state, MAS and Celcom. With such crucial support, such politically linked Bumiputera businessmen have become major corporate players, comparable in standing to some of the most established Chinese businessmen in the country.

Case Study 10: Vincent Tan Chee Yioun

Vincent Tan Chee Yioun, aged 43 in 1996, left school at 16 to work as a bank clerk when his father's business ventures failed. Tan also sold insurance part-time for American International Assurance, a career which proved to be more successful; by the age of 23 he was an agency manager. Around this time Tan started several small companies involved in general insurance, trading, property development and credit.

Tan first gained national prominence in 1981, when he won the Malaysian franchise for the leading American fast-food outlet, McDonald's. Tan incorporated Golden Arches Restaurant Sdn Bhd to assume control of the McDonald's franchise. By 1990 the US-based McDonald's Corporation owned 49 per cent of Golden Arches, while Tan owned 26 per cent. The remaining 25 per cent was held by Mohamad Shah Abdul Kadir, the son of Abdul Kadir, a former UMNO minister. Since the company commenced business in April 1982, it registered consistent losses until 1990 (*Malaysian Business* 1/1/92). In 1982 Tan became managing director of McDonald's Malaysia; the number of McDonald's outlets nationwide has spiralled since then. Tan reportedly asks for and gets a million ringgit from a franchise holder for the opening of each new outlet (*Malaysian Business* 16/3/90; *Asian Wall Street Journal* 6/11/89).

Tan's most important acquisition was in May 1985, when his investment holding company, B&B Enterprise Sdn Bhd, was, ostensibly as part of Malaysia's privatisation efforts, awarded the right to acquire 70 per cent of the lucrative gaming entity Sports Toto Bhd. This lottery operator, incorporated by the government in 1969 to generate funds for the country's sports budget, then fully owned by the government's holding company, Ministry of Finance Incorporated, under the jurisdiction of the then Finance Minister Daim. The *Far Eastern Economic Review* (31/8/89) quotes Tan as insisting that the sale of Sports Toto was 'the only favour he has ever received from the government'. The privatisation of Sports Toto came under severe criticism since it was not open to bidding (see *Asiaweek* 29/7/88). In 1986, through another holding company, Nautilus Corporation Sdn Bhd, Tan obtained a licence to operate another gaming entity, Ascot Sports, the only off-course betting centre operator in Malaysia for English and Australian horse races; Ascot Sports, which began operations in 1988, ceased operations in June 1990 (*Asiaweek* 23/9/88; *The Star* 9/6/90).

After getting control of Sports Toto, B&B Enterprise sold 10 per cent of its stake in the company for RM4 million to Melewar Corporation Bhd, a company controlled by Tunku Abdullah, the younger brother of the ruler of Negeri Sembilan and a close associate of Prime Minister Mahathir. When the Sports Toto shares were publicly listed in July 1987 at an offer price of RM2, its closing price on its first day of trading was RM9.55, almost five times its offer price! In the process, B&B Enterprise's stake in the company was reduced to 45 per cent, while Melewar owned 7.5 per cent, and the government retained 30 per cent of equity (*The Star* 12/5/88). A month later, in August 1987, Tan swapped his stake in Sports Toto for a substantial stake in the Berjaya Corporation Bhd, a minor publicly listed manufacturing concern in which he already had an interest; the eight Berjaya Corporation shares for one Sports Toto share swap increased his stake in the Berjaya Corporation significantly (*Far Eastern Economic Review* 17/9/87).

The following year, in June 1988, Tan swapped his Berjaya Corporation shares for a controlling stake in the loss-making, publicly listed Raleigh Bhd (later renamed Inter-Pacific Industrial Group), which had been Daim's flagship company before his ministerial appointment. By September 1986, after Mahathir had issued a directive that all his cabinet ministers divest their corporate holdings, Daim was believed to be looking for a buyer for his equity in Raleigh. It was reported that Tan had acquired the Inter-Pacific stake from Daim's associates who were holding the company's equity in trust for the minister (see *Asiaweek* 19/1/90). One month before the share swap, in another controversial deal, the government sold its remaining 30 per cent stake in Sports Toto to Inter-Pacific in May 1988 (*The Star* 12/5/88). Apart from acquiring the Berjaya Corporation and Sports Toto, Inter-Pacific also acquired a stake in Prudential Assurance Sdn Bhd, which it later publicly listed. To finance these acquisitions, Inter-Pacific declared a then unprecedented seven-for-two rights issue (*The Star* 20/9/88). It received acceptances of only 61.3 per cent, meaning that the underwriters had to pick up the remaining rights issues (*Far Eastern Economic Review* 10/11/88).

In January 1989, ostensibly as part of a rationalisation exercise, the Berjaya Corporation bought all of Inter-Pacific's equity in Sports Toto, raising its stake in the gaming company to almost 90 per cent (*The Star* 1/2/89). At the same time the Berjaya Corporation also acquired a 17 per cent stake in TV3, another highly profitable company in which UMNO companies owned a majority stake. By the end of 1989 Inter-Pacific, then substantially under the control of B&B Enterprise, had a 57 per cent stake in the Berjaya Corporation, which owned 93.25 per cent of Sports Toto's equity (*New Straits Times* 22/10/89). The Inter-Pacific Industrial Group was renamed the Berjaya Group, the Berjaya Corporation was renamed Berjaya Industrial Bhd, and Sports Toto was renamed Berjaya Leisure Bhd in September 1991.

Since then, the Berjaya Group has become one of the country's most active corporate raiders. It has diversified extensively and has acquired and sold stakes in some major publicly listed entities including Prudential Assurance Bhd, South Pacific Textiles Industries Bhd (later renamed Berjaya Textiles), Far East Asset Bhd (renamed Berjaya Sports Toto), Singer Holdings (M) Bhd (subsequently renamed Berjaya Singer), IGB Corporation Bhd, Magnum Corporation Bhd, Taiping Consolidated Bhd, Dunlop Estates Bhd, Malayan United Industries Bhd (MUI), SIG Holdings Bhd (renamed Berjaya South Island Bhd), and Tropical Veneer Company Bhd (renamed Intiplus Bhd).

Some of the important unlisted concerns the Berjaya Group has bought into include a 20.5 per cent stake in Star Publications (M) Bhd, which publishes the popular English tabloid, *The Star*. The equity in Star Publications was acquired from IGB Corporation by Berjaya Industrial (*Business Times* 21/12/90). In September 1994 Tan relinquished around half of his 20.5 per cent stake in Star Publications to Tengku Adnan Tengku Mansor, an UMNO supreme council member and a director of publicly listed Berjaya Singer Bhd, controlled by the Berjaya Group; Adnan also owns a Malay bi-weekly, *Watan*. Tan, however, owns another English daily, *The Sun*, through Fikiran Abadi Sdn Bhd, which also publishes a business monthly, *Corporate World* (*Malaysian Industry* August 1993). In 1995 Mutiara Telecommunications Sdn Bhd, a private limited company owned by Tan, was awarded a licence to launch Malaysia's fourth mobile telecommunications service (*Malaysian Business* 1/6/95).

Apart from this, through Berjaya Leisure, the Group acquired a 25 per cent stake in Sri Damansara, a highly lucrative property development concern, from Land & General, controlled by Wan Azmi Wan Hamzah (*The Star* 16/11/90). The Berjaya Group has also ventured overseas and been involved in the takeover of some foreign companies. But it has sold its stake in TV3, for a profit of RM17 million, to the Johore SEDC, and has reduced its stakes in Berjaya Textiles by 26 per cent, in Berjaya Leisure to 54.7 per cent, in Berjaya Sports Toto to 4.36 per cent, and in Taiping Consolidated to 14 per cent. The Berjaya Group's more than 55 per cent stake in Taiping Consolidated was reduced to around 14 per cent in 1992 when the listed company's equity was sold to Suleiman Manan (see *Malaysian Business* 16/6/90; *The Star* 28/5/91; *New Straits Times* 8/1/92).

The Berjaya Group has also been at the centre of some bitter business disputes, most notably when it bought into Magnum Corporation, controlled by T. K. Lim's Multi-Purpose Holdings, and MUI, controlled by Khoo Kay Peng. After the divestment of apparently lucrative assets by Magnum Corporation, Tan got embroiled in a heated public debate with Lim. The Berjaya Group and Berjaya Leisure then acquired a massive 32.9 per cent stake in Magnum Corporation, precipitating the belief that a hostile takeover was imminent before, in a surprising turn of events, divesting the entire equity to the cash-rich publicly listed Dunlop Estates Bhd, also a member of the Multi-Purpose Holdings Group. In the process, the Berjaya Group and Berjaya Leisure made a capital gain of RM43.8 million (*New Straits Times* 6/12/90).

Khoo Kay Peng had built up MUI from a small toothbrush manufacturer into a diversified corporation by going on a massive acquisition drive from 1975. Apart from manufacturing, MUI is now involved in banking and finance, trading, hotels, property development and tertiary education (*Malaysian Business* 16/6/91). In October 1991, after acquisition of an almost 30 per cent stake in MUI – the equity was bought through the Berjaya Corporation (10 per cent) and Berjaya Leisure (20 per cent) – the Berjaya Group had to sell Sports Toto (M) Sdn Bhd, which owns the Sports Toto gaming operations, to Berjaya Sports Toto (formerly Far East Asset); the Finance Ministry had issued a directive to the Berjaya Group to divest its gaming interests when it acquired a majority stake in MUI (*Business Times* 29/10/91). Meanwhile MUI acquired a 38 per cent stake in the Berjaya Group, creating an interlocking network between these companies in an attempt to gain the upper hand in the dispute.

It was suggested that the dispute between Tan and Khoo was encouraged by powerful UMNO leaders because Khoo, known to have once been a close associate of Razaleigh, was believed to have helped finance the former Finance Minister's Semangat 46 in the 1990 general elections (see *Far Eastern Economic Review* 15/8/91). In what appeared to be an attempt to dispel these rumours and ingratiate himself with the new UMNO leadership, Khoo helped appoint two people close to the then Deputy Prime Minister Ghafar Baba as directors of Pan Malaysia Rubber Industries Bhd (PMRI), a publicly listed company indirectly controlled by MUI. In June 1991 Khoo resigned as director of PMRI in favour of Mohd Ibrahim Mohd Zain, the chairman of the Bank Kerjasama Rakyat Malaysia and a close associate of Ghafar. A month later Mohd Tamrin Abdul Ghafar, Ghafar Baba's son, was also appointed to the board of PMRI (see *Malaysian Business* 16/4/92). Tamrin, then a member of parliament, was then also director of a number of other listed companies, such as Mycom Bhd and Gadek Bhd, as well as chairman of the government-controlled MARA; he, however, relinquished most of these appointments after his father's defeat by Anwar Ibrahim in the contest for UMNO's deputy presidency.

Despite Vincent Tan's acquisition of MUI, there was apparently some reluctance by the Berjaya Group's Berjaya Leisure to divest its lucrative Sports Toto gaming operations. This gaming operation was sold to Far East Asset, an ailing property company, for RM600 million. The amount was settled through a cash payment of RM209.03 million and the issue of 390.97 million Far East Assets convertible unsecured loan stock valued at RM1 each. Berjaya Leisure, however, was to sell the entire 390.97 million loan stock to Berjaya Leisure shareholders, Far East Asset's minority shareholders, and through private placement in the market. Although there was no explicit stipulation by the authorities that the Berjaya Group could not retain a certain segment of Far East Asset's shares, it was argued that this requirement was implicit in the original conditions of sale for Berjaya Leisure's gaming operations (see

Business Times 14/7/92). In November 1992, however, Berjaya Leisure announced its acquisition of a 12.95 per cent stake in Far East Asset, thus allowing it to have indirect control over the Sports Toto gaming operation (*New Straits Times* 18/11/92). In May 1993 Far East Asset was renamed Berjaya Sports Toto.

Before Berjaya Leisure's acquisition in Far East Asset, it was disclosed that a substantial shareholder with a 12 per cent stake in Far East Asset was Tengku Adnan Tengku Mansor, then the national treasurer for UMNO Youth and a close associate of Vincent Tan; in 1993 Adnan was elected into UMNO's Supreme Council. Adnan, a director of Berjaya Singer, another listed company controlled by the Berjaya Group, also acquired more than 10.5 per cent of Tan's 20.5 per cent stake in Star Publications, which publishes *The Star*, the best-selling English daily in the country (see *Malaysian Business* 1/9/92; *Far Eastern Economic Review* 6/10/94).

In 1993 Tan was again the main beneficiary of a major privatised contract when Indah Water Konsortium Sdn Bhd, a consortium led by his Berjaya Group, was awarded a RM6 billion sewerage contract which entailed, apart from the refurbishing and upgrading of existing sewerage systems, the planning and construction of new systems; the privatised contract had a concession period of 28 years (Cheong, 1995: 236–9). Having no experience in the construction of such sewerage facilities, the Berjaya Group was expected to rely heavily on its main partner in Indah Water, Northwest Water Ltd, the leading British water treatment company, to implement the contract. Among the other shareholders of Indah Water were the police co-operatives, Koperasi Polis DiRaja Bhd and Lembaga Tabung Angkatan Tentera (LTAT).

By December 1994, however, Indah Water was bought for a price of RM450 million, or RM15 per share, by Prime Utilities Bhd (formerly Berjaya South Island Bhd) then under the majority control of the politically well-connected Ahmad Sebi Abu Bakar. Eighty per cent of Indah Water's equity was acquired through a share swap from Berjaya Industrial (20 per cent), Northwest Water (25 per cent), Koperasi Polis DiRaja (20 per cent), and AIMS Worldwide (M) Sdn Bhd (15 per cent); the remaining 20 per cent Indah Water equity held by LTAT was acquired for RM90 million (Cheong 1995: 236–9). The privatised sewerage contract had enabled Tan to acquire an interest in another listed company, while retaining his interest in the lucrative project. In view of the manner of such corporate deals and the extent to which he actively participates in the management and operation of government-awarded contracts and projects, Tan's business style has been questioned by many critics. His company's actual role in the privatised sewerage contract, for instance, has been subject to criticism in both political and business circles.

The controversial manner in which Vincent Tan obtained his majority stake in the privatised Sports Toto gaming operations (which was crucial to the speedy build-up of his vast corporate empire and his takeover of the Berjaya Group owned by Daim), the way in which he was awarded the privatised Sports Toto and the sewerage project, and the swiftness with which he has been able to conglomeratise the Berjaya Group have been major reasons why he has not been able to shrug off market speculation that he has the backing of powerful politicians or that he may even be a proxy for certain political interests. Tan, however, has attempted to link his Berjaya Group conglomerate in powerful alliances with two other major Chinese conglomerates, the MUI Group and the IGB Group, which collectively could have become a major force in many sectors of the economy; the deal, however, fell through after acrimonious and well-publicised differences among them on how the alliance should develop (see *Asian Wall Street Journal* 4/7/90).

IGB had acquired a 20 per cent stake in Berjaya Group by late 1989 from Vincent Tan and the Berjaya Corporation, reportedly because Tan had amassed almost RM200 million in personal debt amidst a welter of transactions leading to the takeover of the Berjaya Group and the transformation of the company into a conglomerate (*Asian Wall Street Journal* 6/11/89). IGB's acquisition of the Berjaya Group equity was also believed to be part of an amalgamation exercise involving IGB, the Berjaya Group and MUI. In fact the dispute between the Berjaya Group and MUI began after Khoo Kay Peng refused to buy IGB's 20 per cent stake in MUI after the proposed amalgamation fell through. Tan was subsequently in the news after his disputes with another Chinese corporate figure, T. K. Lim. He has, in fact, been more successful in his business deals with Bumiputera businessmen, such as Wan Azmi Wan Hamzah through Sri Damansara, Tengku Adnan Tengku Mansur through Berjaya Sports Toto and Berjaya Singer, Suleiman Manan through Taiping Consolidated, and Ahmad Sebi through Prime Utilities.

Malaysian Business (16/4/1992) estimated the corporate assets owned by Tan in early 1992, through the Berjaya Group, at RM856.3 million. His brother, Danny Tan Chee Seng, also owns equity worth RM800.12 million in companies in the Berjaya Group conglomerate; the Tan brothers' combined ownership of listed company stock amounted to around RM1.7 billion, built up within barely a decade. In terms of ownership of listed stock by its directors, they were among the richest, next only to Quek Leng Chan of the Hong Leong Group and Halim Saad of the Renong Group. It should be noted that this does not include

Figure 5.4   Vincent Tan's Berjaya Group

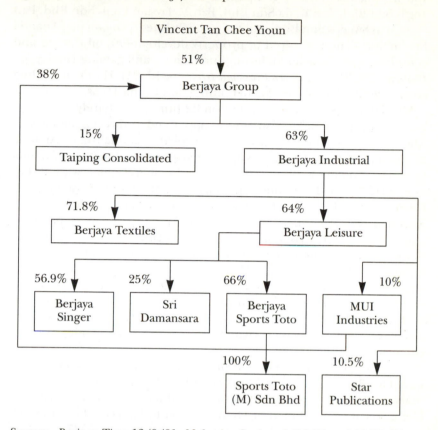

Sources: *Business Times* 13/9/91: *Malaysian Business* 1/10/91 and 16/12/93

Tan's ownership of local private companies and foreign property and corporate equity. Vincent Tan's corporate holdings through Berjaya Group in 1992 are shown in Figure 5.4.

Case Study 11: T. Ananda Krishnan

A Sri Lankan Tamil from Kuala Lumpur and son of a civil service clerk, T. Ananda Krishnan was born on 1 April 1938. A graduate of political science and economics from University of Melbourne, he also obtained a Masters degree in Business Administration from Harvard University. Operating through a myriad companies, such as his US-based companies, Pacific States Investment Ltd, Pexco Holdings, and Worldwide Sports & Entertainment, his Manila-based company, Exoil Trading Ltd,

and his Malaysian-based companies, MAI Holdings Sdn Bhd, Usaha
Tegas Sdn Bhd, Seri Kuda Sdn Bhd, Pan Malaysian Pools Sdn Bhd, Pan
Malaysian Sweeps Sdn Bhd, and the publicly listed Tanjong plc, Ananda
Krishnan is mainly involved in property development, oil trading and
consultancy, satellites and telecommunications, and gaming (*Malaysian
Business* 1/7/91; *Far Eastern Economic Review* 5/12/91). His main holding
companies in Malaysia are MAI Holdings and Usaha Tegas.

MAI Holdings was incorporated on 22 June 1988. Barely two weeks
later, on 4 July, Ananda Krishnan was appointed its director, along with
Khoo Teng Bin and T. Puvanesvari, probably a relative of Ananda
Krishnan; Ooi Boon Leong was appointed alternate director to Ananda
Krishnan. Ananda Krishnan was then major shareholder, with all but
one share of MAI Holdings' paid-up capital of RM1.5 million. By
February 1991 Khoo and Ooi had resigned as directors, while T. Maya
Krishnan was appointed to the board; Maya Krishnan is probably
another of Ananda Krishnan's relatives. MAI Holdings' share capital by
this time had also increased to RM6 million, with Ananda Krishnan still
holding all but one share. MAI Holdings, an investment holding
company, only commenced business in 1989. By the end of 1990 MAI
Holdings had investments worth RM4.24 million and two wholly owned
subsidiaries, Pacific Fortune Sdn Bhd and Fanuc Resources Sdn Bhd.
These two companies wholly owned equity in a number of minor private
companies.

Usaha Tegas was incorporated on 5 June 1984; its original directors
were Ooi Boon Leong and Khoo Teng Bin. Dormant for the first few
years, and then wholly owned by MAI Holdings, one million shares of
Usaha Tegas were allotted in October 1986 to Sports & Lotteries Systems Ltd, a London-based company. Although by June 1987 First City
Resources Sdn Bhd had two million shares, Sports & Lotteries was again
listed as the sole shareholder in 1988; the ultimate holding company,
however, was listed as Southwide Trading Ltd of Hong Kong. By this
time also, Usaha Tegas had a few wholly owned subsidiaries: Perkhidmatan Usaha Tegas Sdn Bhd, involved in telecommunications, as well as
Pan Malaysian Pools, Pan Malaysian Sweeps, and Big Sweep Sdn Bhd, all
of which were dormant then. By 1990 Pacific States Investments was
listed as the ultimate holding company of Usaha Tegas, which was by
then a highly profitable entity after its venture into the gaming industry.

Reportedly a close friend of Prime Minister Mahathir and for a long
time a low-profile director of Bank Negara (between 1982 and 1987)
and the government-owned Petronas, Ananda Krishnan first gained
national prominence in 1991 when he was disclosed as a director of Seri
Kuda, a company involved in a multi-billion ringgit development project
involving 39 hectares of former Selangor Turf Club prime land situated

in the heart of Kuala Lumpur (*New Straits Times* 18/6/91). So massive is the scale of the project, known as the Kuala Lumpur City Centre, that it has been touted as 'the single largest new real estate development in the world' (*Malaysian Business* 1/10/92).

Seri Kuda was incorporated on 30 January 1989 as an investment holding company. Apart from Ananda Krishnan, those who have served as directors of Seri Kuda include Ooi Boon Leong, Tunku Ahmad bin Tunku Yahya of Sime Darby, Ronald Khoo, a prominent lawyer, and Tunku Mahmud bin Tunku Besar Burhanuddin. Although at the end of 1989, the major shareholders of Seri Kuda were Ronald Khoo and Tunku Ahmad bin Tunku Yahya with 750,000 shares each, since then Seri Kuda has had numerous shareholders. The company's main share-holders in June 1991 were MAI Holdings (one million shares), Ronald Khoo and Tunku Ahmad (each of whom held 750,000 shares in trust, although it was not stated for whom), Adamwell Company Ltd of Hong Kong (500,000 shares), three Dutch companies – Solaro N.V. (600,000 shares), Taiheiyou Hotel & Shisan N.V. (700,000 shares), and Taiheiyou Kaihatsu N.V. (700,000 shares) – and a series of obscure companies. Apart from this, MAI Holdings also held 25 million preference shares and Usaha Tegas another 75 million preference shares in Seri Kuda.

The diverse number of shareholders of Seri Kuda, which includes trustees and obscure companies, frustrates attempts to estimate accurately Ananda Krishnan's stake in the company; one local daily suggested that his total equity in Seri Kuda in June 1991 was 30 per cent; meanwhile Petronas had emerged as a partner in the development project around this time, taking a 51 per cent stake in Seri Kuda (see *New Straits Times* 18/6/91). On 31 January 1992 Azizan bin Zainal Abidin, Hamzah Bakar and Mohd Hassan Marican, all directors of Petronas, were appointed to Seri Kuda's board.

Seri Kuda's involvement in the Kuala Lumpur City Centre project can be traced back to 1989, when it acquired the racecourse from the Selangor Turf Club for RM110 million. Later the authorities redesignated the land for commercial and residential development after an application by Seri Kuda (*Far Eastern Economic Review* 13/6/91; *Investors Digest* July 1992). Seri Kuda's company accounts state that the contract for the project was 'aborted and rescinded', but the company later 'entered into a Trust Deed under which terms it acquired, subject to certain conditions, the development land as trustee for its wholly owned subsidiaries who are beneficiaries under the Trust Deed'. The identities of the beneficiaries were not revealed. It is possible that the rescinding of the original contract and the involvement of Petronas in the project were the result of financing requirements as well as criticisms from various quarters, including UMNO members, of Ananda Krishnan's majority control of the project. In fact so strong were the criticisms that at the 1992 UMNO General Assembly both Prime Minister Mahathir and Finance Minister Anwar Ibrahim had to explain Ananda Krishnan's involvement in the Kuala Lumpur City Centre project (see *New Straits Times* 9/11/92).

Seri Kuda was not Ananda Krishnan's first lucrative business interest in Malaysia. In September 1988 the sale of Big Sweep lottery operations was privatised to another of his companies, Pan Malaysian Sweeps, controlled by his holding company, Usaha Tegas (*New Straits Times* 16/2/89). The licence for the Big Sweep lottery had originally been held by the Selangor, Perak and Penang Turf Clubs, though they were allowed to sell the lottery only to members. After Pan Malaysian Sweeps took over the Big Sweep lottery, however, it was given permission to sell the tickets to the public from 1 February 1989. This caused some uproar as its more lucrative prizes began to adversely affect sales of the Welfare Ministry's Social Welfare Lottery (*New Straits Times* 16/2/89).

The Big Sweep Lottery was not the only privatised operation to benefit Usaha Tegas. Under another privatisation scheme in January 1989, the Totalisator Board of Malaysia appointed Usaha Tegas to manage the NFO. The Totalisator Board, a statutory body which organises and regulates horse-racing totalisators, had been in operation since 1961. The NFO was, in turn, managed by the turf clubs until 1988, before the appointment of Usaha Tegas. The NFO's management was undertaken by Usaha Tegas' wholly owned entity, Pan Malaysian Pools, a company incorporated in July 1988. The NFO operated two gaming activities: the '3-Digit', introduced in 1961, and the '1+3 Digit', brought out by Pan Malaysian Pools in September 1989. These numbers-forecast gambling operations, it should be stressed, did not include the Big Sweep lottery operations already controlled by Pan Malaysian Sweep.

When the Social Welfare Lottery, run by the Welfare Ministry, ceased to operate in late 1990, the Big Sweep lottery became the only legal lottery ticket operation in Peninsular Malaysia; though there are a few lottery ticket operations in East Malaysia, particularly in Sabah. By April 1990, 30 per cent of Pan Malaysian Pools' equity had been sold to Bumiputeras (*New Straits Times* 6/11/91; *Malaysian Business* 16/11/91). The highly lucrative lottery operations, which made Pan Malaysian Pools very profitable, were the basis for a share swap which gave Usaha Tegas control of an ailing, suspended listed entity, Tanjong plc.

Tanjong was incorporated in England as Tanjong Tin Dredging Ltd in January 1926, and was involved in tin-mining. In February 1974 Tanjong was listed on the KLSE. As the company's mining leases had expired and since it was not involved in any other activity, Tanjong got permission to suspend trading of its shares in late 1987. Tanjong was then under the control of Tien Ik Enterprise Sdn Bhd, a company controlled by the family of business tycoon Robert Kuok (KLSE 14 1988: 1226–8; *New Straits Times* 3/6/91).

On 13 February 1991 a Hong Kong-based company, Marlestone Investment Ltd, acquired for RM9.69 million a 69.4 per cent stake in Tanjong from Tien Ik Enterprise. Two weeks later, on 27 February 1991, Marlestone entered into an agreement with Pan Malaysian Pools to 'cause and procure Tanjong to acquire the entire issued share capital of PMP (Pan Malaysian Pools)' (*Malaysian Business* 16/11/91). Tanjong was to acquire Pan Malaysian Pools for a massive RM332.5 million, which was paid for through a swap involving 166,250,000 Tanjong shares priced at RM2 each. It was later admitted that the people behind Marlestone were 'friends of PMP' (*Malaysian Business* 16/11/91). This complicated deal involving Tanjong, Pan Malaysian Pools, Marlestone and Usaha Tegas, eventually led to a back-door listing of Pan Malaysian Pools, with Usaha Tegas in control of the lucrative listed company, Tanjong.

Later, in May that year, after a five-for-one rights issue and a public issue of 17.5 million new Tanjong shares, and a special Bumiputera issue of 14.2 million shares in November 1991, Usaha Tegas emerged with a controlling 33.2 per cent stake; Marlestone's stake in Tanjong was reduced to a mere 0.5 per cent. Tanjong was requoted on the local bourse in December 1991 (*Malaysian Business* 16/11/91). So lucrative were the future prospects of Tanjong that the rights and public issue price of RM2 per share opened trading at a massive premium price of RM6.15, which was the highest premium of all new listings in that year (*The Star* 25/12/91). Within six months, by early June 1992, Tanjong's share price on the KLSE was hovering at almost RM13!

During the reorganisation and takeover of Tanjong, Usaha Tegas was appointed by the Totalisator Board in August 1991 as the sole agent for managing totalisators of race meetings. Under the agreement with the Board, Usaha Tegas would get 45 per cent of the racing totalisator's collections; the Board took 5 per cent, while the remaining 50 per cent went to the Perak, Selangor and Penang turf clubs (*The Star* 3/4/92). In April 1992, around eight months after being appointed to manage the racing totalisator, Usaha Tegas sold its rights to Tanjong's now wholly owned subsidiary, PMP, for RM75 million cash. This meant the centralisation under one company of the NFO and racing totalisators, which substantially increased the profit potential of Tanjong (*New Straits Times* 2/4/92).

In terms of overall control of the gaming sector in Malaysia, Tanjong's subsidiary, Pan Malaysian Pools, has cornered approximately 28 per

Figure 5.5   T. Ananda Krishnan's Corporate Holdings

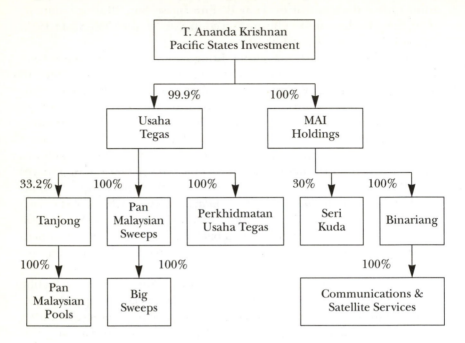

Sources: *Malaysian Business* 16/11/91; *Far Eastern Economic Review* 5/12/91;
            Company records

cent of the industry. The other major companies are Magnum, controlled by Multi-Purpose Holdings (which runs the four-digit lottery)
with 43 per cent; the publicly listed Mycom Bhd (which controls the
Sabah Big Sweep lottery and three-digit draws) with 12 per cent; and
Sports Toto (which also operates a four-digit lottery), controlled by
Vincent Tan, with 17 per cent (*New Straits Times* 24/12/91). As mentioned earlier, through Usaha Tegas' control of Pan Malaysian Sweeps,
which operates the Big Sweep lottery tickets, Ananda Krishnan wields
monopoly over lottery operations in Peninsular Malaysia.

Ananda Krishnan's involvement in the development of the Kuala
Lumpur City Centre project and the fact that he obtained the rights to
a number of lucrative gaming operations – he reportedly secured the
contract over other politically connected companies – appear to
confirm speculation over his close relationship with the Prime Minister
(see *The Star* 24/12/92). Apart from the Seri Kuda and Tanjong deals,
another company in which Ananda Krishnan has a stake, Binariang Sdn
Bhd, is involved in the proposed operation of a RM3.5 billion satellite
project, Measat I, which was launched in 1996. The satellite licence,

issued as part of Malaysia's privatisation initiative, also permits Binariang to operate various telecommunications and broadcasting services (*Far Eastern Economic Review* 26/5/94). Binariang, incorporated on 19 December 1986 as an investment holding company, is wholly owned by MAI Holdings, while its chairman is Hanif Omar, a former inspector-general of police. Among the others who have served as directors of Binariang are Ooi Boon Leong, Khoo Teng Bin and Tunku Mahmud bin Tunku Besar Burhanuddin, who also figure as directors of Usaha Tegas. Ooi and Tunku Mahmud also served as directors of Seri Kuda, while Khoo and Ooi served as directors of MAI Holdings. Figure 5.5 shows the major Malaysian companies controlled by Ananda Krishnan.

The Star (19/5/92) estimated the net worth of Ananda Krishnan's corporate assets – both listed and private, including foreign assets – in 1992 at RM1.8 billion. *The Star's* (19/5/92) tabulation also placed Ananda Krishnan as Malaysia's second wealthiest corporate leader. According to the newspaper's tabulation, the wealthiest local entrepreneur was Lim Goh Tong of Genting Bhd, with corporate assets worth RM2.8 billion, while Loh Boon Siew of Kah Motors Bhd was listed along with Ananda Krishnan at number two, with RM1.8 billion worth of corporate stock each. In fact, according to *The Star's* tabluation, in terms of corporate assets, Ananda Krishnan owned more equity than even Robert Kuok (RM1.7 billion) and Daim Zainuddin (RM1 billion).

6

Liberalisation After 1990?

By the end of the 1980s it was evident that most of the NEP's ambitious goals had been achieved. Poverty in Malaysia had been reduced remarkably to 15 per cent in Malaysia compared to 49 per cent in Peninsular Malaysia and a figure probably exceeding 50 per cent for the whole country in 1970 (Table 6.1); the identification of race or ethnicity with economic function or occupation and sectoral activity had been generally reduced (Table 6.2); and there were many fewer Malay–Chinese disparities in average income as well as ownership of corporate wealth. The accumulation of public sector assets on behalf of Bumiputeras, government regulation of business opportunities and investments, often requiring divestiture to Bumiputeras, privatisation of government assets at discounted prices primarily to Bumiputeras, and other preferential policies for Bumiputera businesses helped to increase the Bumiputera share of equity in publicly listed companies to 19.3 per cent in 1990, compared to a meagre 2.4 per cent share in 1970 (Table 6.3).

Some social features of Malaysia's economy persisted, however, in spite of the rapid changes in the two NEP decades. For example, although the NEP had helped to develop a significant Malay middle class, Bumiputeras still predominated in peasant agriculture and increased their predominance in the public sector. Although the government's attempts to redistribute ownership of corporate stock have been quite effective and several studies have argued that there has been considerable underestimation of the actual size of the Bumiputera share of corporate wealth (see, for example, Fong 1989; Jomo 1990; Tan 1993; Gomez 1990, 1994), income inequality and wealth differences among Bumiputeras have also increased substantially; small farmers still account for most of those living in poverty. Meanwhile the Chinese continue to

Table 6.1 Malaysia: Incidence of Poverty by Ethnic Groups, 1970, 1984, 1990, and 1992 (percentages)

	1970	1976	1984	1990	1992
Peninsular Malaysia					
All ethnic groups	49.3	35.1	18.4	15.0	13.5
Bumiputera	64.8	46.4	25.8	20.8	n.a.
Chinese	26.0	17.4	7.8	5.7	n.a.
Indian	39.2	27.3	10.1	8.0	n.a.
Others	44.8	33.8	22.0	18.0	n.a.
Sabah					
All ethnic groups	n.a.	51.2	33.1	34.3	33.2
Bumiputera	n.a.	82.9	39.2	41.2	n.a.
Chinese	n.a.	5.7	6.2	4.0	n.a.
Others	n.a.	11.4	12.4	6.0	n.a.
Sarawak					
All ethnic groups	n.a.	51.7	31.9	21.0	19.0
Bumiputera	n.a.	85.9	41.6	28.5	n.a.
Chinese	n.a.	14.0	9.3	4.4	n.a.
Others	n.a.	0.1	4.0	4.1	n.a.

Sources: *Third Malaysia Plan, 1976–80;*
Fourth Malaysia Plan, 1981–85;
Mid-Term Review of the Fourth Malaysia Plan, 1981–85;
Mid-Term Review of the Fifth Malaysia Plan, 1986–90;
The Second Outline Perspective Plan, 1991–2000;
Sixth Malaysia Plan, 1991–95;
Mid-Term Review of the Sixth Malaysia Plan, 1991–95.

Table 6.2 Malaysia: Employment by Occupation and Ethnic Group, 1995 (percentages)

Occupation	Bumiputera	Chinese	Indians	Others
Professional & technical	64.3	26.2	7.3	2.2
Teachers & nurses	72.3	20.5	6.6	0.6
Administrative & managerial	36.1	54.7	5.1	4.1
Clerical workers	57.2	34.4	7.7	0.7
Sale workers	36.2	51.9	6.5	5.4
Service workers	58.2	22.8	8.7	10.3
Agriculture workers	63.1	12.9	7.5	16.5
Production workers	44.8	35.0	10.3	9.9

Source: *Seventh Malaysia Plan, 1996–2000*

Table 6.3   Malaysia: Ownership of Share Capital (at par value) of Limited
Companies^a, 1970, 1990, 1995 (percentages)

Ownership group	1970	1990	1995
Bumiputera	2.4	19.3	20.6
Bumiputera individuals & institutions^b	1.6	14.2	18.6
Trust agencies^c	0.8	5.1	2.0
Non-Bumiputera	28.3	46.8	43.4
Chinese	27.2	45.5	40.9
Indians	1.1	1.0	1.5
Others	–	0.3	1.0
Nominee companies	6.0	8.5	8.3
Foreigners	63.4	25.4	27.7

Notes: ^{a} Excludes shares held by federal, state, and local governments.
  ^{b} Consists of investments owned by Bumiputeras as direct investors
    and investments through institutions channelling Bumiputera
    funds such as the Amanah Saham Nasional and the Amanah
    Saham Bumiputera schemes.
  ^{c} Refers to shares held through trust agencies such as Pernas,
    PNB and the SEDCs.

Sources: Third Malaysia Plan, 1976–80; Seventh Malaysia Plan, 1996–2000

dominate certain sectors, such as wholesale and retail trade, despite the
considerable inroads by Bumiputeras, especially through state enterprises. As a community, Indians have failed to make any significant gains
in ownership and control. While conceding that poverty is still widespread among Bumiputeras, non-Malay political leaders in the Barisan
Nasional began to argue in the late 1980s that poor non-Bumiputeras
had benefited least from the NEP.

The Thus despite its achievements, the extent to which the NEP's over-
riding goal of achieving 'national unity' – usually interpreted as improved inter-ethnic relations – had been attained is highly questionable;
in fact inter-ethnic relations were arguably worse in 1990 than in 1970.
S. Samy Vellu, president of the Malaysian Indian Congress, acknowledged
in 1990 that Indians were more marginalised and alienated than ever
before. The Malaysian Chinese Association had also become more
vocal in criticising UMNO politicians' preoccupation with constraining
Chinese accumulation of wealth to develop Bumiputera wealth. Furthermore, regional grievances had become more pronounced, not only in
Sabah and Sarawak but also on the East Coast of Peninsular Malaysia,
especially Kelantan.

The objectives of post-1990 economic development policy were first set
out by Mahathir in February 1991, two months into the post-NEP period,

when he presented his 'Vision 2020' plan. Containing nine central strategic challenges, the plan's main goal was for Malaysia to achieve 'fully developed country' status by the year 2020, mainly by accelerating industrialisation, growth and modernisation. This apparent policy volte-face from the NEP's redistributive priorities was hardly surprising. Since the early 1980s, Mahathir's government had emphasised growth, modernisation and industrialisation as national economic priorities, and the NEP had been quietly 'put on hold' from 1986, ostensibly because of the urgent need to respond to the recession.

Vision 2020's nine main objectives were to establish:

1 a united, peaceful, integrated and harmonious Malaysian nation;
2 a secure, confident, respected and robust society committed to excellence;
3 a mature, consensual and exemplary democracy;
4 a 'fully moral' society with citizens strongly imbued with spiritual values and the highest ethical standards;
5 a culturally, ethically and religiously diverse, liberal, tolerant and unified society;
6 a scientific, progressive, innovative and forward-looking society;
7 a caring society with a family-based welfare system;
8 an 'economically just' society with inter-ethnic economic parity; and
9 a 'fully competitive, dynamic, robust, resilient and prosperous' economy.

The policy also envisaged a more competitive, market-disciplined, outward-looking, dynamic, self-reliant, resilient, diversified, adaptive, technologically proficient and entrepreneurial economy with strong industrial links, productive and knowledgeable human resources, low inflation, exemplary work ethics and strong emphasis on quality and excellence.

In mid-1991 the government announced a new National Development Policy (NDP) – in conjunction with a ten-year Second Outline Perspective Plan (OPP2) for 1991–2000 – as well as the Sixth Malaysia Plan (6MP) for 1991–1995. Hence while the OPP2 and 6MP were supposed to provide medium-term economic policy perspectives, Vision 2020 provided the long-term objectives. The new economic development policy shift away from the redistributional objectives associated with the NEP were obvious. In fact Vision 2020 reiterated some of the major policy changes introduced by Mahathir during his tenure as prime minister, especially as the economic liberalisation undertaken since the mid-1980s encouraged the private sector – at the expense of the public sector – with privatisation and some deregulation.

Understandably, there has been some enthusiasm, especially on the part of non-Bumiputeras, for Vision 2020's explicit commitment to forging a Malaysian nation (bangsa Malaysia) transcending existing ethnic identities and loyalties. But whereas the NEP sought national unity in improved inter-ethnic relations, ostensibly to be realised by achieving inter-ethnic (especially Malay–Chinese) economic parity, Vision 2020's 'developed country' goal stresses an equally narrow, materialistic and economistic emphasis on growth.

Other differences, however, are more suggestive of the new approach and priorities. While the NEP envisaged progressive government intervention and a redistributive welfare role for the state, Vision 2020 has sought to shift primary responsibility for human welfare back to the family. With cuts in public expenditure, the costs of social services like education and health have been increasingly transferred to consumers in the form of higher university fees, payments for school amenities, hospital charges and medicine fees. Among its various other objectives, Vision 2020 still emphasises achieving inter-ethnic economic parity, implying that this is what is meant by economic justice. Unlike the NEP, however, the NDP document also expresses concern about relative poverty, and hence income inequality, both between and within ethnic groups.

The poverty rate is projected to decline from 17.1 per cent in 1990 to 7.2 per cent by the year 2000, with increased employment outside agriculture. The OPP2 estimated that 143,100 households, or about 4 per cent of the population, were in the hard-core poor category in 1990, many of whom would need direct transfers to be able to enjoy the basic necessities of life.

The OPP2 also claims that growth with effective governmental redistributive policies has been responsible for substantial improvements in income distribution – with the Gini coefficient going down from 0.513 in 1970 to 0.445 in 1990. Like other government documents, however, the 1991 documents do not indicate how distributional policies have had this impact. Official data suggests, for example, that the greatest reduction in income inequalities occurred between 1984 and 1987, possibly as a result of the differential consequences of the recession. But the OPP2 (1991b: 17) also acknowledges that 'income disparities within the Bumiputra community are higher than among other ethnic groups'.

Noting that the Malaysian economy grew by an average of 6.9 per cent over the twenty-year NEP period, Vision 2020 set a target average growth rate of 7 per cent for the next three decades. This would almost double the GDP in every decade, which would make it almost eight times larger in 2020 than it was in 1990. With a 2.5 per cent rate of population growth, however, per capita GDP would be only four times as much in 2020 compared to 1990. The NDP document also envisaged a 7 per cent growth rate for the OPP2 period (1991–2000), while the 6MP envisaged a 7.5 per cent annual growth rate for 1991–95, which has been exceeded by almost one percentage point.

In line with the Vision 2020 assumptions, the OPP2 projects an average growth rate of 7 per cent, higher than the 6.9 per cent of the first OPP period (1971–90). This projection, however, ignores the considerable, but unsustainable, contribution to growth from resource rents, especially from petroleum, timber and natural gas, during the first OPP period. While the economic boom since 1987 has been led by manufacturing, it has also been heavily reliant on foreign investments, especially from East Asia, and favourable international trade conditions, both of which may not continue indefinitely. Furthermore, it has already begun to run up against infrastructure, skill, labour and other constraints, while fuelling inflationary pressures in a near full employment situation.

In spite of Malaysia's impressive growth record, especially since the late 1980s, it remains to be seen whether these ambitious growth targets are realistic. The Malaysian economy has diversified considerably from the time when rubber and tin were the economic pillars of the colonial economy. Within the primary sector, petroleum and gas have raised mining's contribution, while palm oil, cocoa and pepper have diversified Malaysian export-oriented agriculture. With import substitution in the early 1960s and mid-1980s, and export-oriented industrialisation booming in the 1970s and since the late 1980s, manufacturing has become the single largest sector in the Malaysian economy, with services growing correspondingly.

Yet Malaysia's economic reliance on non-renewable natural resources has grown and continues to be high. Throughout the 1980s, for example, petroleum and timber contributed the highest export earnings. With agricultural production growing more modestly, manufacturing and services will have to grow at much higher rates to compensate for sluggish growth in the primary sector, especially as the timber industry goes into decline with the impending exhaustion of commercially accessible forests. The export-oriented industrial sector's reliance on foreign investments, technology and market access, and Malaysia's limited success in developing its own industrial and technological capacity as well as moving into greater value-added manufacturing renders industrialisation vulnerable and constrains its potential contribution. The contribution of the burgeoning public sector to growth, especially in the 1970s and early 1980s, also has to be considered.

To its credit, the government recognises a number of problems plaguing Malaysian industrialisation: manufacturing's narrow base, weak industrial links, insignificant local supply of intermediate products, inadequate development of indigenous technology, too little value-added, rising production (especially labour) costs, infrastructural bottle-necks, serious shortages of skilled personnel, the need for diversification of products as well as markets, problems raised by protectionism, trade blocs, managed trade, domestic private sector performance and the need for agrarian reform as well as resource and environmental protection.

In so far as it approves of various liberalisation measures, Vision 2020 represents a partial return of the pendulum to the relatively *laissez faire* policies of the first dozen years after Independence in 1957 from the government intervention and expanded public sector of the next decade and a half under the NEP. Vision 2020 therefore represents a reiteration and consolidation of the policy changes undertaken from the mid-1980s. While not representing new policy changes in a real sense, it nonetheless made economic policies already in place more explicit, coherent and legitimate.

In a longer perspective then, one might well argue that the 1991 announcements of Vision 2020, OPP2 and the 6MP have confirmed, consolidated and reiterated the economic policy changes which began much earlier in the mid-1980s. Whereas the earlier policy changes were often justified as temporary responses to the recession and as con-cessions to revive the economy, the post-1990 policy announcements were legitimised as the imperatives of rapid modernisation, the promise of a good life in the future, and the rapid growth and industrialisation that have occurred since the late 1980s.

Whether Vision 2020 adequately addresses the main contemporary challenges faced by Malaysian society is a different question. It has certainly shifted attention away from the previous narrow emphasis on inter-ethnic distributional concerns without abandoning them altogether. It has also given priority to the challenge of late industrial-isation without seeming oblivious of human welfare. Yet despite a wide-spread desire for change and reform among Malaysians, it cannot be claimed that there is a shared vision of an alternative yet.

However, the marginalisation and downgrading of distributional considerations as well as other non-economic concerns in favour of a growth and industrialisation fetish is unlikely to resolve the complex problems continuing to divide and destabilise Malaysian society. Also, without the stability achieved through mutually acceptable compromise, it may be difficult to ensure the socio-political stability necessary for rapid industrialisation and growth. And as well as this, as recent discus-sion of resource, environmental, and moral issues suggests, human wel-fare is unlikely to be secured in the future by economic growth alone.

Both plan documents, especially the 6MP, seem to take cognisance of problematic issues pertaining to regional and other non-ethnic inequalities, on women, on Indians and other smaller minorities, and on the environment. It remains to be seen how much of this is mere rhetoric and what will actually be done. But the key question of accountability – for example, in terms of institutional checks and balances, monitoring and availability of information to the public – highlighted by criticism from various quarters, especially in the second half of the 1980s, is still conspicuous, this time only by omission.

The NDP claims that it maintains the basic strategies of the NEP while making four main policy shifts. With the NDP, there is to be much more of a focus on hard-core poverty (those earning less than half the poverty-line income), and on relative poverty, that is inequalities in income and wealth. More attention is to be given to the rapid development of a Bumiputera Commercial and Industrial Community (BCIC). The NDP also emphasises growth led by the private rather than the public sector to achieve restructuring. Finally, more attention is to be given to human resource development to achieve the country's growth and distributional objectives.

Interestingly, while the 30 per cent equity restructuring target has been reiterated, no specific time frame has been set for its achievement. The OPP2 (1991b: 17) states that

> past efforts aimed at creating a BCIC have met with the least success. Equity ownership alone will have little impact on promoting effective Bumiputera participation in the economy if the newly acquired wealth is not retained and enlarged and if they have limited experiences in business operation ... The system of quotas, licences and other special assistance which has been implemented to help them ... will continue to be necessary in the nineties until the economic imbalances are corrected.

Emphasising 'balanced development in order to establish a more united and just society', the OPP2 (1991b: 5) developmental priorities for the 1990s are to

- strike an optimum balance between the goals of economic growth and equity;
- ensure a balanced development of the major sectors of the economy so as to increase their mutual complementarities to optimise growth;
- reduce and ultimately eliminate the social and economic inequalities and imbalances in the country to promote a fair and more equitable sharing of the benefits of economic growth by all Malaysians;
- promote and strengthen national integration by reducing the wide disparities in economic development between states and between the urban and rural areas in the country;

- develop a progressive society in which all citizens enjoy greater material welfare, while simultaneously imbued with positive social and spiritual values, and an increased sense of national pride and consciousness;
- promote human resource development including creating a productive and disciplined labour force and developing the necessary skills to meet the challenges in industrial development through a culture of merit and excellence without jeopardising the restructuring objectives;
- make science and technology an integral component of socio-economic planning and development, which entails building competence in strategic and knowledge-based technologies, and promote a science and technology culture in the process of building a modern industrial economy; and
- ensure that in the pursuit of economic development, adequate attention will be given to the protection of the environment and ecology so as to maintain the long-term sustainability of the country's development.

Balanced development is considered crucial for ensuring stable growth, minimising social conflict, promoting racial harmony and enhancing national unity. The OPP2 argues that this development strategy is premised on four considerations:

- that growth with equity would help ensure a fair and equitable distribution of national wealth;
- that balanced development would promote social and political stability;
- that high moral values and positive attitudes would create a responsible, resilient, progressive and caring society; and
- that prudent natural resource and ecological management would ensure sustainable development.

Except for the recent emphasis on environmental concerns, these objectives are, by and large, a reiteration of the rationale underlying the post-1969 NEP and Rukunnegara (National Ideology).

Table 6.4 sums up the major macro-economic and sectoral planning targets for the OPP2, contrasting them with OPP1 targets and achievements. As the table elaborates, the sectoral targets see a continued relative decline of agriculture, mining and construction, in favour of manufacturing and (presumably private sector) services during the OPP2 period. Both exports and imports are expected to grow more slowly than GDP, unlike during the period 1971–90, and also by much less than was the case during the OPP1 period. Trends since 1991 and continued reliance on export-oriented industrialisation and foreign investment underline doubts about whether these projections are realistic. Although not necessarily unfeasible, there are no clear policy measures to raise the savings rate (as a share of GNP) from 30.3 per cent in 1990 to 35.2 per cent in 2000, as targeted in Table 6.4.

Table 6.4 Malaysia: Outline Perspective Plan Targets and Achievement, 1991–2000

	Target OPP1 (1971–90)	Achieved OPP1 (1971–90)	Target OPP2 (1991–2000)
(I) *Macro-economic targets*	(% p.a.)	(% p.a.)	(% p.a.)
GDP (real)	8.0	6.7	7.0
Export (real)	7.1	9.2	6.3
Import (real)	5.2	10.0	5.7
Employment	3.3	3.4	3.1
Labour force	3.1	3.3	2.9
Unemployment rate[a]	3.6	6.0	4.0
	Target 1990	Achieved 1990	Target OPP2
Share of GNP (%)			
Savings	16.5	30.3	35.2
Investment	22.3	35.1	34.6
	Target 1990	Achieved 1990	Target 2000
(II) *Sectoral targets*			
Share of GDP (%)			
Agriculture & forestry	19.7	18.7	13.4
Mining[b]	2.6	9.7	5.7
Manufacturing	26.2	27.0	37.2
Construction	4.7	3.5	3.5
Services	48.3	42.3	45.4
Import duties less bank service charges	−1.5	−1.2	−5.2
Share of total employment (%)			
Agriculture & forestry	35.1	27.8	20.0
Mining[b]	1.5	0.6	0.5
Manufacturing	16.8	19.5	23.9
Construction	3.6	6.4	7.4
Services	43.0	45.7	48.2

Notes: [a] End of period
[b] Includes petroleum and gas

Source: OPP2, p. 90; Table 3.10

In this longer perspective then, it can be argued that the new economic initiatives announced in 1991 – Vision 2020, OPP2, and 6MP – have consolidated and reiterated the economic policy changes which began earlier, especially in the mid-1980s, and have been legitimised in terms of the imperatives of rapid modernisation, the promise of a better future, and the rapid growth and industrialisation record from the late 1980s.

7

Politics, Policies and Patronage

Rents, Redistribution and Restructuring

With the commendable objectives of Vision 2020, the NDP, the OPP2 and the 6MP as well as the more 'Malaysian-oriented' – as distinct from the NEP's 'Bumiputera-oriented' – vein of these policies, government practices of according preferential treatment to Bumiputeras have changed during the 1990s but arguably not diminished. Rents in various forms (discounted privatisations, overpriced contracts, permits and licences, special loan and credit facilities, as well as subsidised training and education opportunities) continue to be extensively provided by the government, now ostensibly in order to create competent Bumiputera entrepreneurs. But even the government has admitted that after twenty years of the NEP, genuine and competent indigenous entrepreneurs have failed to emerge in satisfactory numbers. The fact that the most influential and wealthy Malaysian businessmen by the early 1990s were also those most closely associated with the Prime Minister and Daim Zainuddin suggests that the creation and disbursement or allocation of these rents have been crucial for continued political hegemony as rent-financed patron–client relations continue to be important in Malaysian politics.

Although the NEP gave way in 1991 to a new generation of policies that appear to further consolidate the growth, industrialisation, liberalisation and privatisation initiatives begun in the mid-1980s, the NEP emphasis on restructuring wealth along ethnic lines continues to shape implementation of the government's new policies. While Vision 2020 and the NDP involve greater economic and cultural liberalisation and are less ethnic and redistributive in orientation, fundamental changes in the implementation of these new policies have been slow in coming since all the main political parties in the Barisan Nasional continue to make political appeals along ethnic lines. Furthermore, in view of the prominence still accorded the question of ownership by ethnicity, differences on public and private ownership in Malaysia's political economy will remain contentious.

Privatisation, part of Malaysia's liberalisation package, appears to have been especially abused for the development and consolidation of politically linked businessmen. With the UMNO-led Barisan Nasional firmly consolidated in power and periodically relegitimised by increasingly gerrymandered national elections, and with amendments to the national constitution to curb the powers of the judiciary and the constitutional monarchs, giving the UMNO leadership greater hegemony over the state, the political sphere has been reorganised to serve their interests and priorities better. This has involved the transfer of assets, other sources of income and significant control of the national economy to the politically influential.

Despite this, the creation and deployment of rents in the Malaysian economy so far point to a combination of different forces at work. Rents have also been created and allocated in ways that encourage investments in new productive activities which have contributed to the diversification of the national economy from its colonial inheritance, as well as various industrialisation campaigns, including export promotion, import substitution and heavy industrialisation. Investments in agriculture and tourism have also been induced.

In this regard, the availability of resource rents – most notably from petroleum, petroleum gas, tin and timber – has been very significant for growth, exports, government revenue and hence fiscal capacity, allowing the government a greater degree of latitude than that enjoyed by most other economies and governments in the world. It could be argued that such wealth of resources, Malaysia's relatively small population, and poor fiscal discipline gave rise to a 'soft budget constraint' which not only allowed, but even encouraged, various public sector extravagances. Such fiscal irresponsibility seemed to increase with greater state intervention and the greater availability of resource rents from the mid-1970s until the economic and political crises of the mid-1980s, when new policies to address the resulting fiscal and debt problems became imperative. The growth of the public sector was also accompanied by other interventions, which had a cumulative crowding-out effect (with specific ethnic undertones, discouraging non-Malay investment), that was reflected in significant capital flight and declining private investments from the mid-1970s, and especially in the early 1980s.

The other important goal of the creation and deployment of rents in Malaysia has been redistribution, especially along inter-ethnic lines.

It appears, however, that this ethnic agenda has served as a smokescreen which has obscured significant private accumulation by the politically well connected, especially with privatisation and other policies associated with economic liberalisation since the mid-1980s. With increasing Malay hegemony in the 1970s, the role of the predominantly Malay bureaucracy was significantly enhanced, only to give way to an increasingly assertive executive and a more politically influential rentier business community since the 1980s. After all, since the NEP-inspired 1970s, the allocation of such rents has ostensibly been intended primarily to enhance redistribution along inter-ethnic lines and to promote the development of Bumiputera capitalists. This has enabled the Bumiputera share of corporate wealth to rise significantly from 2.4 per cent in 1970 to 20.6 per cent in 1995 (see Table 6.3); of this 20.6 per cent, Bumiputera individuals held 18.6 per cent and trust agencies the balance.

More importantly, the share held by Bumiputeras had risen appreciably from 2.4 per cent in 1970 to 18.7 per cent in 1983, just over a decade after the start of the NEP, before rising merely by 0.6 per cent over the next seven years to 19.3 per cent in 1990; by 1995 this figure had increased by just another 1.3 per cent to 20.6 per cent (see Table 6.3). Thus while the Bumiputera corporate shareholding figure in 1990 was considerably short of the NEP's 30 per cent target, actual Bumiputera corporate power is probably underestimated by these figures because of the strategic nature of Bumiputera shareholding.

Yet although yielding handsome pecuniary returns, substantial profits and capital gains, the business operations of most Bumiputeras – and some non-Bumiputeras – benefiting from government-allocated rents are mainly non-entrepreneurial, unless one stretches the definition of entrepreneurship beyond recognition. Commenting on Malay businesses in 1994, Daim Zainuddin criticised their continued dependence on the state for protection, their subsidy mentality, and their lack of business focus, before harshly concluding that 'their minds are confused' (*New Straits Times* 28/6/94). There is probably much justification for these criticisms since most politically connected businessmen have tended to concentrate their rent-appropriating activities in the relatively protected import-substituting manufacturing, services, and other non-tradables such as real property, construction and infrastructure, while others have gained mostly from often complex paper-shuffling, asset-stripping and other similar corporate manoeuvres, rather than from significant gains in productivity or international competitiveness.

A comparison of businesses in different eras reflects the changing nature of business expansion of most new rentier capitalists. Whereas the companies which developed during the colonial and pre-NEP

post-Independence periods were more inclined to expand in a particular field of business and only diversify into related fields, the
contemporary conglomerate style of growth, especially pronounced in
the last decade, involves mergers, acquisitions and asset-stripping, with
scant regard for relevant experience and expertise. This change reflects
the greater attention to financial accumulation rather than the difficult
but ultimately necessary development of internationally competitive
productive capacities.

Exacerbating the problem of the unproductive business preferences
and practices of the 'new rich' is the fact that increasing conglomeratisation has led to increasing concentration of stock ownership and
monopolisation of the economy. The influential broadcasting as well as
newspaper and magazine publishing industries have been consolidated
under the control of a few businessmen with strong ties to powerful
political figures, while the UMNO-linked Renong Group has cornered
highway construction and related activities (see Gomez 1994). There is
also some concentration of the financial and property development
sectors within a diminishing network of interconnected companies,
through joint stock control and interlocking directorships, further enhancing the concentration of wealth-generating activities in the hands
of a select group. Such concentration also reflects the development of
an economy increasingly dominated by politicised oligopolies; although
the market still operates, it does so in conditions strongly influenced by
the state.

Moreover, given the executive's ascendant political position, the
extent to which the bureaucracy has been able to function independently in the implementation of state policies has been significantly
circumscribed; rather, the interests of politicians have created an
irresistible momentum encouraging greater political patronage. Without much transparency, such abuses are not obvious to the public.
Furthermore, continued ethnic political mobilisation, the economic
boom since the late 1980s, full employment and significant trickle-down
have enhanced the regime's legitimacy.

In the process, a few genuine entrepreneurs, mainly Chinese, have
survived and grown in the interstices of the system, often despite rather
than because of state support. Thus although Chinese equity ownership
increased significantly from 27.2 per cent in 1970 to 44.9 per cent in
1990 (see Table 6.3), for many, survival and expansion requires by-
passing the state rather than the state intervention on which the crony
rentiers thrive.

Although Chinese capital has continued to develop despite the constraints of the NEP, it appears to have lost its once powerful grip on the
economy. This somewhat reduced Chinese economic influence was

reflected in the decline of the MCA's most prominent investment company, Multi-Purpose Holdings, which was nearly taken over by companies linked to UMNO. Chinese capitalists also found that they either had to establish links with Malay patrons, capitalists or politicians, or fund UMNO, to develop their businesses. The new Chinese capitalists who emerged in the 1980s – Vincent Tan Chee Yioun, Danny Tan Chee Sing, Ting Pek Khiing, Robert Tan Hua Choon, T. K. Lim – are seen to be closely associated with leading Malay politicians rather than independent businessmen; there is much unverified speculation that some of these men have operated as business proxies for certain UMNO leaders, particularly Daim.

Elections, Accommodation and Investments

Despite this situation of Malay dominance in politics and business, senior UMNO leaders have noted that such unproductive corporate activities and concentration of economic power have occasionally strained relations between the UMNO-dominated state and both Chinese and foreign big business; these leaders are also aware of the likely repercussions of the swift and avaricious advance of politically well-connected Malay businessmen on Chinese business interests in general. Perhaps recognising that this could impair the Mahathir government's desire to promote Malaysian business interests regardless of ethnicity ('Malaysia Incorporated'), the executive appears to have become somewhat more restrained in continuing blatantly to favour the Malay business elite. By providing rentier opportunities to some Chinese and Indian businessmen, the state has also managed to reduce dissent among the non-Malay communities (see Gomez 1996a). The impressive economic recovery since 1987 and government efforts to liberalise, deregulate and de-emphasise the NEP – long desired by most non-Bumiputeras – have swung significant Chinese sentiment to the Barisan Nasional since late 1988, and especially after 1990, and was reflected in the impressive Barisan Nasional victory in the April 1995 general election (see Table 7.1).

In the 1990 general election, when the opposition had presented a strong challenge, the Barisan Nasional managed to win only 127 of the 180 (or 70.5 per cent) parliamentary seats; in the 1995 general election, however, the ruling coalition lost only 30 parliamentary seats (securing 84.3 per cent of the seats). In terms of popular votes, the Barisan Nasional obtained 3,862,694 votes in contrast to the 2,075,822 votes secured by the opposition; the Barisan Nasional thus got 65.05 per cent of the popular vote. Compared to the 53.4 per cent electoral support enjoyed by the Barisan Nasional in 1990, the proportion of popular

Table 7.1 Malaysia: Parliamentary Election Results, 1995 (1990 Parliamentary Election Results in Parentheses)

State	BN		S46		PAS		DAP		PBS	
	C.	W.	C.	W.	C.	W.	C.	W.	C.	W.
Perlis	3	3 (2)	1	– (–)	2	– (–)	–	– (–)	–	– (–)
Kedah	15	15 (14)	6	– (–)	9	– (–)	–	– (–)	–	– (–)
Kelantan	14	2 (–)	8	6 (7)[a]	6	6 (6)	–	– (–)	–	– (–)
Terengganu	8	7 (6)	4	– (1)	4	1 (1)	–	– (–)	–	– (–)
Penang	11	8 (5)	2	– (–)	2	– (–)	8	3 (6)	3	– (–)
Perak	23	23 (19)	9	– (–)	5	– (–)	11	– (4)	–	– (–)
Pahang	11	11 (10)	6	– (–)	3	– (–)	2	– (–)	–	– (–)
Selangor	17	17 (11)	11	– (–)	3	– (–)	3	– (3)	–	– (–)
Negeri Sembilan	7	7 (7)	3	– (–)	2	– (–)	3	– (–)	–	– (–)
Kuala Lumpur	10	6 (3)	2	– (–)	2	– (–)	6	4 (4)	–	– (–)
Sarawak	27	26 (21)	–	– (–)	–	– (–)	6	1 (2)	3	– (–)
Sabah	20	12 (6)	–	– (–)	1	– (–)	4	– (–)	20	8 (14)
Labuan	1	1 (1)	–	– (–)	–	– (–)	–	– (–)	1	– (–)
Malacca	5	4 (4)	2	– (–)	3	– (–)	2	1 (1)	–	– (–)
Johore	20	20 (18)	11	– (–)	4	– (–)	5	– (–)	1	– (–)
Total		162 (127)		6 (8)		7 (7)		9 (20)		8 (14)

Note: [a] One Semangat 46 parliamentarian later crossed over to the Barisan Nasional.   C – Contested   W – Won

Source: Gomez 1996a

support it won in 1995 increased by almost 12 percentage points. This impressive increase in support for the Barisan Nasional was mainly attributed to the significant Chinese support that the ruling coalition managed to secure (see Gomez 1996a).

Since government leaders are aware of the importance of Chinese and foreign capital for sustaining growth, and particularly continued industrialisation, privatisation, especially for investments, has been actively promoted. Yet despite Malaysia's campaign to secure foreign investments – between 1990 and 1992, foreign ownership of corporate equity rose substantially from 25.1 per cent to 32.4 per cent – there has been limited state subservience to foreign and Chinese capital (see Jesudason 1989).

Enhancing the confidence of UMNO leaders is the current electoral set-up, which virtually guarantees the party's hegemony in the Barisan Nasional. In addition, UMNO's dominance in the executive, its control of state patronage and the media through business organisations and stringent government regulation, together with the impaired independence of the judiciary and the monarchies, all reinforce UMNO hegemony. In these circumstances the question that arises is whether the rapidly changing socio-economic conditions, such as the growth of a multi-ethnic middle class, the resentments of less favoured business interests, and the growing cultural and lifestyle disparities are bringing about tensions within the authoritarian state and its relationship with civil society which may lead to the development of more democratic tendencies. To some extent this has transpired, particularly with the emergence and consolidation of Semangat 46 and the opposition coalition it leads. But with the economic boom since the late 1980s and in view of Semangat 46's lack of access to patronage, some of its leaders and members have been rejoining UMNO, including party president Tengku Razaleigh Hamzah. The opposition coalition has also been weakened after PBS's loss of control of Sabah in the 1994 state elections. Even the DAP has found it difficult to retain some of its traditional urban strongholds because of the impressive economic recovery since 1987 (see Gomez 1996a).

Despite this, in view of the factionalism within UMNO – as evidenced by the party's contentious 1993 elections and growing discord among second-echelon party leaders – the centralisation of political power among its top leaders and their business links raise questions about how conflicts between these factions could affect the corporate sector. The attempts by corporate figures to tie up with influential politicians and the use of political patronage to develop new rentier businessmen can also exacerbate tensions among rival business interests. This is likely to

impede the development of a more dynamic, entrepreneurial and progressive capitalism in Malaysia.

It is also likely that such conflicts among the elite will become sharper
and more severe as resources become scarce, especially after the most
lucrative candidates for privatisation are distributed. With the current
level of distrust among rival factions and their common desire for
control over the state for their own benefit, the likelihood of further
political problems is great. Since there is little consensus and insufficient resources to satisfy all groups, those who are marginalised fear
with much justification that they will be permanently denied access to
the spoils and what they may perceive as their fair share of rents; this
may heighten the political tensions, which may have a spillover effect
on the economy given the close ties between politics and business in
Malaysia.

In addition, while the implementation of policies like the NEP and
privatisation has exacerbated rentier activity, the post-1990 economic
initiatives, despite their more subdued ethnic rhetoric, also do not
involve reforms required to bring about a more equitable distribution
of the economic resources and welfare. However, as the development of
participatory democratic institutions will be crucial to ensuring greater
transparency and accountability in governance, public policy-making
and administration, it is unlikely that this will happen in the near future
given the current economic prosperity, the declining influence of
opposition parties, and the continued centralisation of power in the
hands of the UMNO leadership.

Bibliography

Abdul Aziz Abdul Rahman, 1993. 'Privatisation in Malaysia: Some Observations of the Divested GOEs', in Hara Fujio (ed.), *Formation and Restructuring of Business Groups in Malaysia*, Tokyo: Institute of Developing Economies

Adam, Christopher and William Cavendish, 'Background', in Jomo K. S. (ed.), *Privatizing Malaysia*

Alavi, Rokiah, 1987. The Phases of Industrialisation in Malaysia, 1957–1980. MA thesis, University of East Anglia

Amsden, Alice, 1990. *Asia's Next Giant: South Korea and Late Industrialisation*, New York: Oxford University Press

Anand, Sudhir, 1982, *Inequality and Poverty in Malaysia*, New York: Oxford University Press for the World Bank

Anek Laothamatas, 1989. *Business Associations and the New Political Economy of Thailand: From Bureaucratic Polity to Liberal Corporatism*, Boulder: Westview Press

Anuwar Ali, 1992. The Role of the State and Market Mechanisms in Malaysia. Paper presented at the Second East-Asia and East-Central Europe Conference, Budapest, 22–30 April

Arasaratnam, Sinnappah, 1980. *Indians in Malaysia and Singapore*, Kuala Lumpur: Oxford University Press

Awang Adek Hussein, 1992. 'Recent Developments in the Malaysian Financial System', *Journal of Economic Cooperation Among Islamic Countries* 13 (3–4): 109–35

Bach, Robert L., 1975. 'Historical Patterns of Capitalist Penetration in Malaysia', *Journal of Contemporary Asia* 6: 458–76

Banks, Jeffrey S. and Eric A. Hanushek (eds) 1995. *Modern Political Economy: Old Topics, New Directions*, Cambridge: Cambridge University Press

Bello, Walden and Stephanie Rosenfeld, 1990. *Dragons in Distress: Asia's Miracle Economies in Crisis*, London: Penguin Books

Bhagwati, Jagdish N., 1982. 'Directly Unproductive, Profit-seeking (DUP) Activities', *Journal of Political Economy* 90 (51): 988–1002

Blomqvist, Ake and Sharif Mohammad, 1986. 'Controls, Corruption, and Competitive Rent-Seeking in LDCs', *Journal of Development Economics* 21: 161–180

Bowie, Alasdair, 1988a. 'Redistribution with Growth? The Dilemmas of State-sponsored Economic Development in Malaysia', *Journal of Developing Societies* IV: 52–66

Bowie, Alasdair, 1988b. *Crossing the Industrial Divide: State, Society and the Politics of Economic Transformation in Malaysia*, New York: Columbia University Press

Brawley, Mark R., 1993. 'Regime Types, Markets, and War: The Importance of Pervasive Rents in Foreign Policy', *Comparative Political Studies* 26 (2)

Brown, Robert, 1994. *The State and Ethnic Politics in Southeast Asia*, London: Routledge

Bruton, Henry J., 1992. *The Political Economy of Poverty, Equity and Growth: Sri Lanka and Malaysia*, New York: Oxford University Press

CARPA, 1988. *Tangled Web: Dissent, Deterrence and the 27 October 1987 Crackdown in Malaysia*, Sydney: Committee against Repression in the Pacific and Asia

Case, William, 1993. 'Semi-Democracy in Malaysia: Withstanding the Pressures for Regime Change', *Pacific Affairs* 66 (2)

Chan Kwok Bun and Claire Chiang, 1994. *Stepping Out: The Making of Chinese Entrepreneurs*, Singapore: Simon & Schuster (Asia)

Chandra Muzaffar, 1979. *Protector?: An analysis of the concept and practice of loyalty in leader–led relationships within Malay society*, Pulau Pinang: Aliran

Chandra Muzaffar, 1982. 'The 1982 Malaysian General Election: An Analysis', *Contemporary Southeast Asia* 4 (1): 86–106

Chang, Ha-Joon, 1994. *The Political Economy of Industrial Policy*, Basingstoke: Macmillan

Chee, Stephen, 1991. 'Consociational Political Leadership and Conflict Regulation in Malaysia', in Stephen Chee (ed.), *Leadership and Security in Southeast Asia: Institutional Aspects*, Singapore: Institute of Southeast Asian Studies

Cheong, Sally, 1990a. *Corporate Groupings in the KLSE*, Petaling Jaya: Modern Law Publishers & Distributors

Cheong, Sally, 1990b. *Bumiputera Controlled Companies in the KLSE*, Petaling Jaya: Modern Law Publishers & Distributors

Cheong, Sally, 1992. *Chinese Controlled Companies in the KLSE — Industrial Counter*, Petaling Jaya: Corporate Research Services Sdn Bhd

Cheong, Sally, 1993. *Bumiputera Controlled Companies in the KLSE*, 2nd edn, Petaling Jaya: Corporate Research Services Sdn Bhd

Cheong, Sally, 1995. *Changes in Ownership of KLSE Companies*, Petaling Jaya: Corporate Research Services Sdn Bhd

Cho, George, 1990. *The Malaysian Economy: Spatial Perspectives*, London: Routledge

Chong Kwang Yuan, 1982. 'Trade and External Relations', in E. K. Fisk and H. Osman Rani (eds), *The Political Economy of Malaysia*, Kuala Lumpur: Oxford University Press

Clad, James, 1989. *Behind the Myth: Business, Money and Power in South East Asia*, London: Unwin Hyman Ltd

Clapham, Christopher, 1982. *Private Patronage and Political Power*, London: Frances Pinter

Conybeare, John A., 1982. 'The Rent-Seeking State and Revenue Diversification', *World Politics* 35: 25–42

Cook, Paul and Martin Minogue, 1990. 'Waiting for Privatization in Developing Countries: Towards the Integration of Economic and Non-Economic Explanations', *Public Administration and Development* 10: 389–403

Cowan, L. Gray, 1990. *Privatization in the Developing World*, New York: Greenwood Press

Coyne, John and Mike Wright, 1985. *Management Buy-Outs*, London: Croom Helm

Coyne, John, 1986. 'Divestment by Management Buy-Out: Variant and Variety', in John Coyne and Mike Wright (eds), *Divestment and Strategic Change*, Oxford/New Jersey: Philip Allan/Barnes & Noble Books

Craig, James, 1988. 'Privatisation in Malaysia: Present Trends and Future Prospects', in Paul Cook and Colin Kirkpatrick (eds), *Privatisation in Less Developed Countries*, Brighton: Harvester Press

Crouch, Harold, Lee Kam Hing and Michael Ong (eds) 1980. *Malaysian Politics and the 1978 Election*, Kuala Lumpur: Oxford University Press

Crouch, Harold, 1989. 'Money Politics in Malaysia', in Jomo K. S. (ed.), *Mahathir's Economic Policies*, Kuala Lumpur: Insan

Crouch, Harold, 1992. 'Authoritarian Trends, the UMNO Split and the Limits to State Power', in Joel S. Kahn and Francis Loh Kok Wah (eds), *Fragmented Vision: Culture and Politics in Contemporary Malaysia*, Sydney: Allen & Unwin for Asian Studies Association of Australia

Crouch, Harold, 1993a. 'Malaysia: Neither Authoritarian nor Democratic', in Kevin Hewison, Richard Robison and Garry Rodan (eds), *Southeast Asia in the 1990s: Authoritarianism, Democracy and Capitalism*, Sydney: Allen & Unwin

Crouch, Harold, 1993b. 'Malaysia: Do Elections Make a Difference?'. Paper presented at the Elections in Southeast Asia: Meaning and Practice? Conference, The Woodrow Wilson Center, Washington DC, 16–18 September

Crouch, Harold, 1994. 'Industrialization and Political Change', in Harold Brookfield (ed.), *Transformation with Industrialization in Peninsular Malaysia*, Kuala Lumpur: Oxford University Press

Deyo, F. C., (ed.), 1987. *The Political Economy of the New Asian Industrialism*, Ithaca: Cornell University Press

Donahue, John D., 1989. *The Privatization Decision: Public Ends, Private Means*, New York: Basic Books

Ekelund, Robert B., Jr and Robert Tollison, 1981. *Mercantilism as a Rent-Seeking Society: Economic Regulation in Historical Perspective*, College Station: Texas A&M University Press

Evans, Peter B., Dietrich Rueschemeyer and Theda Skocpol (eds) 1985. *Bringing the State Back In*, Cambridge: Cambridge University Press

Fong Chan Onn, 1989. *The Malaysian Economic Challenge in the 1990s: Transformation for Growth*, Singapore: Longman

Funston, N. J., 1980. *Malay Politics in Malaysia: A Study of the United Malays National Organisation and Party Islam*, Kuala Lumpur: Heinemann Educational Books

Galal, Abdul, 1986. A Theory of Capital Utilization in Public Enterprises with an Application to Egypt. PhD thesis, Boston University

Gale, Bruce, 1981. *Politics and Public Enterprise in Malaysia*, Petaling Jaya: Eastern University Press

Gale, Bruce, 1985. *Politics and Business: A Study of Multi-Purpose Holdings Berhad*, Petaling Jaya: Eastern Universities Press

Gellner, Ernest, 1977. 'Patrons and Clients', in Ernest Gellner and John Waterbury (eds), *Patrons and Clients in Mediterranean Societies*, London: Gerald Duckworth & Co.

Gereffi, Gary, 1990. 'Big Business and the State', in Gary Gereffi and Donald Wyman (eds), *Manufacturing Miracles: Paths of Industrialization in Latin America and East Asia*, Princeton: Princeton University Press

Gill, Ranjit, 1985. *The Making of Malaysia Inc.: A Twenty-five Year Review of the Securities Industry of Malaysia and Singapore*, Petaling Jaya: Pelanduk Publications

Golay, Frank H., Ralph Anspach, M. Ruth Pfanner and Elizabeth B. Ayal, 1969. *Underdevelopment and Economic Nationalism in Southeast Asia*, Ithaca: Cornell University Press

Gold, Thomas B., 1986. *State and Society in the Taiwan Miracle*, Armonk: M. E. Sharpe

Gomez, Edmund Terence, 1990. *Politics in Business: UMNO's Corporate Investments*, Kuala Lumpur: Forum

Gomez, Edmund Terence, 1991a. *Money Politics in the Barisan Nasional*, Kuala Lumpur: Forum

Gomez, Edmund Terence, 1991b. 'Malaysia's Phantom Privatisation', *Asian Wall Street Journal* 8/5/91: 8

Gomez, Edmund Terence, 1993. 'Anwar's Men Gain Media Control: The Management Buy-Out of NSTP and TV3', *Aliran Monthly* 13 (2): 2–6

Gomez, Edmund Terence, 1994. *Political Business: Corporate Involvement of Malaysian Political Parties*, Cairns: Centre for Southeast Asian Studies, James Cook University

Gomez, Edmund Terence, 1996a. *The 1995 Malaysian General Elections: A Report and Commentary*, Singapore: Institute of Southeast Asian Studies

Gomez, Edmund Terence, 1996b. 'Electoral Funding of General, State and Party Elections in Malaysia', *Journal of Contemporary Asia* 26 (1): 81–99

Gomez, Edmund Terence, 1996c. 'Philanthropy in a Multiethnic Society: The Case of Malaysia', in Tadashi Yamamoto (ed.), *Emerging Civil Society in the Asia Pacific Community*, Tokyo/Singapore: Japan Center for International Exchange/ Institute of Southeast Asian Studies (revised edn)

Gullick, John and Bruce Gale, 1986. *Malaysia: Its Political and Economic Development*, Petaling Jaya: Pelanduk Publications

Haggard, Stephan, 1990. *Pathways from the Periphery: The Politics of Growth in the Newly Industrializing Countries*, Ithaca: Cornell University Press

Haggard, Stephan and Robert F. Kaufman (eds) 1992. *The Politics of Economic Adjustment*, Princeton: Princeton University Press

Haggard, Stephan and Steven B. Webb (eds) 1994. *Voting for Reform: Democracy, Political Liberalization, and Economic Adjustment*, New York: Oxford University Press

Haggard, Stephan and Robert F. Kaufman (eds) 1995. *The Political Economy of Democratic Transitions*, Princeton: Princeton University Press

Halim Salleh, Johan Saravanamuttu, Khoo Kay Jin and Muhammad Ikmal Said, 1991. 'Dasar Ekonomi Baru dan Persepsi Etnik di Kalangan Pemimpin Pertubuhan', *in Dasar Ekonomi Baru dan Masa Depannya*, Kuala Lumpur: Persatuan Sains Sosial Malaysia

Harris, Nigel, 1986. *The End of the Third World: Newly Industrializing Countries and the Decline of an Ideology*, London: Penguin Books

Hasan Haji Hamzah, 1990. *Mahathir: Great Malaysian Hero*, Kuala Lumpur: Media Printext (M) Sdn Bhd

Head, David, 1990. 'The Relevance of Privatization to Developing Economies', *Public Administration and Development* 10: 3–18

Henig, Jeffrey R., 1989. 'Privatization in the United States: Theory and Practice', *Political Science Quarterly* 104 (4): 649–70

Heng Pek Koon, 1988. *Chinese Politics in Malaysia: A History of the Malaysian Chinese Association*, Singapore: Oxford University Press

Heng Pek Koon, 1992. 'The Chinese Business Elite of Malaysia', in McVey (ed.), *Southeast Asian Capitalists*

Herman, Edward S., 1982. *Corporate Control, Corporate Power*, Cambridge: Cambridge University Press

Hewison, Kevin, Richard Robison and Garry Rodan (eds) 1993. *Southeast Asia in the 1990s: Authoritarianism, Democracy and Capitalism*, Sydney: Allen & Unwin

Hing Ai Yun, 1984. 'Capitalist Development, Class and Race', in Syed Husin Ali (ed.), *Ethnicity, Class and Development, Malaysia*, Kuala Lumpur: Persatuan Sosial Sains Malaysia

Hing Ai Yun, 1987. 'The Financial System and Industrial Investment in West Malaysia', *Journal of Contemporary Asia* 17 (4): 409–35

Ho Ting Seng, 1990. 'The Financial Industry of Malaysia: Towards a New Era of Technological Change'. MIER Discussion Papers, 33

Holton, Robert J., 1992. *Economy and Society*, London: Routledge

Horii, Kenzo, 1991. 'Disintegration of the Colonial Economic Legacies and Social Restructuring in Malaysia', *The Developing Economies* 29 (4): 281–313

Horowitz, Donald L., 1985. *Ethnic Groups in Conflict*, Berkeley: University of California Press

Hua Wu Yin, 1983. *Class & Communalism in Malaysia: Politics in a Dependent Capitalist State*, London: Zed Books

Huntington, Samuel P., 1971a. 'Political Development and Political Decay', in Claude E. Welch, Jr (ed.), *Political Modernization: A Reader in Comparative Political Change*, Belmont: Wadsworth Publishing Co.

Huntington, Samuel P., 1971b. 'The Change to Change: Modernization, Development, and Politics', *Comparative Politics* 3 (3): 283–322

Huntington, Samuel P., 1991. *The Third Wave: Democratization in the Late Twentieth Century*, Norman: University of Oklahoma Press

Huntington, Samuel P. and Joan M. Nelson, 1976. *No Easy Choice: Political Participation in Developing Countries*, Cambridge: Harvard University Press

Ismail Kassim, 1979. *Race, Politics and Moderation: A Study of the Malaysia Electoral Process*, Singapore: Times Books International

Ismail Md Salleh, 1991. 'The Privatisation of Public Enterprises: A Case Study of Malaysia', in Geeta Gouri (ed.), *Privatisation and Public Enterprise: The Asia-Pacific Experience*, New Delhi: Oxford and IBH Publishing Co. Ltd

Jesudason, James V., 1989. *Ethnicity and the Economy: The State, Chinese Business and Multinationals in Malaysia*, Singapore: Oxford University Press

Johnson, Chalmers, 1987. 'Political Institutions and Economic Performance: The Government–Business Relationship in Japan, South Korea and Taiwan', in F. C. Deyo (ed.), *The Political Economy of the New Asian Industrialism*, Ithaca: Cornell University Press

Jomo K. S., 1988. *A Question of Class: Capital, the State, and Uneven Development in Malaya*, Singapore: Oxford University Press

Jomo K. S. (ed.), 1989. *Mahathir's Economic Policies*, Kuala Lumpur: Insan

Jomo K. S., 1990. *Growth and Structural Change in the Malaysian Economy*, London: Macmillan

Jomo K. S., 1991. 'Whither Malaysia's New Economic Policy?', *Pacific Affairs* 63 (4): 469–99

Jomo K. S. (ed.), 1993. *Industrialising Malaysia: Policy, Performance, Prospects*, London: Routledge

Jomo K. S., 1994. *U-Turn?: Malaysian Economic Development Policies After 1990*, Cairns: Centre for Southeast Asian Studies, James Cook University

Jomo K. S. (ed.), 1995. *Privatizing Malaysia: Rents, Rhetoric, Realities*, Boulder and London: Westview Press

Jomo K. S. and Ishak Shari, 1986. *Development Policies and Income Inequality in Peninsular Malaysia*, Kuala Lumpur: Institute for Advanced Studies, University of Malaya

Jomo K. S. and Chris Edwards, 1993. 'Malaysian Industrialisation in Historical Perspective', in Jomo K. S. (ed.), *Industrialising Malaysia*

Jones, Leroy and Fadil Azim Abbas, 1992 Malaysia: Background, Malaysian Airlines, Kelang Container Terminal, Sports Toto. Paper presented at a World Bank conference, The Welfare Consequences of Selling Public Enterprises, Washington DC, 11–12 June

Jones, Susan K., 1991. 'The Road to Privatization', *Finance & Development* March: 39–41

Junid Saham, 1980. *British Industrial Development in Malaysia 1963–71*, Kuala Lumpur: Oxford University Press

Kamal Salih and Zainal Aznam Yusoff, 1989. 'Overview of the NEP and Framework for a Post-1990 National Economic Policy: Options', *Malaysian Management Review* 24 (2): 13–61

Kasper, Wolfgang, 1974. *Malaysia: A Study in Successful Economic Development*, Washington DC: American Enterprise Institute for Public Policy Research

Kennedy, Laurel, 1995. 'Telecommunications', in Jomo K. S. (ed.), *Privatizing Malaysia*

Khan, Mushtaq Husain, 1989. Clientelism, Corruption and Capitalist Development: An Analysis of State Intervention With Special Reference to Bangladesh. PhD thesis, University of Cambridge

Khong Kim Hoong, 1984. *Merdeka! British Rule and the Struggle for Independence in Malaya, 1945–1957*, Kuala Lumpur: Insan

Khong Kim Hoong, 1991. *Malaysia's General Election 1990: Continuity, Change, and Ethnic Politics*, Singapore: Institute of Southeast Asian Studies

Khoo Boo Teik, 1994. Mahathir Mohamad: A Critical Study of Ideology, Biography and Society in Malaysian Politics. PhD thesis, Flinders University

Khoo Kay Jin, 1992. 'The Grand Vision: Mahathir and Modernisation', in Joel S. Kahn and Francis Loh Kok Wah (eds), *Fragmented Vision: Culture and Politics in Contemporary Malaysia*, Sydney: Allen & Unwin for Asian Studies Association of Australia

Khoo Kay Kim, 1988. 'Chinese Economic Activities in Malaya: A Historical Perspective', in Manning Nash (ed.), *Economic Performance in Malaysia: The Insider's View*, New York: Professors World Peace Academy

Khor Kok Peng, 1983. *The Malaysian Economy: Structures and Dependence*, Kuala Lumpur: Maricans

Kirkpatrick, Colin, 1993. 'Some Background Observations on Privatisation', in V. V. Ramanadham (ed.), *Privatisation in Developing Countries*, London: Routledge

Koh, Woosung, 1990. Government Policies, Foreign Capital, State Capacity: A Comparative Study of Korea, Indonesia and Malaysia. PhD thesis, Northern Illinois University

Krueger, Anne O., 1974. 'The Political Economy of the Rent-Seeking Society', *American Economic Review* 64 (3): 291–303

Kuala Lumpur Stock Exchange, 1988. *Annual Companies Handbook*, vol. 14, KLSE

Kuala Lumpur Stock Exchange, 1991. *Annual Companies Handbook*, vol. 17, Books I and II, KLSE

Kuala Lumpur Stock Exchange, 1993. *Annual Companies Handbook*, vol. 19, Books I and II, KLSE

Lee H. P., 1995. *Constitutional Conflicts in Contemporary Malaysia*, Kuala Lumpur: Oxford University Press

Lee Kam Hing, 1987. 'Three Approaches in Peninsular Malaysian Chinese Politics: The MCA, the DAP and the Gerakan', in Zakaria Haji Ahmad (ed.), *Government and Politics in Malaysia*, Singapore: Oxford University Press

Lee Kam Hing and Michael Ong, 1987. 'Postcolonial Democracies: Malaysia', in Myron Weiner and Ergun Ozbudun (eds), *Competitive Elections in Developing Countries*, Durham: Duke University Press

Leeds, Roger S., 1989. 'Malaysia: Genesis of a Privatization Transaction', *World Development* 17 (5): 741–6

Leigh, Michael, 1992. 'Politics, Bureaucracy, and Business in Malaysia: Realigning the Eternal Triangle', in Andrew J. MacIntyre and Kanishka Jayasuriya (eds), *The Dynamics of Economic Policy Reform in South-East Asia and the South-West Pacific*, Singapore: Oxford University Press

Lent, John A., 1991. 'Telematics in Malaysia: Room at the Top for a Selected Few', *Ilmu Masyarakat* 18: 17–50

Leys, Colin, 1975. *Underdevelopment in Kenya: The Political Economy of Neo-Colonialism, 1964–1971*, London: Heinemann

Lijphart, Arend, 1977. *Democracy in Plural Societies: A Comparative Exploration*, New Haven: Yale University Press

Lim, David, 1973. *Economic Growth and Development in West Malaysia*, Oxford University Press: Kuala Lumpur

Lim Chong-Yah, 1967. *Economic Development of Modern Malaya*, Kuala Lumpur: Oxford University Press

Lim Kit Siang, 1986. *BMF: Scandal of Scandals*, Kuala Lumpur: DAP

Lim Kit Siang, 1987. *The $62 Billion North–South Highway Scandal*, Kuala Lumpur: DAP

Lim Kit Siang, 1992a. *Samy Vellu and Maika Scandal*, Kuala Lumpur: DAP

Lim Kit Siang, 1992b. *Battle for Democracy in Malaysia*, Kuala Lumpur: DAP

Lim Lin Lean and Chee Peng Lim (eds) 1984. *The Malaysian Economy at the Cross-roads: Policy Adjustment or Structural Transformation*, Kuala Lumpur: Malaysian Economic Association & Organisational Resources Sdn Bhd

Lim, Linda Y. C. and L. A. Gosling (eds) 1983. *The Chinese in Southeast Asia*, vol. 1, Singapore: Maruzen Asia

Lim Mah Hui, 1981. *Ownership and Control of the One Hundred Largest Corporations in Malaysia*, Kuala Lumpur: Oxford University Press

Lim Mah Hui and William Canak, 1981. 'The Political Economy of State Policies in Malaysia, *Journal of Contemporary Asia* 11 (2): 208–24

Lim Mah Hui, 1983. 'The Ownership and Control of Large Corporations in Malaysia: The Role of Chinese Businessmen', in Lim and Gosling (eds), *The Chinese in Southeast Asia*

Lim Mah Hui, 1985. 'Contradictions in the Development of Malay Capital: State, Accumulation and Legitimation', *Journal of Contemporary Asia* 15 (1): 37–63

Lim Mah Hui, 1989. Reflections on the Implementation and Consequences of the New Economic Policy. Paper presented at the 41st Annual Meeting of the Association of Asian Studies, Washington, DC, 17–19 March

Limlingan, Victor Simpao, 1986. The Overseas Chinese in ASEAN: Business Strategies and Management Practices. PhD thesis, Harvard University

Lin See Yan, 1989. 'Malaysian Capital Market: Current Situation and Prospects', in *Central Banking in an Era of Change*, Kuala Lumpur: Bank Negara Malaysia

Lindblom, Charles E., 1977. *Politics and Markets: The World's Political-Economic Systems*, New York: Basic Books Inc.

Loh Kok Wah, F., 1981. 'Ethnicity and Loyalty: Chinese Education and Other Issues', in Loh Kok Wah, Phang Chung Nyap and J. Saravanamuttu, *The Chinese Community and Malaysia–China Ties: Elite Perspectives*, Tokyo: Institute of Developing Economies

Loh Kok Wah, 1982. *The Politics of Chinese Unity in Malaysia: Reform and Conflict in the Malaysian Chinese Association 1971–1973*, Occasional Paper No. 70, Singapore: Institute of Southeast Asian Studies

Low Kam Yoke, 1985. 'The Political Economy of Restructuring in Malaysia: A Study of State Policies with Reference to Multinational Corporations'. MEc thesis, University of Malaya

MacIntyre, Andrew, 1991. *Business and Politics in Indonesia*, Sydney: Allen & Unwin for Asian Studies Association of Australia

MacIntyre, Andrew and Kanishka Jayasuriya (eds) 1992. *The Dynamics of Economic Policy Reform in South-East Asia and the South-West Pacific*, Singapore: Oxford University Press

Mackie, Jamie, 1992. 'Changing Patterns of Chinese Big Business in Southeast Asia', in McVey (ed.), *Southeast Asian Capitalists*

Mahathir Mohamad, 1981. *The Malay Dilemma*, Singapore: Times Books International

Mahathir Mohamad, 1984. 'Malaysia Incorporated and Privatisation: Its Rationale and Purpose', in Bruce Gale (ed.), *Malaysia Incorporated and Privatisation*, Kuala Lumpur: Pelanduk Publications

Mahathir Mohamad, 1989. 'New Government Policies', in Jomo K. S. (ed.), *Mahathir's Economic Policies*, Kuala Lumpur: Insan

Malaysia, 1971. *Second Malaysia Plan, 1971–1975*, Kuala Lumpur: Government Printers

Malaysia, 1976. *Third Malaysia Plan, 1976–1980*, Kuala Lumpur: Government Printers

Malaysia, 1981. *Fourth Malaysia Plan, 1981–1985*, Kuala Lumpur: Government Printers

Malaysia, 1984. *Mid-Term Review of the Fourth Malaysia Plan, 1981–1985*, Kuala Lumpur: Government Printers

Malaysia, 1986. *Fifth Malaysia Plan, 1986–1990*, Kuala Lumpur: Government Printers

Malaysia, 1989. *Mid-Term Review of the Fifth Malaysia Plan, 1986–1990*, Kuala Lumpur: Government Printers

Malaysia, 1991a. *Sixth Malaysia Plan, 1991–1995*, Kuala Lumpur: Government Printers

Malaysia, 1991b. *Second Outline Perspective Plan, 1996–2000*, Kuala Lumpur: Government Printers

Malaysia, 1991c. *Privatization Masterplan*, Economic Planning Unit, Kuala Lumpur

Malaysia, 1993. 'Privatisation in Malaysia', in V. V. Ramanadham (ed.), *Privatisation in Developing Countries*, London: Routledge

Malaysia, 1994. *Mid-Term Review of the Sixth Malaysia Plan, 1991–1995*, Kuala Lumpur: Government Printers

Malaysia, 1996. *Seventh Malaysia Plan, 1996–2000*, Kuala Lumpur: Government Printers

Mansor Md Isa, 1993. 'Newly Emerged Bumiputera Businesses in Malaysia: The Case of Sapura Holdings', in Hara Fujio (ed.), *Formation and Restructuring of Business Groups in Malaysia*, Tokyo, Institute of Developing Economies

Mauzy, Diane K., 1979. 'A Vote for Continuity: The 1978 General Elections in Malaysia', *Asian Survey* 19 (3): 281–96

Mauzy, Diane K., 1983. 'The 1982 General Elections in Malaysia: A Mandate for Change?', *Asian Survey* 23 (4): 497–517

Mauzy, Diane K., 1987. 'Malaysia in 1986: The Ups and Downs of Stock Market Politics', *Asian Survey* 27 (2): 231–41

Mauzy, Diane K., 1993. 'Malaysia: Malay Political Hegemony and "Coercive Consociationalism"', in John McGarry and Brendan O'Leary (eds), *The Politics of Ethnic Conflict Regulation*, London: Routledge

McChesney, Fred S., 1988. 'Rent Extraction and Rent Creation in the Economic Theory of Regulation', in Charles K. Rowley, Robert D. Tollison and Gordon Tullock (eds), *The Political Economy of Rent-Seeking*, College Station: Texas A&M University Press

McKenzie, Richard B. and Dwight R. Lee, 1991. *Quicksilver Capital: How the Rapid Movement of Wealth Has Changed the World*, New York: Free Press

McVey, Ruth, 1992. 'The Materialization of the Southeast Asian Entrepreneur', in Ruth McVey (ed.), *Southeast Asian Capitalists*, Ithaca: Cornell University Press

Means, Gordon P., 1970. *Malaysian Politics*, London: University of London Press

Means, Gordon P., 1991. *Malaysian Politics: The Second Generation*, Singapore: Oxford University Press

Mehmet, Ozay, 1988. *Development in Malaysia: Poverty, Wealth and Trusteeship*, Kuala Lumpur: Insan

Mehmet, Ozay, 1990. *Islamic Identity and Development: Studies of the Islamic Periphery*, Kuala Lumpur: Forum

Milne, R. S. and Diane K. Mauzy, 1980. *Politics and Government in Malaysia*, Singapore: Times Books International

Milne, R. S., 1981. *Politics in Ethnically Bipolar States: Guyana, Malaysia, Fiji*, Vancouver: University of British Columbia Press

Milne, R. S., 1986. 'Malaysia – Beyond the New Economic Policy', *Asian Survey* 26 (12): 1366–82

Milne, R. S., 1991. 'The Politics of Privatization in the ASEAN States'. *ASEAN Economic Bulletin* 7 (3): 322–33

Milne, R. S., 1992. 'Privatization in the ASEAN States: Who Gets What, Why, and With What Effect?', *Pacific Affairs* 65 (1): 7–29

Milne, Stephen, 'Corporatism in the Asean Countries', *Contemporary Southeast Asia*, 5 (2): 172–83

Mohd Fauzi Haji Yaacob, 1988. 'The Development of Malay Entrepreneurship Since 1957: A Sociological Overview', in Manning Nash (ed.), *Economic Performance in Malaysia: The Insider's View*, New York: Professors World Peace Academy

Mohd Sheriff bin Mohd Kassim, 1991. 'Privatization: Performance, Problems and Prospects', in Lee Kiong Hock and Shyamala Nagaraj (eds), *The Malaysian Economy Beyond 1990: International and Domestic Perspectives*, Kuala Lumpur: Persatuan Ekonomi Malaysia

Moore, Chris, 1990. 'Displacement, Partnership and Privatization: Local Government and Urban Economic Regeneration in the 1980s', in Desmond S. King and Jon Pierre (eds), *Challenges to Local Government*, London: Sage Publications

Morgan, David R. and Robert E. England, 1988. 'The Two Faces of Privatization', *Public Administration Review* November/December: 979–87

Mullard, Chris and Martin Brennan, 1978. 'The Malaysian Predicament: Towards a New Theoretical Frontier', *Journal of Contemporary Asia*, 8: 341–53

Ness, Gayl D., 1967. *Bureaucracy and Rural Development in Malaysia*, Berkeley: University of California Press

North, Douglass C., 1990. *Institutions, Institutional Change, and Economic Performance*, New York: Cambridge University Press

Olson, Mancur, 1982. *The Rise and Decline of Nations: Economic Growth, Stagflation, and Social Rigidities*, New Haven: Yale University Press

Ong, Michael, 1987. 'Government and Opposition in Parliament: The Rules of the Game', in Zakaria Haji Ahmad (ed.), *Government and Politics of Malaysia*, Singapore: Oxford University Press

Pang Eng Fong, 1983. 'Race, Income Distributions, and Development in Malaysia and Singapore', in Lim and Gosling (eds), *The Chinese in Southeast Asia*

Parmer, J. Norman, 1964. 'Malaysia', in George M. Kahin (ed.), *Government and Politics in Southeast Asia*, Ithaca: Cornell University Press

Paul, Samuel, 1985. 'Privatization and the Public Sector', *Finance & Development*, December

Phang Chung Nyap, 1981. 'The Malaysian Chinese Press and the Malaysian Chinese Community', in Loh Kok Wah, Phang Chung Nyap and J. Saravanamuttu, *The Chinese Community and Malaysia–China Ties: Elite Perspectives*, Tokyo: Institute of Developing Economies

Pollak, Peter, 1980. 'Malaysian Exports of Merchandise', in Kevin Young, Willem C. F. Bussink and Parvez Hasan (eds), *Malaysia: Growth and Equity in a Multi-Racial Society*, Baltimore: Johns Hopkins University Press

Puthucheary, James J., 1960. *Ownership and Control in the Malaysian Economy*, Singapore: Eastern Universities Press

Puthucheary, Mavis, 1978. *The Politics of Administration: The Malaysian Experience*, Kuala Lumpur: Oxford University Press

Puthucheary, Mavis, 1987. 'The Administrative Elite', in Zakaria Haji Ahmad (ed.), *Government and Politics of Malaysia*, Singapore: Oxford University Press

Puthucheary, Mavis, 1989. 'The NEP and Privatisation: Conflicts in Economic Policy', in V. Kanapathy (ed.), *The Mahathir Era: Contributions to National Economic Development*, Petaling Jaya: International Investment Consultants

Pye, Lucien W., 1985. *Asian Power and Politics: The Cultural Dimensions of Authority*, Cambridge: Harvard University Press

Rachagan, Sothi, 1984. 'Ethnic Representation and the Electoral System', in S. Husin Ali (ed.), *Ethnicity, Class and Development in Malaysia*, Kuala Lumpur: Persatuan Sains Sosial Malaysia

Rachagan, Sothi, 1987. 'The Apportionment of Seats in the House of Representatives', in Zakaria Haji Ahmad (ed.), *Government and Politics in Malaysia*, Singapore: Oxford University Press

Rachagan, Sothi, 1993. *Law and the Electoral Process in Malaysia*, Kuala Lumpur: University of Malaya Press

Ranis, Gustav, 1992. 'The Role of Governments and Markets: Comparative Development Experience', in Louis Putterman and Dietrich Rueschemeyer (eds), *State and Market in Development*, Boulder: Lynne Rienner

Rao, V. V. Bhanoji, 1980. *Malaysia: Development Pattern and Policy 1947–1971*, Singapore: University of Singapore Press

Rasiah, Rajah, 1995. 'State intervention, rents and Malaysian industrialization', in John Borrego, Alejandro Alvarez and Jomo K. S. (eds), *Capital, the State and Late Industrialization: Comparative Perspectives from the Pacific Rim*, Boulder: Westview

Ratnam, K. J., 1965. *Communalism and the Political Process in Malaya*, Kuala Lumpur: University of Malaya Press

Ratnam, K. J. and R. S. Milne, 1967. *The Malaysian Parliamentary Election of 1964* Singapore: University of Malaya Press

Robison, Richard, 1986. *Indonesia: The Rise of Capitalism*, Sydney: Allen & Unwin for Asian Studies Association of Australia

Robison, Richard, 1988. 'Authoritarian States, Capital-Owning Classes and the Politics of Newly Industrializing Countries: The Case of Indonesia', *World Politics* 41 (1): 52–74

Robison, Richard, 1990. The Dynamics of Authoritarianism: Theoretical Debates and the Indonesian Case. Paper presented at the Asian Studies Association of Australia Conference, Brisbane, Australia

Robison, Richard, Kevin Hewison and Garry Rodan, 1993. 'Political Power in Industrialising Capitalist Societies: Theoretical Approaches', in Kevin Hewison, Richard Robison and Garry Rodan (eds), *Southeast Asia in the 1990s: Authoritarianism, Democracy and Capitalism*, Sydney: Allen & Unwin

Robison, Richard, Kevin Hewison and Richard Higgott (eds) 1987. *Southeast Asia in the 1980s: The Politics of Economic Crisis*, Sydney: Allen & Unwin

Roff, William, 1967. *The Origins of Malay Nationalism*, Kuala Lumpur: University of Malaya Press

Rogers, Marvin L., 1985. 'Political Involvement and Political Stability in Rural Malaysia', *Journal of Commonwealth and Comparative Politics* 28: 226–50

Rowley, Charles, 1985. 'The Relationship between Economics, Politics and the Law in the Formation of Public Policy', in R. C. O. Matthews (ed.), *Economy and Democracy*, London: Macmillan

Rueschemeyer, Dietrich, Evelyne Huber Stephens and John D. Stephens, 1992. *Capitalist Development and Democracy*, Cambridge: Polity Press

Rugayah Mohamed, 1994. 'Sino-Bumiputera Business Cooperation', in Hara Fujio (ed.), *The Development of Bumiputera Enterprises and Sino-Malay Economic Cooperation in Malaysia*, Tokyo: Institute of Developing Economies

Rugayah Mohamed, 1995. 'Public Enterprises', in Jomo K. S. (ed.), *Privatizing Malaysia*

Sankaran Ramanathan and Mohd Hamdan Adnan, 1988. *Malaysia's 1986 General Election: The Urban-Rural Dichotomy*, Singapore: Institute of Southeast Asian Studies

Saravanamuttu, Johan, 1987. 'The State, Authoritarianism and Industrialization: Reflections on the Malaysian Case', *Kajian Malaysia* 5 (2)

Schatzl, Ludwig H., 1988. 'Economic Development and Economic Policy in Malaysia', in Ludwig H. Schatzl (ed.), *Growth and Spatial Equity in West Malaysia*, Singapore: Institute of Southeast Asian Studies

Schermerhorn, R. A.,1970. *Comparative Ethnic Relations*, New York: Random House

Schumpeter, Joseph A., 1943. *Capitalism, Socialism and Democracy*, London: Allen & Unwin

Self, Peter, 1993. *Government by the Market: The Politics of Public Choice*, London: Macmillan

Sen, Anupam, 1982. *The State, Industrialization and Class Formations in India: A Neo-Marxist Perspective on Colonialism, Underdevelopment and Development*, London: Routledge & Kegan Paul

Shamsul A. B., 1986. *From British to Bumiputera Rule: Local Politics and Rural Development in Peninsular Malaysia*, Singapore: Institute of Southeast Asian Studies

Shamsul A. B., 1988a. 'Political Change and Economic Development', in Manning Nash (ed.), *Economic Performance in Malaysia*, New York: Professors World Peace Academy

Shamsul A. B., 1988b. 'The Battle Royal: The UMNO Elections of 1987', *Southeast Asian Affairs*, Singapore: Institute of Southeast Asian Studies

Shapiro, Helen, 1990. 'Rent-Seeking or Rent Redistribution? Automobile Firms and the Brazilian State', in F. Desmond McCarthy (ed.), *Problems of Developing Countries in the 1990s*, vol. 1, World Bank Discussion Papers No. 97, Washington DC: World Bank

Shapiro, Helen and Lance Taylor, 1992. 'The State and Industrial Strategy', in Charles K. Wilber and Kenneth P. Jameson (eds), *The Political Economy of Development and Underdevelopment*, Singapore: McGraw-Hill Inc.

Sieh Lee Mei Ling, 1992. 'The Transformation of Malaysian Business Groups', in McVey (ed.), *Southeast Asian Capitalists*

Skocpol, Theda, 1980. 'Political Response to Capitalist Crisis: Neo-Marxist Theories of the State and the Case of the New Deal', *Politics and Society* 10 (2): 155–201

Snodgrass, Donald K., 1980. *Inequality and Economic Development in Malaysia*, Kuala Lumpur: Oxford University Press

Stenson, Michael, 1980. *Class, Race and Colonialism in West Malaysia: The Indian Case*, Brisbane: University of Queensland Press

Strauch, Judith, 1978. 'Tactical Success and Failure in Grassroots Politics: The MCA and DAP in Rural Malaysia', *Asian Survey* 18 (12): 1280–94

Stubbs, Richard, 1979. 'The United Malays National Organization, the Malayan Chinese Association, and the Early Years of the Malayan Emergency, 1948–1955', *Journal of Contemporary Asia* 10: 77–88

Sulaiman Mahbob (ed.), 1992. *Issues in Recent Malaysian Economic Growth*, Kuala Lumpur: Arena Ilmu Sdn Bhd

Supian Haji Ali, 1988. 'Malaysia', in G. Edgren (ed.), *The Growing Sector: Studies of Public Sector Employment in Asia*, New Delhi: ILO-ARTEP

Tan Boon Kean, 1993. The Role of the Construction Sector in National Development: Malaysia. PhD thesis, University of Malaya

Tan Tat Wai, 1982. *Income Distribution and Determination in West Malaysia*, Kuala Lumpur: Oxford University Press

Toh Kin Woon, 1989. 'Privatisation in Malaysia: Restructuring or Efficiency?', *ASEAN Economic Bulletin* 5 (3): 242–58

Tollison, Robert D., 1987. 'Is the Theory of Rent-Seeking Here to Stay?', in Charles K. Rowley (ed.), *Democracy and Public Choice*, Oxford: Basil Blackwell

Toye, John, 1987. *Dilemmas of Development: Reflection on the Counter-Revolution in Development Theory and Policy*, Oxford: Blackwell

Vickers, John and George Yarrow, 1988. *Privatization: An Economic Analysis*, Cambridge: MIT Press

Vining, Aidan R. and Bryan J. Poulin, 1989. 'Will Corporatisation and Partial Privatisation Work', *Public Sector* 12 (4)

von Thadden, Ernst-Ludwig, 1990. 'On the Efficiency of the Market for Corporate Control', *Kyklos* 43 (4): 635–58

Wade, Robert, 1990. *Governing the Market: Economic Theory and the Role of Government in East Asian Industrialization*, Princeton: Princeton University Press

Wang Gungwu, 1991. *China and the Chinese Overseas*, Singapore: Times Academic Press

Wang Gungwu, 1993. *Community and Nation: China, Southeast Asia and Australia*, Sydney: Allen & Unwin

White, John, 1988. 'Privatization and the State-Owned Enterprises; Logic or Ideology?', *Public Sector* 11 (1/2): 19–22

Whynes, David K. and Robert A. Bowles, 1981. *The Economic Theory of the State*, Oxford: Martin Robertson

Wilson, Graham K., 1985. *Business & Politics: A Comparative Introduction*, London: Macmillan

World Bank, 1989. *Malaysia: Matching Risks and Rewards in a Mixed Economy*, Washington DC: World Bank

World Bank, 1993. *The East Asian Miracle: Economic Growth and Public Policy*, New York: Oxford University Press

Yasuda Nobuyuki, 1991. 'Malaysia's New Economic Policy and the Industrial Coordination Act', *The Developing Economies* 29 (4), 330–49

Yeoh Kok Kheng, 1987. A Study of the Malaysian Chinese Economic Self-Strengthening (Corporatisation) Movement – With Special Reference to MPHB, Other Communal Investment Companies and Cooperatives. MEc thesis, University of Malaya

Yeoh Oon Kheng, Michael, 1988. 'The Chinese Political Dilemma', in *The Future of Malaysian Chinese*, Kuala Lumpur: Malaysian Chinese Association

Yoshihara, Kunio, 1988. *The Rise of Ersatz Capitalism in South-East Asia*, Kuala Lumpur: Oxford University Press

Zainal Aznam Yusof, 1991. 'Distributional Policies and Programmes: The Malaysian Experience', in Lee Kiong Hock and Shyamala Nagaraj (eds), *The Malaysian Economy Beyond 1990: International and Domestic Perspectives*, Kuala Lumpur: Persatuan Ekonomi Malaysia

Zakaria Haji Ahmad, 1989. 'Malaysia: Quasi-Democracy in a Divided Society', in Larry Diamong, Juan J. Linz and Seymour Martin Lipset (eds), *Democracy in Developing Countries*, vol. 3, Boulder: Lynne Rienner

Zakaria Haji Ahmad, 1993. 'Malaysia in an Uncertain Mode', in James Morley (ed.), *Driven by Growth: Political Change in the Asia-Pacific Region*, New York: M. Sharpe

Zysman, John, 1983. *Governments, Markets and Growth*, Ithaca: Cornell University Press

Newspapers and Magazines

Asian Wall Street Journal, Hong Kong
Asiaweek, Hong Kong
Berita Harian
Borneo Post
Business Times
Business Times, Singapore
Corporate World
Far Eastern Economic Review, Hong Kong
Hak (Newsletter: Suara Rakyat Malaysia)
Investors Digest
Malaysian Business
Malaysian Industry
New Straits Times
New Sunday Times
See Hua Daily
The Edge
The Observer, London
The Star
The Straits Times, Singapore
The Sun
Utusan Malaysia
Watan
Wawancara

Index

Abdul Kadir Jasin, 68
Abdul Mulok Awang Damit, 132
Abdul Rahman, Tunku, 22
Abdul Rashid Abdul Manaff, 148
Abdul Rasip Haron, 113, 114
Abdul Razak Hussein, 22, 23
Abdul Taib Mahmud, 110, 113
Abdullah Ahmad Badawi, 126
Abdullah, Tunku, 59, 92, 153
Abu Bakar Noor, 106
Abu Talib Othman, 47
Adam, Christopher and William
    Cavendish, 25
Adamwell Company Ltd, 161
Adnan Tengku Mansur, Tengku, 157, 158
Advance Synergy Bhd, 57, 70–1
Ahmad Nazri Abdullah, 68
Ahmad Saad, 96
Ahmad Sebi Abu Bakar, 57, 70, 121, 125,
    126, 157, 158
Ahmad Tunku Yahya, Tunku, 90, 94, 119,
    121, 125–6, 140, 161
Ahmad Zahid Hamidi, 146
AIMS Worldwide (M) Sdn Bhd, 157
Air Asia Sdn Bhd, 82, 95
airport project in Sepang, 98
Alliance, 20–2
    formation of, 10–12, 14
Alpine Resources Sdn Bhd, 148, 152
Amalgamated Steel Mills Bhd, 143
Amanah Saham Bumiputera (ASB), 31,
    35–6, 39
Amanah Saham Nasional (ASN), 31, 34–7,
    38, 39
Ampang Hotel Sdn Bhd, 145
Ampang Investments Pte Ltd, 145

Ananda Krishnan, T., 82, 88, 93, 121, 138,
    159–65
Angkatan Belia Islam Malaysia (ABIM), 73,
    126
Angkatan Keadilan Rakyat (Akar), 136
Antah Biwater Sdn Bhd, 91
Antah Holdings Bhd, 91, 119
Anuar Othman, 50, 52
Anwar Batcha bin Ibram Ghaney, 66, 68
Anwar Ibrahim, 57, 58, 59, 64, 68, 69, 70,
    71, 73, 82, 92, 94, 96, 99, 112, 124–7,
    128, 129, 156, 162
Aokam Perdana Bhd, 106, 119
Arab Malaysian Group, 119
Arnah Murni Sdn Bhd, 148, 149, 150
Aseam Bankers, 61
Asia Bank International Merchant
    Bankers, 61
Asia Lab Sdn Bhd, 96
Asian political culture, 3–4
Asian Development Bank, 79
Ascot Sports, 92, 153
Au Metalvest Sdn Bhd, 96
Austral Amalgamated Bhd, 108, 119
Austral Enterprises Bhd, 38
Automobile Citroen (France), 94, 125
Azizan bin Zainal Abidin, 161
Azman Hashim, 119
Azmi Jaafar, 96

Baharuddin Mohd Arip, 114
Bakti Kilat Sdn Bhd (renamed UMBC
    Holdings Sdn Bhd), 57, 58
Baktimu Sdn Bhd, 55, 106
Bakun Dam, 83, 98, 110–15, 129
Ban Hin Lee (BHL) Bank Bhd, 67, 70, 71

Bandar Raya Developments Bhd, 55
Bank Bumiputra (M) Bhd, 21, 38–9, 55,
    61, 79, 103, 108, 129
Bank Kerjasama Rakyat Malaysia, 156
Bank Negara, 56, 58, 59, 60, 61, 62, 64, 65,
    90, 94, 133–4, 143, 150, 160
Bank of Commerce Bhd (BCB), 62, 103
Bank of Nova Scotia, 64
Bank of Tokyo (M) Bhd, 65
Bank Pembangunan (M) Bhd, 37
Bank Simpanan Nasional Bhd, 65, 146
Banking Act (1973), 64
Banking and Financial Institutions Act
    (1989), 58, 64, 65, 70
banking sector 60–6
Barisan Nasional, 3, 4, 5, 22–3, 26, 39, 44,
    47, 56, 72, 121, 130–7, 168, 177, 178,
    181–3
  gerrymandering, 3
  multi-ethnic, multi-party coalition, 2, 10
Basir Ismail, 82, 103, 108, 119, 145, 149
Bata (M) Bhd (*renamed* FCW Holdings
    Bhd), 114–15
Batu Kawan Bhd, 38
B&B Enterprise Sdn Bhd, 92, 153
Bedrod Bhd, 66
Bell Telephone, 73
Benta Bhd, 125
Berita Harian Group, 68
Berjaya Corporation Bhd (*renamed* Berjaya
    Industrial Bhd), 73, 153–4, 155, 156
Berjaya Group Bhd (*formerly named* Raleigh
    Bhd, Inter-Pacific Industrial Group
    Bhd), 54, 70, 82, 92, 96, 138, 139, 148
  as corporate raider, 154–8
Berjaya Industrial Bhd, *see* Berjaya
    Corporation Bhd
Berjaya Leisure Bhd (*formerly named* Sports
    Toto (M) Bhd), 154, 155, 156–7, 164
Berjaya Singer Bhd (*formerly named* Singer
    Holdings (M) Bhd), 47, 154
Berjaya South Island Bhd (*formerly named*
    SIG Holdings Bhd; *renamed* Prime
    Utilities Bhd), 154
Berjaya Sports Toto Bhd (*formerly named*
    Far East Asset Bhd), 154, 156–7
Berjaya Textiles Bhd (*formerly named* South
    Pacific Textile Industries Bhd), 154,
    155
Big Sweep lottery, 93
Big Sweep Sdn Bhd, 160, 161
Binariang Sdn Bhd, 82, 93, 165
Biwater Ltd, 66, 91
BMF scandal, 102
Bolton Properties, 56
Bombay, 82

Borneo, 130
Bosnia-Herzegovina, 132
Britain, 79
  and colonialism, 1, 10–11,
  and anti-colonialism, 2,
  and economic development, 10, 13, 91
  and political development, 10–12
Brunei, 74
Bumiputera Commercial and Industrial
    Community (BCIC), 173
Bumiputeras, private wealth accumulation,
    53
Bumiputra Malaysia Finance (BMF), 38, 79
Bumiputra Merchant Bankers Bhd, 103

Capital Issues Committee (CIC), 42, 43,
    103
Capitalcorp Securities Sdn Bhd, 103
Celcom Sdn Bhd, 82, 95, 148, 150–1
Cement Industries of Malaysia (CIMA), 87
Cement Manufacturers Sarawak Bhd, 34,
    87
Chan, Dick, 138
Cheng, William, 94
Chia, Eric, 72, 102
China, 66
Chinese business, 44–5, 60, 62, 99, 120,
    129
  accumulation of wealth, 18
  and industrialisation, 16
  and legislation, 41–2, 44
  business community, 12, 21, 40, 43–9,
    71–2, 119, 136, 137–8
  dominance, 168
  ownership of economy, 19
  political support, 132
  reduced influence, 181
  ties with Malay political elite, 48
Chong Kok Lim, 106–5
Citibank Bhd, 65
Clearway Sdn Bhd, 114
Cold Storage Bhd, 56, 103, 106, 108, 119,
    123, 145–7
concentration of wealth/ownership, 1,
    100, 117, 180
  among Bumiputeras, 53
consociationalism, 21–3
Consolidated Plantations Bhd, 38
Construction and Supplies House Bhd,
    132
Cooperative Central Bank, 64
Credit Corporation (M) Bhd (CCM), 125
cronyism, 25, 27, 51, 99
Crouch, Harold, 2
Cycle & Carriage Bintang Bhd, 103, 145
Cycle & Carriage Ltd, 103, 108, 119, 145–7

Daim Zainuddin, 53–6
  associate of Dr Mahathir, 99, 123
  associates favoured in business, 112, 113,
    114
  business dealings, 33, 57, 67, 69, 79, 91,
    105, 106, 119, 139, 145, 154
  close associates, 50, 52, 59, 61, 103, 110,
    129, 132, 146, 148, 149, 177
  control of UMNO company, 122
  economic philosophy, 80, 179
  family ties with business, 46, 93, 139
  one of 'new rich', 26
  protégés, 26, 62, 92, 93, 94, 107–8, 124,
    125
  wealth, 165
  UMNO leader, 181
Damansara Realty Bhd, 123
D&C Finance, 62
D&C Mitsui Merchant Bank Bhd, 62, 123,
    143, 149
Dataprep Holdings Bhd, 119
Datuk Keramat Holdings Bhd, 57, 58–9,
    61, 123
Daza Sdn Bhd (renamed Tekal), 55, 106
Democratic Action Party (DAP), 104, 122,
    183
Development & Commercial (D&C) Bank,
    57, 61–2
Diamond League Sdn Bhd, 115
directly unproductive profit-seeking
    (DUP), 6
Diversified Resources Bhd, 93–4, 119, 125
Dunlop Estates Bhd, 110, 154

economic development, 4, 12–15
  post-Independence, 15–21
  post-NEP, 168, 171–4
economic recession (mid-1980s), 77
Edaran Otomobil Nasional Bhd (EON),
    46, 87, 94
Ekran Bhd, 83, 110–11, 113–16
elections, 3,
  10 May 1969, 21
  April 1995, 181
  1990, 181
  general election results
  Sabah state elections, 130–7
EMC Logistics Bhd, 48
Employees' Provident Fund (EPF), 110
Eurocrest Sdn Bhd, 92, 108
export-oriented industrialisation (EOI),
    17, 24, 40, 171

Faber Group Bhd, 50, 54, 55, 96, 145, 146
Fanuc Resources Sdn Bhd, 160
Far East Asset Bhd, see Berjaya Sports Toto
    Bhd

FCW Holdings Bhd, 115
FCW Industries Sdn Bhd, see Federal
    Cables, Wires & Metal Manufacturing
    Bhd
Federal Cables, Wires & Metal
    Manufacturing Bhd (FCW) (renamed
    FCW Industries Sdn Bhd), 113, 114
Federal Industrial Development Authority
    (FIDA) (renamed Malaysian Industrial
    Development Authority), 17
Federal Land Development Authority
    (FELDA), 15, 31
Fibroceil Manufacturing Sdn Bhd, 68
Fikiran Abadi Sdn Bhd, 155
Fima Corporation, 105
Fima Metal Box Bhd (formerly Metal Box),
    102
Finance Ministry, 94, 102, 112, 124, 156
First City Resources Sdn Bhd, 160
Fleet Group Sdn Bhd, 52, 54, 55, 67, 73,
    91, 95, 105, 123, 148, 151
Fleet Holdings Sdn Bhd, 51–2, 54, 122
Fleet Trading & Manufacturing Sdn Bhd,
    55
Food Industries of Malaysia (FIMA), 30
Foreign Investment Committee (FIC), 42,
    43
Free Trade Zone Act, 18

Gadek Bhd, 94, 119, 125, 140, 156
Gagasan Rakyat, 130
General Corporation Bhd, 47
General Lumber, 139
Genting Bhd, 47, 82, 165
George Town Holdings Bhd, 59
Gerakan Rakyat Malaysia (Gerakan), 22,
    39, 61
Ghafar Baba, 47, 68, 69, 119, 124, 125, 126,
    156
Golden Arches Restaurant Sdn Bhd, 153
Golden Hope Plantations Bhd, 38
Golden Plus Holdings Bhd, 125
Golf Associates Sdn Bhd, 107
Goodyear (M) Bhd, 32
Gracom Sdn Bhd, 108
Grand Care Sdn Bhd, 125
Granite Industries Bhd, 106, 115, 123, 127
Guoco Group, 66
Guthrie Ropel, 56

Halim Saad, 50, 51, 52, 55, 69, 115, 119,
    121, 123, 125, 129, 158
Hamzah Abu Samah, 48
Hamzah Bakar, 161
Haniff Omar, 47, 165
Hanoi, 82

Harun Idris, 54
Hassan bin Chik Abas, 93, 106, 107
Hatibudi Sdn Bhd, 97, 106
Health Ministry, 96, 97
Heavy Industries Corporation of Malaysia
    (HICOM), 30, 39, 68, 78, 81, 82, 87,
    90, 94, 95, 110, 119, 125
Hewlett-Packard, 74
Highlands & Lowlands Bhd, 32
Ho Hup Construction Bhd, 98
Hong Kong, 66, 82
Hongkong Bank, 65
Hong Leong Bank Bhd (*formerly named*
    MUI Bank Bhd), 65, 70, 71, 154
Hong Leong Credit Bhd, 66, 67, 70
Hong Leong Finance Bhd, 70
Hong Leong Bank Bhd, *see* MUI Bank Bhd
Hong Leong Group, 48, 50, 65, 66–72,
    129, 138, 143
Hong Leong Industries Bhd, 66
Hotel Properties Ltd, 145
Hume Industries Bhd, 66–7
Hyatt Saujana Hotel, 108

Ibrahim Abdul Rahman, 126
Ibrahim Mohamed, 119
Ibrahim Saad, 96, 126
Idris Hydraulic Bhd, 56, 57, 64, 125, 127
IGB Corporation Bhd, 154, 155, 158
import-substituting industrialisation (ISI),
    16–17, 40
Indah Water Konsortium Sdn Bhd, 92–3,
    157
Independence (1957), 10, 13, 14, 16, 19,
    24, 172
independent power producer (IPP)
    licences, 82
Indonesia, 74, 130
Industrial Coordination Act (1975), 41–2,
    43, 44, 45, 47, 79
Industrial Oxygen Incorporated Bhd, 56,
    126
industrialisation, 16–18, 77–8, 171–2, 177,
    183
Internal Security Act, 2, 135
International Monetary Fund, 79
Inter-Pacific Industrial Group Bhd
    (*renamed* Berjaya Group Bhd)
Investment Incentives Act (1968), 17, 42
Investments Promotion Act (1986), 79
Ishak bin Ismail, 63, 125
Island & Peninsular Bhd, 32, 38
Ismail Abdul Rashid, 66, 67

J. & P. Coats (Manufacturing) Sdn Bhd,
    143–4

Jaguh Mutiara Sdn Bhd, 66–7
Jakarta, 82
Jalan Kuching–Jalan Kepong flyover, 83,
    93, 106
Jamil Mohamed Jan, 95
Jasa Kita Bhd, 113, 114
Jernih Insurance Corporation Sdn Bhd,
    103
Johore SEDC, 103, 155
Juara Perkasa Corporation Bhd (JPC)
    (*renamed* R.J. Reynolds Bhd)

Kadazans, 130–1
Kah Motors Bhd, 165
Kajang community, 112
Kamaruddin Jaffar, 57, 125–6
Kamaruddin Mohamad Nor, 125–6
Kamunting Bhd, 46, 93, 138
Kayan community, 112
Kee Yong Wee, 44
Kedah Cement, 87
Kedah SEDC, 107
Kegiatan Makmur Sdn Bhd, 103, 104
Kelang Port Container Terminal (KCT),
    86, 87
Kelantan, 21, 53, 138
Kenyah community, 112
KFC Holdings (M) Bhd, 34, 125
Khalid Haji Ahmad, 68
Khoo Kay Peng, 43, 44, 47, 69–70, 155–6,
    158
Khoo Teck Puat, 60
Khoo, Ronald, 161
Khoo Teng Bin, 160, 165
Kinta Kellas plc, 50, 98
Kitingan, Joseph Pairin, 130, 131, 133, 134
Kitingan, Jeffrey, 131, 134, 135, 136
KK Industries Sdn Bhd (KKI), 83, 96
KL Kepong Bhd, 120
KLOFFE Sdn Bhd, 67
KM Properties Sdn Bhd, 140
Koding, Mark, 136
Komplek Kewangan (M) Bhd, 37
Komtel Sdn Bhd, 73
Konsortium Tongkah, 96
Kontena Nasional Bhd, 32
Koperasi Polis DiRaja Bhd, 157
Koperasi Usaha Bersatu Bhd (KUB), 59,
    73, 123, 125, 140
Koperatif Serbaguna (M) Bhd (KSM), 45
Kota Kinabalu, 64
Kretam Holdings Bhd, 146
Kuala Lumpur City Centre (KLCC), 161,
    162, 164
Kuala Lumpur, 54, 60, 93, 97, 111, 140
Kuala Lumpur light rail transit project, 98

Kuala Lumpur Industries Holdings Bhd, 97

Kuala Lumpur International Airport, 83

Kuala Lumpur-Kepong Bhd, 38

Kuala Lumpur Options and Financial Futures Exchange (KLOFFE), 67

Kuala Lumpur Stock Exchange (KLSE), 65, 82, 87, 133–4

KLSE Composite Index, 128

Kumpulan Fima Bhd (*renamed* Fima Corporation), 82, 98, 100–5, 106, 108–9

Kumpulan Guthrie, 38, 139

Kuok, Robert, 43, 163, 165

Kuok Group, 103

Kurup, Joseph, 136

Kwek family, 66

Kwong Yik Bank Bhd, 60

Kwong Yik Finance, 61

Labuan, Federal Territory of, 132

Labuan water supply project, 86

Land & General Bhd, 57, 67, 105, 119, 120, 139–40, 141–3, 146, 155

Landmarks Bhd, 106, 107, 108, 119, 129

Landmarks Engineering & Development Sdn Bhd, 107

Lee, Alex, 44, 61, 149

Lee, Henry H.S., 61, 149

Lee Kuan Yew, 3,

Lee, Joseph Ambrose, 132

Lembaga Tabung Angkatan Tentera (LTAT), 157

Licenced Manufacturing Warehouses (LMWs)

Lim, David

Lim Goh Tong, 43, 47, 82, 165

Lim, T. K., 46, 47, 93, 110, 121, 138, 155, 158, 181

Linatex Process Rubber Bhd, 64

Lion Group, 94

Loh Boon Siew, 165

Lord President, removal of, 99

Lorrain Esme Osman, 102

Low Keng Huat, 47

Loy Hean Heong, 44, 94

Magnum Corporation Bhd, 141–2, 154, 155, 164

Mahathir Mohamad, 2, 4, 53, 117, 135, 168
  actions as prime minister, 33, 77, 97, 98, 112, 134
  administration, 34, 38
  business dealings, 102–3
  close associates, 54, 56, 59, 61, 73, 92, 93, 94, 96, 99, 164, 177, 113, 140, 153, 160

defence of Krishnan, 162
  patronage, 125
  political/economic philosophy, 3, 80–1
  promotion of Bumiputera capitalism, 117–19
  The Malay Dilemma, 117
  UMNO president, 52, 122, 123, 124, 126, 128, 131
  see also Vision 2020

Mahmud Abu Bekir Taib, 113

Mahmud Tunku Besar Burhanuddin, Tunku, 165

MAI Holdings Sdn Bhd, 160, 165

Maika Holdings Bhd, 46, 62, 83, 91, 114

Majlis Amanah Rakyat (MARA), 21, 37, 83, 95–6, 118, 156

Malakoff Bhd, 69, 82, 96

Malay Chamber of Commerce, 67

Malay College, Kuala Kangsar, 73, 126

Malayan Banking Bhd, 37, 38, 40, 56, 60–1, 139

Malayan Borneo Finance Bhd (MBf) Group, 94, 129, 143

Malayan Cables Bhd, 72

Malayan Communist Party (MCP), 11

Malayan Emergency (1948–60), 11, 45

Malayan Flour Mills Bhd, 48, 56

Malayan Union, 11

Malayan United Industries (MUI) Bhd, 47, 48, 155–6, 158

Malayawata Steel Bhd, 33

Malaysia Airlines Bhd (MAS), 46, 86, 87, 90, 94–5, 119, 120, 129, 149–50, 152

Malaysia Mining Corporation Bhd, 32, 33, 34, 38,

Malaysia Plans
  First (1966–70), 16, 31
  Second (1971–75), 31, 32
  Third (1976–80), 31
  Fourth (1981–85), 31
  Fifth (1986–90), 31
  Sixth (1991–95) (6MP), 65, 169, 171, 172, 176, 177

Malaysia, state of, 2–5, 98–9

Malaysian Airports, 103

Malaysian Chinese Association (MCA), 2, 10, 12, 14, 21, 22, 42, 44–5, 48, 52, 56, 61, 66, 93, 136, 137, 168

Malaysian French Bank Bhd, 47, 57, 106, 139

Malaysian Helicopter Services Bhd (MHS), 94–5, 119, 149–50

Malaysian Indian Congress (MIC), 2, 10, 12, 14, 45–6, 47, 62, 91, 114, 136, 168
  discrimination policy for Indians, 39–40

Malaysian Industrial Development Authority (MIDA), 17, 29
Malaysian International Shipping Corporation Bhd (MISC), 46, 81, 86, 87, 90
Malaysian Pacific Industries Bhd, 66
Malaysian Plantations Bhd, 34
Malaysian Resources Corporation Bhd (MRCB), 68, 69, 82, 92, 96, 127
Malaysian Rubber Development Corporation (MARDEC), 29
Malaysian Tobacco Company Bhd, 34
management buy-outs (MBOs), 82–3, 100–9, 126
Marlestone Investment Ltd, 163
Marubeni Corporation, 74
Maya Krishnan, T., 160
Mayban Assurance, 61
Mayban Finance, 61
Mbf, see Malayan Borneo Finance Bhd
McDonald's, 153
Measat I, 93, 164
Melewar Corporation Bhd, 96, 153
Melewar Group, 59, 82, 92, 119
Merdeka Square project, 113, 140
Metalbox Overseas Ltd (UK), 105
Meridien Best Sdn Bhd, 57, 59
Metro Vision, 82, 96
Metroplex Bhd, 138
Mid-Term Review of the Fifth Malaysia Plan, 78
Minho Bhd, 48
Ministry of Energy, Telecommunications and Posts, 112
Ministry of Finance Incorporated, 32, 39, 61, 68, 92, 102
Ministry of Public Enterprise, 77
Mirzan Mahathir, 68, 119
Mitsui Bank, 61
Mofaz Air Sdn Bhd, 82
Mohamad Azlan Hasim, 103
Mohamad Sarit Haji Yusoh, 125
Mohamad Shah Abdul Kadir, 153
Mohamed Khir Johari, 48
Mohamed Noor Ismail, 103
Mohamed Noor Yusof (Mohamed Noor Azam), 57–8, 59
Mohd Desa Pachi, 105
Mohd Hassan Marican, 161
Mohd Ibrahim Mohd Zain, 156
Mohd Noor Mutalib, 68
Mohd Noordin Daud, 114
Mohd Razali Mohd Rahman, 55, 105–6, 119
Mohd Sofi Abdul Ghafar, 68
Mohd Tamrin Abdul Ghafar, 47, 156

Mokhzani Mahathir, 96, 152
'money politics', 26–7, 120–37
Muda Agricultural Development Authority (MADA), 29
MUI Bank Bhd (renamed Hong Leong Bank Bhd), 64, 69, 70, 71–2
MUI Finance Bhd (renamed United Merchant Finance Bhd), 69
multi-ethnic society, 1–2, 10–12, 75
  ethnic conflict, 3, 19, 21, 22
  inter-ethnic economic inequality, 14, 19–20, 24, 26, 121, 170, 172
  inter-ethnic economic parity, 4, 24, 25, 170
  politics, 12, 88, 130, 132, 170
  preferential treatment of Bumiputeras (Malays), 15, 19, 21, 49; see also NEP
Multi-Purpose Holdings Bhd (MPHB), 45, 47, 55, 57, 66, 93, 110, 142, 155, 164
Muram Dam, 110
Musa Hitam, 56, 123, 124
Mustapha Harun, 61, 131, 135
Mutiara Telecommunications Sdn Bhd, 155
Mycom Bhd, 66, 156, 164

Najib Razak, 146
Nanyang Press Bhd, 33, 66, 67, 96, 140, 145
Nasaruddin Jalil, 94, 125
National Chamber of Commerce, 67
National Development Policy (NDP), 169, 173–6, 177
National Electricity Board, 82
National Land Finance Cooperative Society (NLFCS), 45–6
National Printing Department, Security Printing Branch, 102
National Sports Complex, 97
Nautilus Corporation Sdn Bhd, 92, 153
Negeri Sembilan royal family, 91, 92, 119
Negeri Sembilan SEDC, 69
Nehru, Jawaharlal, 12
Nestlé (M) Bhd, 102
Nestlé SA, 94
New Economic Policy (NEP), 4, 23, 24–53, 75–7, 78, 81, 100, 102, 117, 177
  and political patronage, 24–7, 49, 51, 81, 98
  development of Bumiputera capitalism 1, 19, 21, 23, 24, 25, 27, 32–4, 49–50, 90, 117–19, 143, 166, 179
  emergence of 'new rich', 26, 117–66, 180
  'ethnic bypass', 78

New Economic Policy (continued)
  implementation, 24, 25, 26, 39, 40, 44,
    46, 75, 118, 121, 137
  objectives, 24, 32, 39, 41, 43, 62, 80, 166
  policies on hold, 169
  poverty eradication, 1, 23, 24, 27–29,
    39–40, 166
  public enterprises, 25–7, 29–39, 40, 49,
    79–80, 109, 118
    as vehicle for creating Bumiputera
      capitalism, 80
    incompetence, 76–9, 109
  public sector investment, 75–6
  wealth-restructuring, 24, 25–7, 29–32,
    87, 90, 166, 168, 177
New Straits Times Press (NSTP), 50, 52,
    55, 67, 68, 69, 127, 139
Newco Bank Bhd, 64
Nik Mahmood Nik Hassan, 139
non-government organisations, 111–12
Noraini Zolkifli, 50
North Port Kelang toll road bypass, 83
North–South Highway, 83, 96, 122
Northwest Water (M) Sdn Bhd, 92, 157
Numbers Forecast Totalisator Operation
    (NFO), 93, 162

Official Secrets Act, 2
Ong Beng Seng, 145
Ooi Boon Leong, 160, 161, 165
Orang Asli, 40
Oriental Highland Ltd, 140
Oriental Holdings, 56
Osaka, 82
Outline Prospective Plan (OPP), 24, 27,
    171
(Second) Outline Perspective Plan
    (OPP2), 169, 171, 172, 173–6, 177
Oversea-Chinese Banking Corporation
    (OCBC), 60
OYL Industries Bhd, 66

Pacific Bank Bhd, 103
Pacific Chemicals Bhd, 113, 114, 115, 116
Pacific Fortune Sdn Bhd, 160
Pacific States Investments, 160
Pan Malaysia Rubber Industries Bhd
    (PMRI), 156
Pan Malaysian Pools Sdn Bhd, 93, 160,
    162, 163
Pan Malaysian Sweeps Sdn Bhd, 93, 160, 161
Papua New Guinea, 140
Parkroyal Hotels, 107
Parti Demokratik Sabah (PDS), 135
Parti Demokratik Sabah Bersatu (PDSB),
    135

Parti Bersatu Rakyat Sabah (PBRS), 135
Parti Bersatu Sabah (PBS), 130–6, 183
Parti Islam SeMalaysia (PAS), 22
Parti Melayu Semangat 46, 70, 102, 122,
    130, 137, 156, 183
Pelangi Air Sdn Bhd, 150
Penan community, 112
Penang, 21, 97
Penang Turf Club, 93, 162, 163
Pengkalan Industrial Holdings Bhd, 132
Peninsula Gas Utilization (PGU), 97
Peninsula Springs Sdn Bhd, 67
Pensions Trust Fund, 90, 150
People's Progressive Party (PPP), 22
Perak, 21
Perak Turf Club, 93, 162, 163
Perbadanan Nasional Bhd (Pernas), 21,
    31, 32–4, 35, 37, 39, 49, 56–7, 79, 83,
    103, 118, 140–1, 150
Perbadanan Nasional Shipping Line Sdn
    Bhd, 33
Perdana Merchant Bankers Bhd, 70
Peremba Bhd, 30, 37, 54, 55, 66, 67, 82, 90,
    100, 105–9, 119, 139
Perkhidmatan Usaha Tegas Sdn Bhd, 160
Perlis SECD, 97
Permodalan Bersatu Bhd (PBB), 73, 140,
    142
Permodalan Nasional Bhd (PNB), 31, 32,
    33, 34–9, 59, 60, 61, 77, 83
Pernas International Hotels and
    Properties Bhd (PIHP), 33, 87
Perstima Bhd, 108
Perusahaan Otomobil Nasional Bhd
    (Proton), 87, 94, 120, 125
Petaling Garden Bhd, 34
Petroleum Development Act (1974), 41
Petroliam Nasional Bhd (Petronas), 29, 57,
    61, 79, 90, 103, 160, 161
Petronas Dagangan Bhd (PDB), 81, 87
Petronas Gas Bhd, 38–9, 81
Philippines, the 66, 130
Pioneer Industries Ordinance, 16
political patronage, 1, 4, 5, 6, 25–7, 49, 51,
    52, 121–2, 124
  disadvantages, 99
  abuses, 5, 51
  Malay, 48
Port Kelang, 82
Pradaz Sdn Bhd, 106, 148
Prime Utilities Bhd (formerly named Berjaya
    South Island Bhd), 157
privatisation, 4, 5, 75–116, 119, 121, 166,
    177, 178, 183
  abused, 108
  and political patronage, 4, 91–8, 100–16

as means of promoting Bumiputera
  capitalism, 80
beneficiaries, 99
disadvantages, 87–91, 99–100, 109
forms, 81–5
implementation, 1, 80, 99
justification, 86–7
objectives, 80
politics, 98–100
Privatisation Master Plan 1991, 80, 83, 87
Promet Bhd, 119
Prudential Assurance Sdn Bhd, 154
P. T. Catur Yasa, 74
Public Bank Bhd, 62, 94, 103
Pulau Langkawi, 107
Pulau Pinang, 96
Pusat Pemeriksaan Kenderaan
  Berkomputer Sdn Bhd (Puspakom),
  93
Puvanesvari, T., 160
Pye, Lucien, 3

Quek Leng Chan, 48, 50, 66, 67, 68, 96,
  129, 138, 158

Raleigh Bhd, 154, see Berjaya Group
Rameli Musa, 73
Rashid Hussain, 62, 67, 146, 149
Rashid Hussain Bhd, 62, 67, 142–3
Razaleigh Hamzah, Tengku, 49, 56, 70,
  102, 122, 123, 124, 156, 183
Realmild Sdn Bhd, 68
Renong Bhd, 50, 52, 62, 67, 68, 98, 105,
  119, 123, 127, 129, 180
Renong Group, 69, 115
rents, 4, 5–8, 40
  abuses, 5–6
  and patronage, 6, 49, 51, 121, 177
  distribution, 4, 5–8, 25, 40, 51, 74, 99,
    112, 119, 120
  redistribution, 177–81
  seeking, 4, 5–8, 41, 51, 98
Resorts World Bhd, 47
Rilla Holdings Sdn Bhd, 72
R. J. Reynolds Bhd (formerly named Juara
  Perkasa Corporation Bhd (JPC), 105,
  119, 143–5, 146
R. J. Reynolds Tobacco Company, 143
Road Transport Department, 125
Rohas Sdn Bhd, 120, 143
Rothmans of Pall Mall Bhd, 34
Roxy Bhd, 61–2
Rural and Industrial Development
  Authority (RIDA) (renamed MARA),
  15, 21, 117

Rubber Industry Smallholders
  Development Authority (RISDA), 31
Rukunnegara (National Ideology), 174
RZ Equities Sdn Bhd, 95, 129, 148, 150

Sabah, 21, 28, 40, 61, 130–1, 168
Sabah Forest Industries, 132
Sabah Foundation, 131
Sabah Progressive Party (SAPP), 132, 135
Sabah SECD, 102
Sabah Shipyard Bhd, 126
Samsudin Abu Hassan, 92, 106, 107–8, 112,
  115, 119, 121, 123, 125, 129
Samy Vellu, S., 114, 168
Sanusi Junid, 126
Sapura Holdings Sdn Bhd, 51, 72, 73–4,
  82, 113
Sapura Research Sdn Bhd, 74
Sapura Telecommunications Bhd, 72, 73
Sarawak, 21, 28, 40, 129, 168; see also Bakun
  Dam
  communities, 112
Sarawak Electricity Supply Corporation
  (SESCO), 110
Satellite Network Services (SNS), 92, 108
Saujana Golf and Country Club, 108
Saujana Hotel Sdn Bhd, 108
Saujana Resort (M) Sdn Bhd, 106, 107, 108
Schumpeter, Joseph, 2, 51, 99
second causeway project, 97, 129
Securities Commission, 42, 65, 134
Securities Commission Act (1992), 65
See Hoy Chan Group, 145
Siemens, 73
Selangor, 21
Selangor Turf Club, 93, 160, 161, 162, 163
Seri Angkasa Sdn Bhd, 93, 106
Seri Iras Sdn Bhd, 54, 55, 148
Seri Kuda Sdn Bhd, 160–2, 165
Setron Bhd, 57, 126
Shamsuddin Abduk Kadir, 51, 72–4, 82,
  113
Shariman Tunku Sulaiman, Tunku, 83
Shell Overseas Holdings Ltd, 94
Shuaib Lazim, 59, 113, 140
Sikap Power Sdn Bhd, 69
Sime Darby Bhd, 32, 33, 34, 38, 59, 61, 69,
  82, 161
Sime UEP Bhd, 54, 55, 56, 139
Singapore, 33, 64, 66, 87, 97, 112
Singer Holdings (M) Bhd, see Berjaya
  Singer
Sistem Televisyen (M) Bhd (STMB), see
  TV3
Social Welfare Lottery, 162

Societies Act, 122
South Korea, 87
South Pacific Textile Industries Bhd, *see*
    Berjaya Textiles Bhd
Southern Bank Bhd, 62
Southern Task (M) Sdn Bhd, 97
Southwide Trading Ltd, 160
Spanco Sdn Bhd, 114, 129
Sports & Lotteries Systems Ltd, 160
Sports Toto lottery, 164
Sports Toto (M) Bhd (*renamed* Berjaya
    Leisure Bhd), 81, 86, 87, 90, 92, 142,
    153–4
Sri Alu Sdn Bhd, 106
Sri Damansara Sdn Bhd (*formerly named*
    Multi-Purpose Bersatu Development
    Sdn Bhd), 141–2, 155
Standard Chartered Bank (M) Bhd, 65
Star Publications (M) Bhd, 155, 157
state economic development corporations
    (SEDCs), 29, 31, 35, 37, 49
Subang Merlin Hotel, 55
'subsidy mentality', 25, 81, 118
Subur Rahmat Sdn Bhd, 103
Sulaiman Abdul Rahman Abdul Taib, 113
Suleiman Manan, 155, 158
Sumatra, 74
Sumitomo Electric Industries Ltd, 74
Sungai Wang Plaza, 107
Sungei Selangor Water Supply Scheme, 98
Suniwang Sdn Bhd, 132
Syarikat Maluri Sdn Bhd, 106
Syarikat Permodalan Kebangsaan Bhd
    (SPK), 15, 56
Syarikat Permodalan & Perusahaan Perak
    Bhd (SPPPB), 56, 140
Syarikat Sepatu Timur Sdn Bhd, 120
Syarikat Telekom (M) Bhd (STM), 46, 82,
    87, 89, 90, 114, 148
Syed Kechik, 61
Syed Kechik Foundation, 91

Taiheiyou Hotel & Shisan N.V., 161
Taiheiyou Kaihatsu N.V., 161
Taiping Consolidated Bhd, 154, 155
Taiwan, 87
Tajudin Ramli, 33, 54, 55, 62, 82, 94, 95,
    103, 119, 121, 123, 125, 129, 148–52
Taman Bukit Maluri Sdn Bhd, 54, 55, 106,
    148
Tan & Tan Bhd, 47
Tan Chee Sing, Danny, 158, 181
Tan Chee Yioun, Vincent, 47, 70, 73, 82,
    88, 92, 96, 121, 138, 142, 148, 152–9,
    164, 181
Tan Chin Nam, 43, 47

Tan Chin Tuan, 60
Tan Hua Choon, Robert, 113–15, 129, 181
Tan Koon Swan, 44, 46, 142
Tanjong Bhd, 138, 162–3
Tanjung Layang (M) Sdn Bhd, 125
Tasik Cement, 56
Technology Resources Industries Bhd
    (TRI) (*formerly* Roxy Electric
    Industries), 33, 56, 62, 95, 103, 119,
    123, 149–50
Teh Hong Piow, 94
Telecoms Department, 72, 82
Teledata Sdn Bhd, 73
Teluk Datai Resorts Sdn Bhd, 107
Tenaga Nasional Bhd (TNB), 69, 82, 87,
    90, 110
Tengku Adnan Tengku Mansor, 47, 48,
    155, 157
Teo family, 145
Terengganu, 21
Thatcher government, 91
The Malay Dilemma, see Mahathir, Mohamad
Tien Ik Enterprise Sdn Bhd, 163
Time Engineering Bhd, 66, 68, 97–8, 151–2
Times Publishing Bhd, 55
Ting Pek Khiing, 110, 111, 112, 113–16,
    121, 129, 181
Topgroup Holdings Bhd, 48
Totalisator Board of Malaysia, 93, 162, 163
Tourist Development Corporation (TCD),
    29
Tradewinds (M) Bhd, 33, 87
Tropical Veneer Company Bhd (*renamed*
    Intiplus Bhd), 154
TV3, 3, 50, 56, 58, 68, 69, 73, 74, 82, 86, 87,
    91–2, 126, 127, 154, 155

UBN Holdings, 106
UCM Corporation Bhd, 114
Ukit community, 112
UMBC Holdings Sdn Bhd, 58
Union Bank (Switzerland), 55
Union Paper Bhd, 48
Uniphoenix Corporation Bhd, 119
Uniphone Telecommunications Bhd, 73,
    74
Uniphone Usahasama Sdn Bhd, 73
Uniphone Works Sdn Bhd (*renamed*
    Uniphone), 72
United Asian Bank Bhd (UAB), 62
United Engineers (M) Bhd (UEM), 50, 66,
    68, 96–8, 106, 119, 122, 123, 129
United Industrial Corporation, 62, 143
United Malayan Banking Corporation Bhd
    (UMBC), 33, 34, 38, 40, 56–60, 61, 79,
    103, 106, 123, 143

United Malayan Flour Mills Bhd, 33
United Malays' National Organisation
    (UMNO), 2, 11–12, 14, 22, 26, 39, 51,
    56, 68, 69, 98, 102, 118, 121–33
  alliances with business leaders, 147, 148
  business dealings, 45, 50, 51–3, 54, 59,
    66–7, 122, 123, 127
  companies, 154
  control over allocation of resources, 26
  efforts at capital accumulation, 47
  factionalism, 26, 124–30, 183
  General Assembly, 26, 88, 122, 127, 128,
    162
  hegemony, 5, 7, 22–3, 25, 26, 44, 48, 81,
    117, 121–2, 178, 183
  in Alliance, 10, 14
  leaders' links with business and political
    elites, 53, 57, 73, 99, 156
  leadership, 5, 14, 21, 22, 26, 48, 69, 129,
    181, 183, 184
  members, 5, 161
  members' criticism of privatisations, 88
  Merbok division, 113
  patronage networks, 25, 51–2
  Permatang Pauh division, 96, 125
  politicians, 168
  ruled illegal, 122
  rural base, 14
  UMNO Baru, 122, 128
  UMNO Youth, 112, 124, 145, 157
  Young Turks, 22
United Merchant Finance Bhd (*formerly
  named* MUI Finance Bhd), 70
United Merchant Group Bhd (UMG),
  70–1
United Motor Works Bhd (UMW), 72
United Overseas Bank, 64
United Plantations Bhd, 102, 103
United Sabah National Organisation
  (USNO), 131, 135
United States, 79
Universal Life & General Insurance, 61

University of Malaya, 70, 126
Unza Holdings Bhd, 48
Urban Development Authority (UDA), 29,
  37, 49, 54, 105, 118
Usaha Tegas Sdn Bhd, 160, 161, 163, 165
Usahasama Proton-DRB Sdn Bhd, 94
Utusan Melayu (M) Bhd, 96, 123

Vietnam, 74
Vision 2020, 168–76, 177

WAMY (World Assembly of Muslim Youth),
  126
Wan Ariff Wan Hamzah, 140
Wan Azmi Wan Hamzah, 55, 57, 67, 105,
  113, 119, 120, 121, 123, 125, 138–47,
  141, 155, 158
Wangsa Maju township project, 106
Waspavest Sdn Bhd, 106, 123
Waspavest Group
'Wawasan' (Vision), 126
Wembley Industries Holdings Bhd, 125
west Johore port development, 97
Wiradaya Sdn Bhd, 113
Woodhouse Sdn Bhd, 113
World Bank, 14, 77, 79

Yayasan Bumiputera Pulau Pinang, 96, 126
Yayasan Gerakbakti Kebansaan, 146
Yayasan Pelaburan Bumiputera (YBB), 34,
  35
Yeap family, 67, 70
Yeoh Tiong Lay, 82
Yong Teck Lee, 132, 135
Yoshihara, Kunio, 25
YTL Corporation Bhd, 82
Yung Pui Company Ltd, 145

Zahari Abdul Wahab, 67–8
Zaki Azmi, 148
Zalik Bhd, 66, 67